35. —

MARKETS AND MAJORITIES

MARKETS
AND
MAJORITIES

The Political Economy of Public Policy

STEVEN M. SHEFFRIN

THE FREE PRESS
A Division of Macmillan, Inc.
NEW YORK

Maxwell Macmillan Canada
TORONTO

Maxwell Macmillan International
NEW YORK   OXFORD   SINGAPORE   SYDNEY

The Free Press
A Division of Macmillan, Inc.
866 Third Avenue, New York, N.Y. 10022

Maxwell Macmillan Canada, Inc.
1200 Eglinton Avenue East
Suite 200
Don Mills, Ontario M3C 3N1

Macmillan, Inc. is part of the Maxwell Communication Group of Companies.

Printed in the United States of America

printing number

1 2 3 4 5 6 7 8 9 10

Library of Congress Cataloging–in–Publication Data

Sheffrin, Steven M.
    Markets and majorities: the political economy of public policy/
Steven M. Sheffrin.
        p.   cm.
    ISBN 0-02-928651-4
    1. United States—Economic policy—1981–   2. Economics—Political
aspects—United States.   I. Title.
HC106.8.S483   1993
338.973—dc20   93-21722
                                                                    CIP

To Anjali, who suffered through hours of C-SPAN

CONTENTS

PREFACE

As the United States lurched from one economic crisis to another during the last twenty years, we began to capitalize our woes. Starting with the Energy Crisis, we moved to the Inflation Problem, the Great Recession, the Deficit Problem, the Loss in Competitiveness, and, most recently, the Health Care Crisis. Lower-case letters are an endangered species in our economic discourse.

But our penchant for magnifying our economic problems has deeper roots. Our economic problems appear to be more profound and no longer the type that can be cured by simple solutions proposed by policy technicians. No ivory tower economist or policy analyst can offer the magic solution to our difficulties. Our economic problems today are inseparable from the political and regulatory environments that surround them. Solutions to our crises today necessarily involve the messy and seemingly intractable world of politics and social change.

We in the United States take pride in our federalist system and applaud the economic and policy innovation that originates in the states. Indeed, there have been areas in which the states have shown leadership—for example, in educational reform. But our pressing economic problems are now national in scope: stopping the escalation in health costs, providing security for the elderly, designing environmental regulation, reining in our liability explosion, developing a framework for international trade, and managing our monetary and fiscal affairs.

This book is about our policy problems in these areas. Two important characteristics distinguish the economic problems that are treated here. First, all operate at the intersection of markets and politics. Real or perceived failures of markets lead to government interventions and to the birth of regulatory mechanisms that attempt to control the markets. Government regulation, however, brings its own political obsessions and preoccupations. Policy outcomes are heavily influenced by this dialectic between markets and politics. Second, the important policy issues treated here all fall within the scope of the government in Washington, D.C. Attempts to control, divert, or replace markets all transpire within this hub of politics.

This book develops a disciplined framework built on understanding the dual failures of markets and government regulation. Through analysis of our complex economic policy debates, it illustrates a style of thinking on policy issues that goes beyond rote ideological positions or politically motivated conclusions. Without a framework for policy analysis, all claims on the government seem equally meritorious and power, influence, and raw politics will rule over informed decision making. This situation is the system we have been living with, and it desperately needs to be changed. It is also particulary important now that President Bill Clinton brings an activist predisposition to governing in Washington, D.C.

This book also attempts to bridge a growing gap between economics as it is taught and practiced in the academy and policy analysis as it is practiced in Washington. Both economists and policy analysts have made great intellectual progress in recent years but only on their own separate and largely disjointed agendas. Very few individuals outside Washington are cognizant of many of the dramatic changes that are occurring in the management of our economic affairs. To bridge the gap between economists and policy analysts, I begin each problem area with an analysis of why there is real or perceived market failure. Only after coming to grips with this key issue do I begin the analysis of policy and politics.

The initial draft of the manuscript was written while I was on a sabbatical leave from the University of California, Davis. The first half of the sabbatical was spent at the Institute of Governmental Affairs at Davis. During the second half, I was a visiting scholar at the London School of Economics. Both institutions provided first-class environments for this research. A travel grant from the the University of California, Davis Washington Center was also very useful in this project.

In preparing a book that covers such a diverse set of topics, I was fortunate to have the advice and counsel of many policy experts and economists. Inside the beltway, I benefited from conversations with Henry Aaron, Gary Burtless, Dallas Burtraw, Raymond Kopp, Kathryn Langwell, Steven Long, and Eugene Steuerle. Colleagues and friends at Davis who contributed their insights and expertise included Greg Clark, Rob and Gail Feenstra, Kathy Kling, Art Havenner, Jay Helms, Kevin Hoover, Anjali Sheffrin, and Robert Triest. Ross Eckert of Claremont Mens College and Max Steurer of the London School of Economics helped me clarify some important issues. I am sure that all of them will disagree with at least some parts of the book.

Two individuals were especially helpful in conducting the research for this book. Jennifer Dinsmore demonstrated great ingenuity in finding and organizing a complex body of information on economic policy in many diverse areas. Jean Stratford, the librarian at the Institute of Governmental Affairs, always managed to find the material I needed and pointed me in novel directions. Jean is also the coauthor of the appendix on think tanks and policy sources at the end of the book.

My editors at The Free Press, Peter Dougherty and Bruce Nichols, were trusted sources of advice, suggestions, and criticism as the project developed. Peter encouraged the project from the beginning and Bruce helped shape the manuscript as it neared completion. It was a pleasure to work with such supportive and talented editors.

MARKETS AND MAJORITIES

1
Introduction
When Markets Fail

Lecturing in Eastern Europe in the autumn of 1989, I was asked in a reproachful way why I did not urge the economics of Professor Friedrich Hayek as the alternative to the economic system there so obviously failing. I replied that this was not a design which, in its rejection of regulatory, welfare, or other ameliorating actions by the state, we in the United States or elsewhere in the nonsocialist world would find tolerable.

—John Kenneth Galbraith[1]

The end of the 1980s and the early 1990s marked a victory for democratic society around the world. Dictators in Eastern Europe were overthrown, the Berlin Wall was torn down, and the former Soviet Union began the difficult and dangerous process of fundamental change. As the secrets spilled out from previously closed societies, the truth was even worse than we had imagined: a massive epidemic of AIDS among the poor children of Romania, choking air pollution and retrograde factories in Eastern Europe, and a complete collapse of the economy of the former Soviet Union.

Democracy was a clear winner in this worldwide transformation and became the United States' best export. It also appeared that capitalism would be a big winner. As Marxist professors quickly became unemployed (except in universities in advanced capitalist economies), free marketeers airlifted themselves to Eastern Europe and the newly formed republics in the former Soviet Union. In conferences, speeches, and meetings they preached the virtues of self-interest, the efficiencies of competition, and the productive genius of the market.

But in this euphoria it is easy to forget an important lesson from the experience of modern successful economies. Sometimes markets work, but sometimes they don't.

When markets work well, economic policy is cut and dried: do everything possible to ensure that the private system continues to function freely and without impediments. As an example of successful markets, consider how an Eastern European citizen would view our all-purpose drug and convenience stores. Open all hours and jammed with merchandise, they provide envelopes, toothbrushes, cold remedies, film, greeting cards, and the cornucopia of other items that we just assume will be available. As we learn in beginning economic classes, it is a miracle that this vast variety of items can reach the consumer without any centralized planning or production and with minimal, if any, government oversight.

Markets also operate silently. They allocate goods and services, generate incomes, reward the talented, skilled, and lucky and punish the less talented, less skilled, and unlucky. A myriad of decisions about the allocation of resources and the distribution of resources are quietly made, prompting economists to describe the silent working of markets as part of a grand circular flow. Consumers purchase goods and services from businesses that, in turn, generate incomes—wages and profits—that accrue to workers and investors and are then reinvested in goods and services.

But markets can fail to work. And when they do, the silence ends. When markets fail, governments intervene and impose regulations on the economy. Economic decisions are no longer left to the silent workings of markets but become heavily influenced by politics. The grand circular flow is thus transformed into the noisy and chaotic Washington money-go-round.

When Washington politics meets the free market, a host of new actors, new factors, and obsessions come into play. Considerations of political equity emerge from the silence. Experts, scientific or otherwise, are called in to share their wisdom, opinions, and prejudice. Raw political power and other political considerations begin to influence economic outcomes. And solutions to social problems based on reintroducing markets are viewed with skeptical eyes since problems seem to have arisen in the first place because markets were not working.

It is precisely at this interface of economics and politics, where markets seem to fail, that the grand debates of U.S. economic policy should occur. We should be asking how markets can be reformed or regulated in a sensible way to achieve our goals. Instead, in the Washington money-go-round we find thousands of lawyers and lobbyists, special interests, influence peddlers, self-anointed reformers, regulators, bureaucrats, and ambitious politicians. All are out to promote their narrow interests or those of their constituencies. In this environment, there are few honest dialogues on economic policy. Instead, discussions of policy often become just another pretext for promoting self-interest.

Today U.S. economic policies are made by accommodating the lobbyists and pressure groups. Occasionally policy rises above the fray, such as with the passage of the Tax Reform Act of 1986, which swept many loopholes and sweetheart deals from the tax code. But this exception, a remarkable detour from politics as usual, proves the rule. The Washington money-go-round provides the media with tales of intrigue, power, and influence that titillate the public. Sometimes this mad scramble for economic positioning may seem amusing, but it deflects attention from the very serious business of making our economy work in a time of increased global economic competition.

Special interests thrive in an atmosphere in which there is no consensus or even a general framework for thinking about economic policy. Without any basic ground rules, all claims on government seem equally valid and plausible:

A housing problem? Let's have a subsidy or tax credit.

Your industry is losing out to foreign competitors? Try a tariff, quota, or "voluntary export restraint."

Worried about the burden of caring for the elderly? Let's start a program of federally subsidized long-term care.

Health care costs rising? Let's put price controls on hospitals.

Lists like these can and do continue indefinitely. We currently do not have any framework to sort the good claims from the bad. Instead, we rely on the day to day workings of the Washington money-go-round to sort out these claims. Unfortunately, this means that power, influence, and access will often be decisive over common sense and sound public policy.

Some reformers claim that the real culprit in our economic and political system is the corrosive effect of money in politics. They promote campaign finance reform as the answer to our difficulties. Put everyone on an equal playing field, they say, and then we will have sound economic policy.

But this argument fails in two important respects. First, try as we may, we can never equalize the power of economic interests in our economy. Large, sophisticated interests will find ways to wield their influence. The evils of today—political action committees and soft money—were the byproducts of our previous reform efforts in the 1970s. The law of unintended consequences has worked with a vengeance in campaign finance. Moreover, in a free society it is extremely difficult to place limits on political actions. The Supreme Court has ruled that billionaires are free to spend as much of their own money as they desire to run for office. Wealthy heirs are permitted to set up tax-free foundations to promote their visions of environmentalism. And it is naive to believe that large corporations would not find similar mechanisms to influence political outcomes.

But there is a more fundamental limitation to campaign finance reform as a solution to our economic problems. Even if we could level the playing field, without a general framework for thinking about policy, we still could not separate the good claims from the bad. The same conundrum remains: there are an infinite number of claimants on public resources. Some basic principles are necessary to decide which claims are worthy of societal support.

This book aims to recreate the missing dialogue on economic policy and promote a framework in which to discuss policy rationally. It brings to this task key insights from the science of economics and the art of governance. Through an approach based on understanding the limits of markets and limits of government regulation, it provides a disciplined framework to sort through our difficult economic problems.

To begin this process, it is crucial to understand why markets fail to work. There are four broad reasons why markets do not work well. Markets fail to work when they produce distributional outcomes that are politically unacceptable, when there are pervasive individual uncertainties, when markets are missing, and when collective goods or institutional structures must be provided.

A first and basic reason why markets are perceived not to work well is that they generate distributional outcomes that are not easily accommodated by the political system. In these cases, the markets may work efficiently—that is, they deliver goods and services at minimum costs to the highest bidders without any disruptions—but the political system cannot handle the final outcomes. A good example of this phenomenon is trade policy, a topic analyzed at length in this book. Free international markets are the best way to achieve international specialization and efficient economic outcomes for the world economy. But free trade may hurt some politically powerful domestic interests. These interests often mobilize to impede free trade. Although there are no technical problems with the functioning of markets, the outcomes from market processes are not welcome.

Another instructive example is rent control. In the face of rising rents, existing renters may develop sufficient political clout to impose rent controls in the community. Without rent controls, market rents may rise, but the housing market works smoothly without queues or shortages. Developers produce new housing if it is sufficiently profitable. Rent control disrupts the housing market, creates queues and shortages, and, in the long run, leads to a deterioration of the housing stock as maintenance is deferred and new construction comes to a halt. The housing market in New York City is a classic example of the devastation that can be caused by rent controls. Ironically, housing markets perform technically much better before the imposition of rent control but do not work satisfactorily in the sense of producing politically palatable outcomes.

The next three reasons why markets do not work well fall into the traditional economists' category of "market failure." Economists reserve this term for situations in which markets do not by themselves produce efficient outcomes. It is not simply that the markets produce outcomes that the public finds unacceptable. When economists diagnose market failures, there are technical reasons why the markets do not operate efficiently.

The first cause of market failure involves *uncertainty*. Markets can handle some but not all uncertainties facing individuals. Living is risky—there are illnesses, sudden deaths, broken families, and changing fortunes. Insurance can provide some assistance in this risky world. Medical, life, and automobile insurance can partly cushion individuals from risks.

But there are well-known limits to insurance markets. Take the example of automobile insurance. Suppose a large group of diverse individuals is covered by a single policy and the insurance company is unable to distinguish or not allowed by law to distinguish between members of the group. The good risks in the group (such as stable nonelderly adults) would like to separate themselves from the bad risks (the single, young, and inexperienced) in order to obtain less expensive coverage. To the extent that they succeed, the quality of the remaining insurance pool will deteriorate. This exodus necessarily leads to higher rates for those remaining and increased pressures for other relatively good risks to exit. Economists term this phenomenon "adverse selection." Taken to its extreme, it can lead to the complete breakdown and disappearance of an insurance market. Other problems with insurance markets arise because individuals can take actions or engage in behavior that insurance companies cannot see. Large insurance firms cannot find out if we drink too much at parties, drive too quickly, or engage in unsafe sexual practices. The fact that individuals have information that insurance companies do not is known as "moral hazard" and also limits the extent to which insurance can be provided. Finally, insurance cannot be provided against events that affect the entire society. Just as a firm writing insurance only in Los Angeles could not insure against earthquakes, insurance firms cannot provide coverage against social outcomes, such as a reduction in the rate of productivity growth. Insurance cannot be provided to cushion against a global drought, a fall in future wages, or the generational struggles that will inevitably occur as average lifespans increase.

Our much-debated problems with health care and the Social Security system emerge from precisely these kinds of market failures. Private insurance schemes have not provided everyone with security against illness and aging. Thus the government has instituted elaborate, expensive, and clumsy regulatory schemes, including Social Security, Medicare, and Medicaid. These institutions, in turn, are undergoing radical changes as they try to cope with the same pervasive uncertainties that have bedeviled private insurance.

Pollution provides a classic example of the second basic cause of market failure: *missing markets*. Suppose a company produces steel but pollutes the air. Because there are no markets for clean air, a firm does not have to pay a price for discharging pollutants into the air. If either individuals or the government had a property right in clean air, they would have to be compensated by the firm for the air pollution

curriculum, values, and educational and social priorities out of the public realm and into the politically insulated environment of free markets. Afro-centric or Hindu-centric schools could flourish as easily in this environment as schools that emphasize fundamental Christianity or the Greek and Roman classics. Opponents of choice in education recognize that government regulation brings political considerations into play in a fundamental way and fear free choice in education precisely because it would diminish the political power of the educational establishment.

Raw politics rears its head when markets fail to work. Powerful committee chairmen may protect their regional economic interests at the expense of broader collective interests. Key trade and environmental decisions will be more influenced by elections than economics. Special interest money will flow to politicians to alter outcomes that the markets would have produced. The circular flow of funds takes a detour through the Washington money-go-round.

Moreover, when markets fail to work, there is a natural suspicion of government solutions based on emulating the market or creating new markets, as in school choice. In another example, environmentalists typically distrust solutions to environmental problems based on the idea of creating new economic markets for the environment. Economists often advocate creating markets in pollution rights that have the effect of allowing firms to "pay to pollute." Some environmentalists do not believe these market-based solutions will work in practice. Other environmentalists, like critics of the church in the Middle Ages, feel that these solutions resemble the practice of selling indulgences and should be opposed on moral grounds. In their view, introducing market structures and market incentives can impede or even corrupt the development of a growing environmental consciousness.

In some cases, this suspicion of markets may be justified. Any economist would tell you that overcapacity—say in the steel industry—leads to an industry shakeout and causes prices to fall. Yet, in the medical community, having too many hospitals in any area leads to higher prices for hospital services as hospitals compete for patients by offering new and expensive services. Since insurance policies often pay the entire cost of major operations (after some limited deductibles), patients have no incentives to seek bargain rates. Hospitals, therefore, offer the most expensive, high-tech treatment to lure patients to their facilities. Because the insurance market skews the incentives, competition perversely can lead to higher prices and higher costs.

The impact of insurance policies on hospital costs illustrates an important lesson in economics. Any institution, such as insurance, that changes the incentives in markets can have unintended consequences. The same lesson applies to government regulations. Policies that attempt to cure problems can easily create new ones. Public or private medical insurance can reduce risks for individuals but it can also lead to vast increases in the costs to society.

Finally, the failure of markets brings forth a call for experts of all kinds to enter the policy arena. We are accustomed to economic experts pronouncing on monetary policy or international finance. But missing markets also attract legions of experts. In the environmental area, for example, scientists of all stripes, often with their own personal agendas, debate the dangers of global warming or of species extinction. Often, neither the public nor the Congress is in the position to judge the merits of experts, and this uncertainty promotes an environment where policy effectiveness may be only loosely related to scientific veracity. At times, Washington seems to be inhabited only by experts—and these experts advocate every policy position imaginable. But expert advocates are not politically neutral truth-seekers. In the age of big science and big grants, it is hard to find any politically neutral truth-seekers, even in universities. We should not expect to find them on K Street or Capitol Hill.

Washington, obsessed as it is with equity, experts, raw politics, and the suspicion of markets, naturally can lose sight of the fundamentals of economic performance and economic efficiency. All too often the result is political failure that rivals the failure of markets. Economic policy making operates at the perilous intersection of market failure and political obsessions. Only when legislators and their constituents begin to understand the compound nature of the problem will sensible and effective answers to these vexing questions prevail.

This book examines some of the critical areas where markets fail to work in the U.S. economy. For the most part, attention is focused on those particularly difficult cases in which markets fail to work *and* there are technical market failures in the economists' sense. These are the most interesting cases because public perceptions of the failure of markets coincide with technical difficulties in the market, thus rendering the economic analysis much more difficult. But economic analysis can only achieve a partial understanding of the problems. Because the failure of markets radically changes the policy environment, the analysis must go beyond understanding the pure economics and extend to political factors as well.

Our policy discussions today are paralyzed by reflex ideologies that fail to recognize the dual limits of market and regulatory solutions. On the right, there is a blind spot toward market failure of any kind. With a complete faith in free markets, these partisans can easily view all taxes as impediments to growth and all bureaucrats as parasites living off the private sector. Liberals see failures in markets, but they fail to see the damage that ill-conceived regulatory structures can cause. They are often blind to the biases and distortions caused by bringing politics into economic affairs and by the damage to the economy that can arise in spite of high-minded ideals. The hard left fails to perceive any virtues in the market. For them, government regulation is just a step on the way to centralized control. Sound economic policy must eschew all of these false ideologies.

The strategy followed in subsequent chapters is to first understand why market solutions are inadequate and then understand the logic of the existing regulatory structure and the politics that surround the problems. Only with this background can suggestions for change and reform be understood. This approach contrasts sharply to the reflex debates between ideologues today and often leads in surprising and somewhat unpredictable directions.

The book is divided into three parts that correspond to the three basic technical reasons why markets fail in the economists' sense: pervasive individual uncertainty, missing markets, and the need for collective provisions of goods and institutions. Each part not only highlights why markets may fail in a narrow technical sense but emphasizes the consequences when they fail to work in the broader sense of the term and the subtle interactions between the two. A final chapter summarizes the key conclusions and provides principles for reform.

The first part, "Economic Security and Pervasive Risks," includes the provision of medical care, the Social Security system, and the problems relating to an aging population. As medical expenditures now account for 14 percent of gross national product (GNP) and Social Security taxes now outstrip income taxes for the average worker, there is legitimate concern that our current systems cannot continue without radical restructuring. Chapters 2 and 3 discuss alternative health plans, the equity and solvency of the Social Security system, and demands for long term care for the elderly.

Part II, "Regulation with Missing Markets" focuses on two important areas: the environment and the liability system. In both areas missing markets have led to the development of regulatory systems that have created extensive political controversy. Chapter 4 covers air pollution, global warming, pesticide regulation, and species preservation. Chapter 5, on liability, focuses on the costs and benefits of regulating safety through the tort system and the liability crisis that besets us.

Part III, "The Search for Governmental Structures" covers trade, monetary, and fiscal policy. Although these areas are often treated as basic economic issues, their political aspects make them most interesting and most difficult. In trade policy, the issues revolve around nations that like to promote their exports and protect their imports; in monetary policy, the issues are who should control the money supply and how should it be controlled; and, in fiscal policy, the most interesting issue is how to control our politicians. Basic economic thinking underscores the analysis, but the discussion quickly leads to the political economic aspects of the problems.

The overall approach of this book is summarized in Table 1–1. Policy issues do not emerge in a vacuum—they are generated because of inherent failures either in the market structures or in the political system. These market and political failures give rise to regulatory structures that try to cope with these problems. Regulatory structures are by their very nature imperfect and bring forth new concerns and issues.

Table 1–1 illustrates this dialectic of policy for the areas treated in the book. For example, our health care system is plagued with rising costs and problems of access. Fundamentally, these problems are caused by the inability of insurance markets to process the pervasive risk in the health system. Our most recent regulatory responses have been to promulgate government-sponsored health insurance and impose direct regulations on hospital costs and physician fees. But the health system is still failing, and further regulation and fundamental change stemming from the debate on a national health policy remain possibilities.

The stance toward economic policy taken in this book—identify where markets fail, understand the logic of the regulatory structure, and only then advocate policies that have sound economic and political features—is more difficult and less predictable than conventional economic analysis. Perhaps highly partisan free marketeers or central planners could find solutions compatible with their beliefs in all

Table 1–1

How Economic and Political Issues Intersect

Issue	Economic Problem	Market or Political Failure	Regulatory Structures	Emerging Issues
Health	Rising costs, access	Limits to insurance markets	Regulation of hospital and doctor fees	Further regulation, national health debate
An aging society	Looming medical and support costs	Insufficient private savings and foresight— insurance failures	Social Security, Medicare	Long-term care, control of Medicare
Environment	Clash of economic and environmental interests	Divergence of private and social costs, uncertain science	EPA, pesticides and species acts	Market solutions to problems, balancing economic costs
Liability	Spiralling costs of insurance	Divergence of law from science and responsibility	Tort law	Federal legislation to cap damage awards
International trade	Protectionism	Special interest lobbying	GATT	Regional free trade areas
Monetary policy and international finance	Unemployment and inflation cycles	Uncertainty plus hazy accountability	Federal Reserve	International policy coordination
Fiscal policy	Persistent budget deficits	Lack of fiscal discipline	Budget control acts	New caps on spending and balanced budget laws

areas. This outcome may be the product of either a strong mind or a closed one. For most of the issues presented in this book, it is not difficult to understand the alternative argument. In each chapter I recommend reforms and actions that are based on explicit underlying political and economic assumptions. Thinking through the consequences of these assumptions after an informed analysis of the issues and of the regulatory structures is what is required when markets fail. I am proposing an approach—a style of thinking—that excludes ideologically charged or politically motivated conclusions. Such an approach can discipline policy choices and raise decision making above the Washington bazaar.

The results of these exercises are often surprising. Some centralized government control may be required in medicine, but greater decentralized efforts by nations in their pursuit of free trade may be the best policy. In the environmental area, regulations for air pollution work reasonably well, but those governing pesticides and species preservation are not working well. Few changes are needed in the framework for monetary policy, but the framework for fiscal policy needs substantial reorientation. The final chapter brings together the important themes that emerge from the approach taken in this book. Not all readers will agree with all the conclusions, but I hope they will be forced to think through, in a disciplined way, the political and economic complexities in play when markets fail to work.

To make informed judgments on policy, however, requires the proper intellectual background as well as access to the latest information. To assist readers in thinking through the policy issues, each chapter is followed by some suggested additional readings. To assist in obtaining the latest information, the book concludes with "An Annotated Guide to Washington Think Tanks and Sources of Policy Information." This guide provides an orientation to the intricate world of Washington think tanks, including names, addresses, phone numbers, publications, and political orientations.

Note

1. John Kenneth Galbraith, "Economics in the Century Ahead," *Economic Journal* Jan. 1991: 45.

PART I

Economic Security and Pervasive Risk

Some called it the end of the welfare state. That may have been wishful thinking. But the dramatic repeal of catastrophic health insurance for the elderly in the fall of 1989 indicated that prior assumptions about the future of government spending were not on firm ground.

The catastrophic health insurance bill was signed into law on July 1, 1988, by President Ronald Reagan. In the signing ceremony, he called the act "an historic piece of legislation" that would protect elderly and disabled people from costly acute care that "could wipe out the savings of an entire lifetime." Although this was a new part of the social safety network, it was Ronald Reagan, the most conservative president of this generation, who presided over its passage. Partly for this reason, most observers felt that this act would become a permanent part of the social fabric.

The catastrophic health insurance bill was designed with the best of intentions and brought to bear the latest thinking in the design of social policy. First of all, there appeared to be a need for some type of catastrophic health insurance. Before the act was passed, the only government-provided coverage for the nonpoor elderly was Medicare, Lyndon Johnson's 1965 innovation. However, Medicare had

15

no ceiling on the expenses an elderly person would have to incur because there were cost-sharing requirements for participants. These cost-sharing requirements applied to both the basic coverage (Part A, or Hospital Insurance) as well as to the voluntary program (Part B, or Supplementary Medical Insurance). Faced with a severe illness or accident, an elderly person could lose the savings of a lifetime just to meet the required copayments.

The elderly, of course, recognized this problem with Medicare and turned to the private sector for additional insurance to cover these costs. Lorne Greene and other trustworthy elderly actors were hired to advertise these insurance packages on television. About two-thirds of the elderly enrolled in Medicare purchased this "Medigap" insurance. Another 10 percent of the elderly who were poor qualified for Medicaid coverage that paid their copayments. Thus, roughly 25 percent of the elderly remained without any coverage and at financial risk from a catastrophic illness.

In addition to the lack of complete coverage, several other arguments were given for a public insurance program. Concern was expressed about the prices charged for Medigap insurance, and it was believed that the public sector could provide less expensive coverage. There was also the fear that private companies might limit access to insurance based on factors such as preexisting health problems so that universal coverage could never be achieved by relying on the private sector alone.

Advocates for the elderly saw the opportunity in new legislation to propose additional benefits. Copayments on drugs taken outside the hospital can be significant expenses for the elderly. Even more important were the costs associated with skilled nursing home care. Under Medicare, benefits were provided for skilled nursing home care, but only after an individual had been hospitalized for three days. The catastrophic health insurance law removed this requirement of a prior hospital stay and also provided some additional benefits for drugs.

These additional benefits were fine, but who was to pay for the new services? A number of scholars had concluded that the elderly, as a group, were no longer poorer than the rest of society. In other words, the Social Security program had been successful, and poverty among the elderly was no longer pervasive in the United States. Lawmakers and the public also had grown sensitive to the increasing burdens placed on the working population. Payroll taxes increased regularly throughout the 1980s and real wages for lower-skilled workers declined.

Because of these two factors, lawmakers decided to spread the burden of the new program among the elderly. This move was a dramatic break from prior entitlement programs in which the entire society was asked to bear the burden of the support. But the elderly do not form a homogeneous group. They include the wealthy as well as the poor. Even though all the elderly would be equally entitled to the benefits under the catastrophic program, Congress rejected an administration proposal for a flat fee and decided that the costs of the program should fall more on the relatively well-off elderly.

The mechanism for distributing the burden to the relatively well-off was an income tax surcharge—that is, an additional tax based on the federal income tax that an elderly couple or individual would pay. The surcharge in the initial year would range from zero (for the relatively poor) to $800 per person for the top 5 percent in terms of income. In addition, all the elderly would pay a fixed monthly charge regardless of income.

The elderly did not become fully aware of the financing scheme until after the bill had passed. It quickly created a firestorm, particularly among those who thought they would be paying a substantial surtax. The Congressional Budget Office estimated that about 30 percent of the elderly would pay more in taxes and fees than they would receive in benefits.[1] For many of the elderly, the comparison was more direct. They were already purchasing Medigap insurance and felt that the private sector was providing a better alternative. Moreover, some of the elderly had Medigap coverage as part of their basic retirement package through their pension plan. For them, the superfluous benefits could raise the taxes for a couple by $1600 per year.

The furor over the surcharge surprised the traditional lobbying groups for the elderly, such as the American Association for Retired Persons, with over 30 million members, which initially supported and continued to support the law. A smaller group, the National Committee to Preserve Social Security, with about 5 million members, led the vocal opposition. They engineered a grassroots rebellion that frightened politicians, particularly in the House of Representatives.

Adding to the furor was a "mistake" in the estimates for the costs of the program. The problem arose in estimating the costs for the *skilled nursing home part of the program. Eliminating the requirement of a prior hospital stay of three days before being eligible for benefits dramatically increased the number of eligible individuals. Over half of the newly eligible were already patients in nursing homes.[2]*

The original estimates for the skilled nursing home component failed to incorporate one basic truth of all social welfare programs: increased eligibility will lead to large and often unpredictable increases in the number of individuals enrolled in a program. In this case, the original estimates were far too low. Original estimates for skilled nursing home care in 1990 were $1.4 billion, but were later changed to $4.2 billion!

Proponents for repeal thus had another weapon besides the grassroots rebellion of the elderly. Even if the program were to remain intact, either benefits would have to be decreased or fees and the surcharge increased. The House caved in first and voted overwhelmingly to repeal the catastrophic health law. The Senate tried to preserve some aspects of the program, but by the time all the lawmakers went home for the holidays, the catastrophic health law was just a disturbing memory.

The lawmakers learned some immediate lessons: Don't underestimate the power of the relatively well-off elderly and don't rely fully on the traditional lobbies to convey their views. Don't believe initial cost estimates for entitlement programs, which are as reliable as initial cost estimates from the Pentagon. And, finally, be cautious in any future plans to expand entitlements.

Stepping back from the legislative fury, another set of questions emerge. How did we get into a situation in which medical costs have become increasingly burdensome, with no immediate prospects for relief? What long-run government policies can we adopt to change this trend? Can we restrict our interventions to Medicare and Medicaid, or is wholesale reform of the system required? Then there are the questions about an aging society. Can our Social Security system and Medicare system meet the growing proportion of elderly in the society? Can and will the workers of the future support the elderly?

The next two chapters deal with medical care and the provision of social support for the elderly. The subjects, of course, are not independent. Medical treatment of the elderly poses profound ethical and financial dilemmas, the solutions to which may transform our medical care system. The solvency of our social programs for the elderly also depends on developments in the health care area. Through it all, pervasive risks and uncertainty pose special challenges to the markets for health and the provision of social insurance and test our ingenuity in designing institutions.

Notes

1. *Subsidies Under Medicare and the Potential for Disenrollment Under a Voluntary Catastrophic Program.* (Washington, D.C.: Congressional Budget Office, Sept. 1989).
2. Kenneth Bacon, "Catastrophic Medicare Insurance Plan Generates Skyrocketing Cost Overruns," *Wall Street Journal* (Sept. 18, 1989): A20.

2

The Peculiar World of Medical Economics

Why Is Medicine Special?

Most observers agree that the market for medical services operates differently from ordinary markets for other goods and services. Perhaps the best way to understand some of the key differences is to remind ourselves of what a truly free and unfettered market would look like.

When economists speak of perfect markets they have a number of different ingredients in mind. First of all, there is perfect information on the part of both the buyers and sellers. Everyone in the market understands precisely what commodity is being traded and the quality and full set of characteristics of the good. Second, the good will trade for a single price in the market. If there are different prices, they reflect quality differentials that all parties to the transaction fully recognize.

Economists have even extended the notion of perfect markets to deal with uncertain outcomes. They define each possible outcome in an uncertain world as a different "state of nature" and would require separate markets for each different state of nature. For example, suppose you were planning a trip to climb a mountain. You would climb the mountain regardless of the weather but you would clearly enjoy

21

your trip more if the weather were nice. Perfect markets in this situation would mean that you could make separate contracts contingent on the weather. For example, you might write a contract with a travel agent in which you would receive a payment from them if it rained during your trip, but you would make a payment if it did not rain. This arrangement would essentially allow you to insure against the adverse outcome of inclement weather. Perfect markets with uncertainty require complete markets for all contingencies.

Unfettered markets should also be free of taxes or other government regulations. In the absence of taxes or subsidies, the amount one pays for any commodity is the full cost of the commodity and this amount flows directly to the seller. With no government regulation, sellers are free to enter or exit the market depending on profitability and buyers can purchase commodities of varying qualities. Moreover, prices are freely set in the market and not subject to any external control.

The market for medical services differs dramatically from the idealized picture of perfect markets in almost every dimension. There is pervasive uncertainty without the corresponding contingent markets (you cannot fully insure against general ill health); individuals rarely pay the cost of the commodities they demand; and there is extensive government control over prices, quality, and entry to the market. All these factors profoundly change the operating characteristics of the market.

Nobel Prize-winning economist Kenneth Arrow first emphasized how uncertainty and lack of contingent markets change the nature of medical practice.[1] There are two types of uncertainty in the medical market. First, there is the simple fact that no one can predict the outcome from any given procedure or treatment. In a world of perfect markets, an individual should be able to purchase full insurance against the possibility that, say, a doctor could not cure his or her migraine headaches. Obviously such detailed markets do not exist, so the individual and the doctor find themselves in a situation in which the outcomes are often out of their control.

The second type of uncertainty is that there is an asymmetry of information. In our age of scientific knowledge and rapid technological advances, even the most informed layman will not have the full knowledge of a specialist. In other economic settings, one-sided information can easily lead to exploitation, and this possibility certainly exists in medical care.

Arrow argued that, in the face of these evident market imperfections, institutions would arise to attempt to offset them. In this case, he proposed, trust and delegation emerged to partly offset information problems. In order to avoid exploitation in the market, a code of ethics developed within the medical profession that imposed certain ethical restrictions on the behavior of doctors.

These restrictions limited the ability of the doctor to practice old-fashioned capitalism. Medical advice, for example, was supposed to be totally divorced from self-interest. Treatment was supposed to be based on "objective conditions" and not on financial or other considerations. Limits on advertising were imposed, allegedly to curb competitive instincts. Nonprofit hospitals proliferated that were supposedly less likely to engage in aggressive competition. In sum, physicians were constrained to avoid aggressive profit-maximizing behavior. This restriction fostered trust on the part of patients and allowed them to delegate medical decisions to doctors. Like Plato's Republic, an ethical elite would govern.

This ethical posture had important consequences for the practice and philosophy of medicine. How could doctors successfully convince patients that they were truly acting in their best interests at all times? Arrow suggested that the "safest course to take is to ... give the socially prescribed 'best treatment' of the day."[2] As we are discovering today, the best treatment in all cases quickly leads to problems of expenditure control.

Today's physicians might be quaintly amused by the picture Arrow paints of doctors and hospitals in an oasis free from competition. Doctors and hospitals operate in a tremendously competitive environment as pressures for cost control emanate from the government, employers, and the public. But Arrow's insight is important; the medical community does share an ethos of best practice and will only reluctantly reconsider its traditional dichotomy between technical issues of treatment and cost concerns.

An important second major departure from the competitive market model is the extensive public and private health insurance for medical care. To be sure, not everyone is covered by insurance, and the 36 million Americans not covered raise sharp challenges to our current system. Yet, most Americans are covered by some plan.

It is not just the presence of insurance but the structure of insurance that is so important. For a typical American, on any single trip to the doctor or hospital, only a fraction of the charges come directly out of pocket. Economists have estimated that in 1987 patients paid an average of only about ten cents on the dollar for hospital costs and twenty-six cents on the dollar for visits to the doctor.[3] The effective price of a visit to the doctor or the hospital is just a fraction of the true cost. Naturally this leads to increased demand for medical services. Yet, individuals purchase insurance precisely so that they do not have to pay the full out-of-pocket costs for each hospital or doctor visit. The mixture of deductibles and cost sharing (coinsurance) remains an important policy issue.

The market for insurance does not fit cleanly into the competitive model. Suppose an insurer provided coverage to a wide group of individuals in the market, including the healthy, the sick, the young, and the old. The average cost or premium for the insurance would reflect the composition of the group. Now imagine another insurer that offers a policy to just the young and healthy. This insurer could easily offer the same insurance at a lower cost because its clients are healthier on average. If the young and the healthy purchase from the second insurer (and why shouldn't they?), the premiums of the remaining individuals will have to increase because the remaining group is less healthy and more likely to incur costs. In some circumstances, insurance for the old and less healthy may cease to exist.

Economists call this phenomenon "adverse selection." All insurance schemes must face this problem in one form or another. Above all, there is no presumption that the market for insurance will work efficiently if left to itself.

Recalling the categories of market failure from Chapter 1, it is clear that medicine is primarily afflicted with the first problem, pervasive uncertainty. Not only is there a general lack of information, but there are also important asymmetries in knowledge in the doctor–patient relationship. Insurance can help to mitigate some of these risks, but the pervasive uncertainty and asymmetry of information also limit the scope of insurance markets.

The other major departure from the free market model is the extensive level of government involvement in all aspects of the medical market. First, government is the largest insurer, with the federal government providing Medicare insurance for the elderly and sharing with the states in providing Medicaid insurance for the poor. As discussed in detail in the next section, increases in medical costs have led the government to employ a variety of intrusive measures to control costs. Since 1984, Medicare has provided a fixed amount in advance to reimburse hospitals for each admission, with the amount determined by an elaborate system of diagnostic related groups (DRGs) that tailor the payment to the medical diagnosis. Essentially, this operates as a form of price controls. In addition, starting in 1992, Medicare began to impose its own schedule of fees for doctors. Compared to prior practice, these fees are higher for primary physicians, such as general practitioners, and lower for surgeons and physicians who use specialized procedures.

Governments also help regulate the supply of doctors and hospitals. In some areas, prior permission has been necessary to start a new medical facility. Governments, in conjunction with medical schools and the American Medical Association, control the supply of physicians by certification requirements, size of medical school classes, and policies toward admission of foreign physicians to the United States.

It is important to assert that some deviations from the competitive ideal are to be expected. Most economists do not worry, say, about the market for breakfast cereal just because some consumers are not informed about the ingredients. But such normal deviations from pure market dynamics do not fundamentally destroy the functioning of these markets. The deviations in the medical area, by contrast, are so great that they easily can cause perverse results from competition.

Imagine, for example, an industry in which consumers paid only a small fee for a service that did not reflect the costs of providing the service and in which the firms were fully reimbursed for the costs they incurred. Suppose that auto repairs were paid more or less automatically by your insurance company. It is not difficult to imagine what would happen. Garages would invest in all types of elaborate equipment to attract customers away from their rivals. There would be an escalating war of expenses as they tried every new bell and whistle in their competitive quest. Consumers would certainly enjoy these new high-quality services, but they probably would not be willing to pay for them if they had to incur the full costs. But if a third party, an insurance company, picks up the tab, why not?

According to insurance executives, this is precisely what happens in the medical industry. As an example, hospitals are rapidly entering the market for organ transplants. Having these facilities provides prestige to the hospital and helps it attract other business. Some health care experts see an explosion in the number of hospitals offering transplant services that would far outstrip the availability of donated organs. An inevitable result of this growth in the number of hospitals with transplant facilities is that large numbers of hospitals will perform relatively few transplants. This trend appears to lead both to excess resources tied up in transplant facilities in hospitals and to questionable quality of care in hospitals that do infrequent transplant operations (practice, after all, makes perfect).

In a normal market, this type of excess capacity would lead to price decreases that would eventually force some competitors out of the market. Industry observers often term this "consolidation." In the medical industry, the forces pushing for such consolidation are limited. The government has little influence over organ transplants because relatively few elderly people have these operations. Insurance companies, which pay the bulk of the costs, are starting to become more aggressive. Prudential Insurance, for example, has begun to direct patients to a limited number of centers where they have negotiated sharp discounts for these operations.[4] Nonetheless, compared to direct competition among hospitals, these forces are very weak.

Medical economists sharply disagree even on the most basic issues. In a competitive market, increases in supply will always lead to a reduction in price. Yet, a number of studies find just the opposite—that increases in the supply of physicians raise prices. For example, Victor Fuchs found that the greater the number of surgeons per capita, the more operations they would perform and the higher would be the price. Similarly, Joseph Newhouse found that prices and the number of general practitioners per capita were positively correlated.[5]

These findings do not necessarily mean that a policy to increase supply would raise prices. It is possible that the studies failed to control for a factor that increased demand—for example, the superior quality of the physicians in large cities. Demand for medical services would be higher in large urban areas with their higher-quality physicians and lead to higher prices for health care. If the studies failed to control for this factor, they would incorrectly attribute the higher prices to the greater supply of physicians in urban areas. Despite this possibility, medical economists have devoted considerable time to trying to determine if greater supply increases prices and, if it does, what mechanism is operating.

Two theories have been developed to explain the perceived positive relation between prices and supply. The first theory, known as the "target income hypothesis" suggests that as more physicians come into an area, existing physicians respond by generating more business for themselves. They can do so because their informational advantage over patients allows them to encourage more visits and marginal treatments. Critics of the theory wonder why apparently greedy doctors wait until new entrants come into the market before they increase the demand for own services.

Another theory is based on reputation. Suppose that as more doctors enter an area, it is more difficult to obtain information about any one doctor because fewer of your neighbors or friends now visit the same doctor. With less information about other doctors, you may be less willing to change doctors if your doctor's prices increase. Because patients become less price sensitive in such a market, all doctors can safely raise their prices. Thus greater supply through diminished reputations can lead to increases in prices.

Suspicions about free markets in medicine are certainly abundant. However, we must not stop with considerations of market failure. We must also consider the three key components of political failure as well: an intense preoccupation with equity, a proliferation of experts (i.e., asymmetric political information), and intense political lobbying.

Some Background on Medical Costs and Health

The projections for future expenditures on health in the United States can only be described as frightening. Currently, about 14 percent of GNP is devoted to the health sector, up from about 5 percent before World War II. Government projections estimate that by the year 2000 this figure will increase to approximately 18 percent.[6]

The share of any sector in GNP grows only because expenditures in that sector grow at a faster rate than the rest of GNP. From 1947 to 1987, expenditures in the health sector grew 2.5 percent faster than the rest of the economy. In the latter half of that period, the excess growth of the health sector was even faster, 3.0 percent.

Looking back over this period, it is possible to decompose the excess growth into two components: excess growth in prices (that is, higher inflation in medical care) and excess growth in the quantity or the usages of services. Stanford economist Victor Fuchs estimates that two thirds of the excess growth arose because of excess inflation in the medical care sector, while the remaining one third was from increased usage. These estimates should be treated cautiously. First, increases in the demand for services could have indirectly caused a substantial portion of the increases in prices as the medical sector had to offer higher prices to draw resources away from other sectors of the economy. Inflation in the medical sector cannot be separated from increased demand for its services. Second, expenditure in the health care industry can be accurately measured, but decompositions into price and quantity changes require accurate price indexes. As in all service industries, it is very difficult to measure quality changes. Thus, some of the measured inflation may be improvements in the quality of delivered services.

Nevertheless, thinking separately about excess price and quantity movements provides a useful device for discussing some of the factors leading to the excess growth of expenditure on the health sector. On the price side, growth in the wages of medical personnel and changes in productivity are the two most important factors.

During the entire postwar era, wages of nonphysicians in the health care industry grew more rapidly than wages in the rest of the economy. From 1977 to 1987, wages in the health care sector grew in real terms, while wages in other sectors were falling. The net income of physicians also grew rapidly in this period.

Productivity growth in service industries is less rapid than in manufacturing or agriculture, partly because there is less opportunity for substituting machines for people in delivering services. Productivity growth in health care was substantially lower than in other sectors of the economy. While output in the health care sector grew approximately 1 percent faster than the rest of the economy, employment grew 2.6 percent more rapidly.[7] Thus, output per worker, or labor productivity, grew more slowly in the health care industry than the rest of the economy.

One factor that is sometimes cited to explain lagging productivity is the increase in necessary record keeping that has been required in medicine. This increase arises from two sources. First, detailed records are increasingly required as insurers and other third parties place increasing scrutiny on medical practices. Second, with the threat of malpractice suits always lurking in the background, doctors feel the need to keep detailed records of the treatment of their patients. Malpractice suits rose during the postwar period; hence, more paperwork was needed.

As with price growth, on the quantity side the increase in usage can be attributed to a number of different factors, including increasing demand for care as income grows, the aging of the population, the growth of insurance and third-party payments, and new technological developments that offer additional care options to patients. The quantitative effects of all of these factors are controversial.

In particular, there is considerable disagreement over the role of the elderly in contributing to the demand for medical care. This debate is extremely important because of the rapid growth in the proportion of the elderly population in the next several decades. Between now and the year 2050, the share of the population over 65 will increase from 9 percent to close to 25 percent; the "super-elderly," over 85, now at 1 percent of the population, are estimated to be 5 percent by 2050.

Some investigators have minimized the impact of the growth of the elderly population by examining utilization figures by age at the current time and then projecting them into the future when the age distribution changes. For example, using this method, the Health Care Financing Administration estimates that the change in the age distribution between the years 1986 and 2026 will contribute about .8 percent per year toward additional expenditure for health care.[8] Others offer even lower estimates; William Schwartz, in a discussion of health costs, cites a figure of .2 percent per year between 1987 and the year 2000.[9] In other words, if everyone uses health care at today's proportions, the future increase caused by an aging population is only significant over a period of very many years.

But estimates based on the assumption of constant relative utilization by the elderly may be extremely misleading. Over the last twenty years, the growth of medical expenditures by the elderly on a per capita basis has exceeded the rest of the population by 1.5 percent a year.[10] While the introduction of Medicare and Medicaid coverage may have contributed to this trend, the differential per capita demand for care rose even more sharply following 1976, after government-sponsored insurance coverage had been well established. With a radical change in the role of the elderly in our society, any past projections must be treated rather cautiously. Recall that estimates for the catastrophic health insurance law changed dramatically when seemingly minor changes were made in some of the provisions for nursing home care.

Projections about the future are always speculative, especially in an area in which new technological developments and social trends will surely change the picture. It is clear, however, that in the medium term—the next ten to fifteen years—the share of expenditure on medical care will continue to rise and the possibility remains for even more dramatic increases. This possibly would be acceptable if we were certain that there were true benefits from this additional expenditure. But, unfortunately, the links between health and expenditure are far from direct.

From the nineteenth century to the 1930s, there was a tremendous improvement in the health of Americans. Infant mortality rates fell dramatically. Mortality from other feared diseases, such as tuberculosis, influenza, pneumonia, and diphtheria, also decreased sharply. Virtually none of this decline had anything to do with the practice of medicine. As Jerome Avorn points out, most of the familiar modern medical interventions stem from the second half of the century: antibiotics (widespread use only after World War II), cardiac pacemakers and kidney dialysis (1960s), and coronary heart surgery (1970s).[11] The real hero in this dramatic change in health status was the rise in real incomes that brought better nutrition, water free of sewage, more adequate housing, and better sanitation practices.

Once an economy has reached a certain level of economic development, health becomes only loosely related to income but more closely related to lifestyle patterns. This point was brought out dramatically by Victor Fuchs in a comparison of the health of citizens of Utah and Nevada during the 1960s. The residents of these two Western states had similar degrees of income, education, and urbanization. But Fuchs pointed out that there were dramatic differences in their health. Infant mortality rates were 40 percent higher in Nevada. At other ages, the effects were even greater. For females between the ages of 40–49, the death rate in Nevada was 69 percent greater than Utah.[12]

The explanation for these vast differences did not lie in medical practice. The number of physicians and hospital beds per capita were roughly the same. The difference was in the lifestyles of residents of the two states. Utah was dominated by Mormons, and cigarette and alcohol consumption were relatively low. The Mormon religion stresses stable family life. Nevada, on the other hand, was the mecca for gambling and attracted a less stable and more restless population. Cigarette and alcohol consumption were significantly higher than in Utah. Family relations were also much less stable in Nevada.

Has all our high-tech medicine and expensive care produced anything? Life expectancy increased throughout this century but appeared to plateau in the 1950s and 1960s. By the mid-1950s life expectancy for men appeared stable at 67 years, while there were only slight increases in the lifespans of females. But in 1968, lifespans started to increase again. By 1986 they had increased to 71.3 years for men and 74.8 years for both sexes combined. Lifestyle changes (less smoking and lower-fat diets) probably were part of the reason but so were the interventions of high-tech medicine.

But the increase in life expectancy may not be all good news. It is quite possible that these extra years will be spent in pain and ill-health. Gerontologists are sharply split on this issue. On the one hand there are those who find decreases in mortality associated with increases in morbidity (sickness). In an article entitled "Longer Life But Worsening Health?" Louise Verbrugge found that for a number of killer conditions such as heart disease, diabetes, and hypertension there were distinct trends toward lower mortality rates but rising rates of morbidity (prolonged ill health) in the population. Verbrugge discusses a number of factors that could have contributed to this trend, including more awareness of chronic diseases and a greater social acceptance of individuals claiming disabilities. But she also puts considerable emphasis on improved survival as a cause of increased morbidity. "As mortality rates drop, some people are 'rescued' from death and remain among the living. Most of these 'new survivors' are ill with chronic diseases, though not as ill as those who died. By staying alive longer, they have more years to develop other chronic conditions, both killers and non-killers."[13] She also notes in support of this view that morbidity changes were most dramatic in the 1970s at the same time that changes in mortality were most pronounced.

Other researchers have also drawn pessimistic conclusions. A Canadian statistician noted that from 1951 to 1978, life expectancy increased in Canada by about six years. About half of that gain also appears to have been associated with disabilities of varying severity. One estimate for the United States was even more pessimistic, with three out of every four additional years of life plagued by disabilities.[14]

Avorn notes that not all of the elderly become chronically ill. "It is as if the health of older Americans has been ratcheted up a notch or two in recent decades. While on the one hand, this results in an improvement in health for the non-ill elderly, on the other hand, this ratcheting up will cause many chronically ill people, who otherwise would have died, to remain one notch below death." He notes that a rising tide lifts all boats equally, "including those that otherwise might be resting at the bottom of the harbor."[15]

But there are also optimists, the most prominent of whom is James Fries. Fries developed a "compression of morbidity" thesis that has two essential components. First, better health practices can delay the onset of chronic illness. Second, these same health practices will not appreciably lengthen the lifespan beyond a certain point. Since illness is delayed but life is not extended, the period of sickness or morbidity is compressed.[16]

Underlying Fries's theory is a picture of death. If an individual survives the normal hazards of life to live to old age, he or she will find that, at a certain point, all the life systems will simultaneously fail. People will not die from any illness as such but simply from old age. In support of this view, he cites studies of the elderly that have found it difficult to pinpoint specific pathologies in a significant fraction of cases. Similar studies on long-lived rats had similar conclusions.[17] Fries currently estimates the biological average maximum life span for humans at 85 years.

Fries points to a number of different pieces of evidence in support of his thesis. He notes that differences in male and female life expectancies have started to narrow. This would be expected if males began to engage in fewer risky health practices (less smoking, better diets) and males and females had the same biological lifespan. He also cites a number of studies that find greater effects from lifestyle changes on postponing illness than decreasing mortality.

Future medical expenditures will be highly sensitive to which view of the process of death is correct. If the pessimists are correct, we will see increasing numbers of the elderly in chronic ill health and requiring expensive high-tech medical care. Moreover, this process will continue over time as new death-postponing technologies become available. Nursing home expenses will also increase dramatically.

If the optimists are correct, average life-expectancy will gradually reach a peak and the elderly will spend fewer years suffering from chronic conditions. Age-specific morbidity rates will eventually fall and medical costs for the elderly will not continue to escalate.

Current Trends in the Health Industry

When Kenneth Arrow wrote his article in the 1960s about the health care industry, doctors were sheltered from the world of competition. A doctor or hospital struggling today with third-party reviews or Medicare regulation might dream of the benign environment depicted by Arrow. Competition and regulation has dramatically changed the environment for physicians and hospitals.

Historically, medical insurance developed in this country with Blue

Cross and Blue Shield. Blue Cross was developed and supported by hospitals and promised total hospital care for subscribers. Blue Shield was developed by physicians, and together these programs provided insurance for both physician and hospital visits. These programs did not compete across state lines and received regulatory and tax advantages from the states and federal government. In compensation for these advantages, these insurers were required to take actions in the public interest such as offering policies to individuals at rates set by the states.

In 1977, the Blues and commercial insurers roughly split the market.[18] While some commercial insurers offered plans that featured coinsurance (consumers paying part of their bills) and other cost-sharing mechanisms, the plans that the Blues offered did not feature much cost-sharing. Some investigators have argued that this led to higher medical costs.

Doctors had traditionally offered their services on a fee-for-service basis. They had resisted capitation plans—that is, plans under which doctors would be paid a fixed amount per patient for the entire year. If there were no third-party insurance, both payment schemes would promote economic efficiency in their own way. Under a fee-for-service scheme, consumers would carefully weigh the costs of an extra visit to the doctor; under capitation schemes, doctors would carefully examine the need for additional tests and procedures. But with total third-party insurance, fee-for-service mechanisms break down. Consumers do not care about additional visits to the doctor, while doctors can err on the side of excess caution (i.e., maximum tests and treatments).

Spurred by increases in medical costs, employers began to seek new arrangements that could reduce their growing burden. This trend led to a number of important innovations in the health care industry in the 1980s. First, a larger number of insurers began to offer policies that featured deductibles and coinsurance. These stipulations work to reduce consumer demand, but there are natural limits to this process as consumers do not wish to bear excess risks.

A major innovation was the growth of health maintenance organizations (HMOs). From 1977 to 1987, they increased their share of the market from 2.5 to 11.5 percent. HMOs are essentially capitation plans that provide complete coverage for physician and hospital expenses. One study found that they can deliver care at a cost up to 25 percent less than providers with full insurance operating on a fee-for-service basis.[19] This saving was accomplished through eliminating useless services and unnecessary hospital days. The HMOs were not, however, substantially less costly than plans under which patients faced significant deductibles and coinsurance.

The 1980s also witnessed the growth of "managed care" and utilization review, which often occur within a network of doctors known as preferred provider organizations (PPOs). A PPO provides services at reduced fees to subscribers as long as patients use the services of doctors and hospitals within the organization. In many cases, individuals must see primary physicians who act as the gatekeepers for access to specialists and testing. Decisions by the physicians to seek additional care for their patients are reviewed regularly either by employees of the PPO or, in some cases, by outside firms that specialize in utilization review. PPOs without managed care systems do exist, but competitive forces increasingly push in this direction.

Corporations have taken an increasingly aggressive role in seeking reduced health care costs. In large part, their efforts are due to the rapid rise in health costs as a component of compensation and to the critical role it has played in collective bargaining decisions. Employees of New York's telephone company successfully fought to prevent management from making them pay part of their health care insurance. College professors at Temple University in Philadelphia were less successful. One estimate by unions was that over 30 percent of all their job actions concerned health insurance. Large employers aggressively shop around for health care providers and regularly add and delete coverage options for their employees. Uncompetitive HMOs and commercial insurers can easily disappear under this competition. Health insurers have also taken actions to reduce costs. The General Accounting Office found that insurance companies refused to pay for cancer drugs that they deemed to be unproven.

As the largest payer of insurance claims, the federal government has aggressively attempted to rein in health costs. The initial innovation was a prospective payment system (PPS) for hospital care under Medicare based on diagnoses of conditions, the DRG (diagnostic related groups) system. Under this system, the government pays a fixed sum to a hospital for the care of a patient depending on the diagnostic group to which that patient is assigned. The payment is adjusted for other factors such as local wage rates, teaching obligations of the hospital, provision of care for the poor, and whether the hospital is rural or urban. This system, initiated in 1984, was a sharp change from prior practice in which the government reimbursed audited expenses of the hospital.

The prospective payment system is a sophisticated form of price controls. In the initial years, the reimbursement rates were high and the hospitals profited from the arrangements. In subsequent years, the reimbursement rates have been less generous. In an overall examination of the system, Louise Russell argued that this system reduced the growth of hospital costs relative to what had been predicted before introduction of the controls.[20] Other analysts were less sanguine about the efficiency of the DRG system. First, although expenditures did decrease from predicted values, there was also an unexplained decrease in hospital admissions in 1984. This finding is ironic because most analysts predicted an increase in admissions because they believed hospitals would take advantage of the DRG system to run patients through the hospital to increase their profits. The drop in admissions remains unexplained and thus may be unrelated to the new reimbursement system. It thus seems inappropriate to give the prospective payment system credit for this decrease in costs.

The analysts also pointed out that when reimbursement rates were high in the early years, hospitals were able to increase their capital equipment. Thus, they were able to operate quite profitably even in subsequent years when the reimbursement rates, on the surface, were not as generous. With this ambiguous evidence, it is not obvious that the prospective payment system has effectively reduced costs.

A major issue that emerged was the extent to which the quality of care changed in response to the system. In anticipation of these concerns, professional review organizations (PROs) were set up in each hospital to monitor the quality of treatment. Hospitals apparently responded to the prospective payment system by reducing average days in the hospital for each patient. Emphasis then shifted to home care and nursing home care. One study found that a higher proportion of individuals were discharged to nursing homes after hospitalization and still remained in the homes from six months to a year after discharge. This finding perhaps indicates that there was a decrease in the quality of care within the hospital after the introduction of the system. Unfortunately, very little is known about the effectiveness of alternative treatments, so making assessments of the quality of care is very difficult.

Over the long run, the quality of care will be determined largely by the degree to which Congress and the administration decide to fund the system. Since Medicare spending is a large fraction of the budget, it is also a tempting target for deficit reduction measures. The budget agreement reached for fiscal year 1991 contained $30 billion in cuts to Medicare providers (doctors and hospitals) over five years. The language accompanying the agreement said that these would be cuts in "unnecessary services." Louise Russell felt that when the program was introduced, economies could be found but worried about the long run: "Over the longer term, the loss (in quality) may become more noticeable as the incentives of prospective payment, and the limits placed on hospital resources, have more time to play themselves out."[21] Some analysts doubt whether the prospective payment system will ever be used aggressively to reduce costs. Members of Congress generally have only a limited number of hospitals in their districts and are likely to be strong advocates in protecting these units. There are already special rules for rural hospitals, teaching hospitals, and hospitals that have a large number of poor patients. If Congress can effectively protect hospitals by creating similar exceptions, even apparently tight controls on reimbursement will not be effective.

The federal government through Medicare and Medicaid will continue to exert great control on the medical sector. Controls over reimbursement will affect capital costs for new medical facilities. As part of the 1989 Medicare legislation, Congress decided to change the manner in which it compensated physicians under Medicare. Under the previous system, Medicare paid the lowest of "customary, actual, and reasonable" charges for services. The new system that began in 1992 uses a complex scale to pay physicians that increases payments to physicians who primarily use their cognitive and diagnostic skills and decreases payments to physicians who primarily use procedures (such as surgeons). For example, office visits for a new patient rose from $40 to $47, but payments for the insertion of a pacemaker fell from $811 to $684. In addition, the new rules place sharp limits on the extent to which physicians can charge amounts greater than the Medicare reimbursements. When the system is fully phased in, physicians effectively will be limited to charging patients no more than 10 percent above Medicare reimbursement levels. Thus, there will be tight price controls for any physicians treating any patients covered by Medicare.[22]

What led the government to this seemingly radical system of price controls for doctors? In what way was the market system not functioning correctly? Among many medical economists there was a general belief that existing compensation arrangements paid too much for procedure-oriented medicine. Often, when a new procedure was introduced, the procedure was difficult and costly, and payments from Medicare and other insurers reflected these costs. Over time, as the procedure became more routine and less costly, the fees did not fall, partly because Medicare paid "customary" fees that traditionally had been high. The government created a Physician Payment Review Commission to develop a new fee schedule with these difficulties in mind.

The new fee schedules rely on both a "relative value scale" for physician payments and adjustments for the costs of practice in various geographical areas. The relative value scale is an attempt to arrive at proper physician fees. Developed at Harvard by a team of medical economists, the scheme sets the relative scales based on assessments of time that physicians spend with patients, the difficulties of skills necessary in each specialty, and the time needed to train for a specialty.

This is an audacious undertaking whose historical antecedents include the labor theory of value and Marxian economics; it is a conceptual sister to the principle of comparable worth. Imagine paying baseball players according to the time it takes to train for a position, the relative difficulty of playing first base rather than the outfield, and the relative unpleasantness of being a catcher rather than a second baseman. As in this hypothetical payment scheme for baseball players, there is no adjustment for individual quality among doctors.

The designers of this new fee schedule were worried that when fees for procedures were cut, physicians would respond by generating more business—for example, surgeons would increase their number of operations. To safeguard against the possibility, the law calls for "volume performance standards." These performance standards are nothing but expenditure caps. If total expenditures exceed the expenditure caps, fees will be reduced in subsequent years. Initially, the Physician Payment Review Commission had built into its initial fee schedule a 50 percent offset; that is, if fees were cut by 10 percent they would anticipate an increase in volume of 5 percent. After some vehement protests by physician groups, these offsets were reduced but not eliminated. No adjustments were made for those physicians whose fees were increased. This is another example of the strange world of medical economics. In most industries we would expect suppliers whose prices were cut to reduce supply and those whose prices were increased to increase supply. But even in designing a price control system, medical economics seems to work backwards.

As with all price control schemes, there are limits to its effectiveness without serious changes in resource use. Hospitals may only reluctantly offer certain procedures or find ways to avoid taking certain patients unless they receive sufficient compensation. Changing payment schedules for physicians ultimately will change the quality of individuals attracted to the specialties and to medicine in general. As with all price control schemes, there eventually will be reductions in quality that are not captured by prices.

Increased competitive pressures from managed care, HMOs, utilization reviews, and government controls on hospital and physician fees potentially can reduce medical costs to some degree. Clearly, we would all welcome the end of unnecessary testing and hospitalization, overall defensive medicine, and padding of charges and bills. Yet, even if we changed all care today to the most efficient practice, there would be only limited gains.

Gains from more efficient practice are limited because they are essentially one-time gains. They do nothing to restrain the long-term rate of growth of costs in the system. As efficiency gains are made, they will reduce costs temporarily, but longer-term growth trends will resume. HMOs may be more efficient, but the growth rate of their costs does not differ from other providers.[23] To make progress on health costs in the long run, we must tackle the rate of growth of health care costs.

The Technology Spiral

In a classic assessment of economic growth, Nobel Prize-winning economist Robert M. Solow tried to determine how much of economic growth could be accounted for by the growth in the resources used in production, such as the labor force and capital. He came to the startling conclusion that they only accounted for one-third of measured economic growth. The remaining two-thirds he attributed to technical progress. Economists have reexamined this finding many times, and all conclude that technical progress is certainly a principal component of economic growth.

Medical science, of course, has also witnessed rapid technological advances and improvements in knowledge. Today, a world without antibiotics would be frightening. How would professional sports teams (and amateur athletes, for that matter) operate in a world without arthroscopic surgery? New heart surgery techniques have made coronary bypass operations quite common.

Some technological developments can reduce costs. For example, automated clinical chemical analyzers can save on labor costs from extensive tests. But the vast majority of our technological advances raise costs. A recent study suggested, for example, that Medicare costs were increased about $40 million by new diagnostic imaging techniques and $81 million by blood clot dissolving agents.[24] New drugs are also very costly. Now that AZT has shown some promise in the treatment of AIDS, we face the prospect of spending potentially $5 billion annually just for this drug.[25] A new drug that is very effective against schizophrenia costs nearly $9000 per year per patient. As our biomedical knowledge rapidly multiplies and as the latest spinoffs from computer technology permeate our lives, an infinite stream of further advances seems possible.

In most areas of life we welcome technological advances. Yet many of us fear future progress in medicine if it leads to elaborate and expensive treatments with very little true benefit for overall health. Is there any rational basis for this fear? How can an increase in knowledge and in technological possibilities make us worse off?

In a world with pervasive insurance, improvements in technology can sometimes make us worse off. Suppose, for example, an individual had an insurance policy with some deductibles and coinsurance but with complete protection against catastrophic illness. Any expenses over, say, $1000 would be covered fully by the insurance. Now suppose a new technology is developed that is very useful in a rare disabling (but nonfatal) disease. This technology, however, is very expensive and treatment costs $1,000,000.

Before this treatment was available, the individual had to pay an insurance premium that covered expected costs. At that time, an individual who contracted the rare disease would not be able to be cured. After the discovery of the new technology, the individual could be cured. Because the insurance policy would pay the vast majority of charges, all the expenses over $1000, the individual surely would want the treatment. It appears that the individual is better off.

But, over time, the insurance premium would have to rise to compensate for the extraordinarily expensive treatment that is now available. Thus, in the vast majority of cases in which individuals do not contract this disease, they will be paying additional large premiums.

This result is really no different than paying additional taxes to support the lifestyle of an indulgent king. The only difference is that you have a small probability of becoming the indulgent king (contracting the disease).

If individuals did not know whether they eventually would contract this rare disease, they might prefer to banish the new technology. They might prefer to enjoy the extra money from lower premiums and take a chance that the disease may not befall them. Their response would depend on their attitudes toward risks and money. At some point, almost all individuals would prefer banishing the technology if the costs were sufficiently high.[26]

This story may not be just an academic fable. Although the links between technology and insurance have only begun to be explored, there are clearly some direct interactions.[27] First, new technologies increase the demand for insurance. If there were fewer expensive treatments available, the total need for insurance would be substantially less. Probably more important is that the presence of insurance leads to additional technological innovations. As long as insurance is available, entrepreneurs and high-tech researchers can safely invest their time and dollars in innovations that promise results but are very costly. Biomedical researchers pursuing new drugs also will allocate time and resources to developing expensive products. As long as the market is there for these innovations and is not really constrained by cost, high-cost innovations will be forthcoming.

In other areas of the economy, technical research is often conducted with an eventual goal of cost reducing or profit making. Medical research more closely resembles Pentagon-sponsored research during a military spending binge.

From a social point of view, new procedures should only be introduced when their marginal or incremental benefits exceed their incremental costs. The medical world operates on a very different principle: procedures are introduced when they have positive marginal benefits even if these benefits are less than marginal costs. This means that resources are utilized in medical care even when they are more valuable elsewhere in society.

This ethos of ignoring costs and pursuing all technologies that produce some benefits is deeply ingrained in the medical system. For example, one doctor, complaining about the intrusive nature of Medicare, bemoaned that "for budgetary reasons, only acceptable rather than ideal care is likely to be authorized under national health insurance."[28] How would the doctor define "ideal care"? Presumably as the treatment that is best for the patient's health, regardless of expense. If a diagnostic method produces marginally more reliable results but is dramatically more expensive, the extra cost is irrelevant in determining "ideal care."

This thinking has also been ingrained in our legal system. In an important court case, *Wickline v. California,* the appellate court ruled that third-party payers could be held liable if they denied care and the patient was harmed. The case involved California MediCal (Medicaid), which had denied extended hospital days to a patient. Subsequently, the patient's leg became infected and had to be amputated. The court, while ruling against the patient in this case, did find that third parties could be held responsible for denying benefits, even if the costs of treatment exceeded the benefits.

The court wrote that the benefits entitled to patients should be based on the "usual standards of medical practice in the community." Furthermore, the court also proclaimed that although "we recognize, realistically, that cost consciousness has become a permanent feature of the health care system, it is essential that cost limitation progress not be permitted to corrupt medical judgment."[29] Appeals courts in California have upheld that private third-party insurers can be held liable for actions that result in death or injury. Future courts must interpret when further decisions, perhaps by hospitals or third parties, "corrupt medical judgments." But do these precedents mean that if a new technology that provides some marginal benefit becomes available, third parties will be forced to pay for its use?

As Daniel Callahan has pointed out, there is also an important connection between new technology and use by the elderly. Kidney dialysis was first developed with younger patients in mind (ages 15–50) and this limited market was one of the reasons that Congress supported the program. But now over 30 percent of those on dialysis are over 65. Callahan points to other technologies that have followed a similar pattern, including mechanical ventilation, artificial resuscitation, and artificial nutrition.[30] With Medicare paying the costs for these treatments, new technologies can reach larger and larger numbers of chronically ill patients. Costly interventions that might be reasonable for a younger person, may not be justified for the chronically ill elderly.

The Elderly and Rationing of Care

The elderly consume a large fraction of the health dollar. Medicare is the single largest payer of claims in the country. Currently, over 1 percent of our GNP is devoted to medical care for individuals in the last year of their life. Because the proportion of elderly will grow so dramatically in the next several decades, there naturally has been increasing concern about medical care for the aged.

Daniel Callahan, a medical ethicist, triggered sharp controversy in his book *Setting Limits,* where he advocated the rationing of care to the elderly. Henry Aaron and William Schwartz have studied the process by which care has been rationed in Great Britain.

Before discussing their findings, it is important to be clear on one point. The price system naturally rations goods and services. If the price of a commodity increases, fewer individuals will buy the commodity. This principle is a natural element of the market system. By *rationing,* however, we mean denying individuals the ability to obtain a commodity or service by either refusing to sell it at any price or, in the case of medical care, refusing to provide insurance coverage for treatment.

Henry Aaron and William Schwartz believe that rationing eventually will have to apply to all segments of society, not just the elderly. But how will this system work in practice? To gain some insight into this issue, they looked at the health care system in Great Britain. To measure rationing, they compared technologies and treatments that were commonly used in the United States but were limited in Great Britain. They asked two basic questions: what types of procedures were rationed, and how, in practice, did people accept this rationing?[31]

Aaron and Schwartz found several interesting patterns in the decisions concerning the types of procedures and categories of individuals that were rationed. Services that used specific capital equipment and specialized staff were easier to ration than those that could be provided at any hospital. Services that patients knew little about because they were new were also rationed. Procedures for the elderly were much more likely to be rationed than for others. Cancer treatments were an exception, and Aaron and Schwartz argued that this was because cancer is a very visible and terrifying disease.

Two other important generalizations also emerged from their investigations. Procedures that were likely to claim a greater share of the health budget were much more likely to be rationed than those that would claim a smaller share. Finally, procedures that promised a higher quality of life after treatment were also less likely to be rationed. All of these generalizations seem quite reasonable and understandable. They do not, however, pass any rigorous cost–benefit tests.

Perhaps the most interesting questions are how rationing works in practice and how individuals come to accept this as part of the course. The key to rationing lies in the fact that access to all hospital and advanced care must be through a primary physician who acts as gatekeeper. The primary physician knows the system and which advanced procedures have long waiting lists and which ones would eventually be denied to certain individuals. Through interactions with patients, the physician can influence expectations about what types of care are likely or unlikely. For many patients, expectations formed at this stage influence their demands for care. Not all patients will be satisfied by the judgment of a primary physician. Some will try to work the system and obtain direct access to a specialist, and others will seek treatment in the private sectors that coexist (even in the hospitals) with the state system.

In the United States, recent discussions of rationing have focused on a proposed Oregon plan that would extend medical treatment to a much larger group of the poor but limit the operations and procedures that would be allowed. In brief, their proposed plan develops a master list of procedures and programs and ranks these by cost and effectiveness. This list would be used to decide which treatments would be available to the poor and which ones would not. The cutoff point for treatments and procedures would depend on the budget for Medicaid. The plan has the virtue of extending care to the entire group of the poor, but it does so by limiting the types of treatment that are available.

The Oregon plan naturally has come under strong criticism. Indeed, it was at least temporarily prohibited by the federal government, which must approve changes in Medicaid, because it was perceived to discriminate against the disabled. Other critics argued that only the politically powerless were included in the plan because the elderly were excluded. The state has responded by attempting to modify the plan to meet federal objections. They continue to point out that they are trying to extend their tax dollars to the entire population of the poor and not only to the 40 percent they cover now.

Interestingly, Aaron and Schwartz also have attacked the plan.[32]

Their main point is that the proposed classifications are much too crude and fail to take into account the varying severity of illnesses or other patient-specific characteristics. As an example, individuals with kidney failure are all lumped together, despite the fact that age, response to dialysis, and related diseases are all key factors in determining whether a treatment is appropriate. Even prenatal care, which is given a very high ranking in the plan, needs closer scrutiny as there are limits to the number of beneficial visits.

Are these simply initial glitches in the plan, or are all systematic attempts to draw explicit lines going to fail? Perhaps the key in Britain is that there is a general silence, indeed a social obfuscation, about aspects of the problem. No one talks explicitly about the rationing of care. In the United States, would people be willing to get by with social obfuscation? Advocate groups, lawyers, and politicians will insure that we will not. Aaron and Schwartz, Callahan, and the Oregon plan have all initiated a long debate on the topic.

Another Problem: The Uninsured

The cost escalation in the health system would be bad enough even if everyone were covered with health insurance. But about 36 million Americans do not have any insurance at all. While the government supplies insurance through Medicare and Medicaid and some people buy health insurance on their own, the majority of the insured derive their benefits either through their own employer or the employer of a member of the family.

The tax system encourages employers to provide insurance coverage as part of overall compensation by excluding these benefits from employees' taxable income. Yet, despite this incentive, not all firms provide health insurance. There are a number of reasons for this. Small firms or individuals typically find coverage more expensive because the insurance companies have less scope for risk spreading and worry about the poor risk profiles from employees of small firms. A second reason is that health insurance is a relatively large percentage of the compensation for low-wage workers, who may prefer direct payments over fringe benefits. This factor is particularly important for part-time workers. One statistic emphasizes the importance of employer-provided health insurance. If all family members of employed workers were insured, the number of uninsured would drop by 85 percent.[33]

The profile of the uninsured is somewhat surprising. All demographic groups have over 70 percent of their population covered by health insurance. The elderly, through Medicare, have virtually universal coverage. Employees of small firms, the unemployed, and those with incomes less than 150 percent of the poverty line are all disproportionately represented among the uninsured. For example, 27 percent of this latter group lack insurance. Still, 10 percent of all full-time workers do not have insurance.

The presence of a significant percentage of uninsured poses social problems beyond the obvious hazards to the uninsured themselves. When individuals lack insurance, they typically forego preventive care. When they become very ill, they tend to go to emergency room clinics where care is expensive. And because they failed to seek care early in their illness, costly complications often ensue. Pregnant women who do not have adequate prenatal care give birth to babies who also require more expensive medical interventions.[34]

Some of these additional costs are carried by public agencies and some by charity. But some fraction of these costs is passed through to the rest of the health system and raises rates for insurance. As insurance rates rise, some individuals opt not to buy insurance, thereby exacerbating the problem.

Many people believe that all the poor are covered under Medicaid; however, this is a misconception. Unlike Medicare, which applies nationally, Medicaid is a joint federal–state program in which states have considerable discretion. States must offer hospital care, physician services, and other specified care to certain groups in the population. These groups include AFDC recipients (mothers of dependent children), recipients of SSI (a part of social security that pays benefits to the poor, blind, and disabled) and several other smaller groups. The states may extend benefits to the "medical needy" and, within limits, decide on rules for determining who is needy. The federal government reimburses the states from between roughly 50 to 75 percent of costs.

The provision of services under Medicaid varies considerably between states both in the services and the percentage of the poor who are covered. For example, most states require individuals to sell their assets before they can qualify for nursing home care. Six states, however, do not require the elderly to sell their homes before obtaining coverage under Medicaid. Only 40 percent of the poor qualify for Medicaid and the percentage varies between states. Moreover, states have differing policies for the length of stays in hospitals and for copayments. In 1986, the nationwide average expenditure for a resident of a state was $169, but this figure varied from $462 in New York to $63 in Wyoming.[35]

Coverage for those eligible for Medicaid is also effectively limited because many physicians refuse to see Medicaid patients. Reimbursement rates for hospital and physicians are determined by the states and can be as low as one half the level of payments under Medicare. Hospitals and physicians claim that the reimbursement rates for these patients fall short of their costs. For a doctor, the "costs" of seeing a patient depend on the revenue the doctor could obtain by seeing non-Medicaid patients and, in this sense (what economists call "opportunity costs"), their costs do exceed Medicaid fees. Medicaid patients have been denied access to care by some doctors and hospitals, but the extent varies across the country and by medical specialty.

The practice of states paying lower fees to Medicaid providers may end. The U.S. Supreme Court ruled in 1990 that Medicaid providers could sue if the payments they received were too low. Over time, as more providers bring lawsuits, states will be forced to raise their payments; however, they will respond in part by trimming nonrequired services and by reducing the proportion of their poor population that has coverage. The states will be squeezed by both the courts and the federal government, which has been increasing their mandates. For example, states now must provide coverage to families for one year after they leave welfare and to pregnant women and children whose incomes can exceed the poverty line.

Some of the difficulties that the states are facing can be illustrated by the recent experience of New Jersey. Insurance rates for health care had been skyrocketing, and proposed rate increases for 1991 for Blue Cross/Blue Shield were 50 percent for individuals and 25 percent for families. As costs rose, a significant proportion of individuals became uninsured and sought treatments directly in hospitals. Hospital bills were taxed to provide for an Uncompensated Care Trust fund that covered the bills of the uninsured. But the trust fund had a large and growing debt, and there was a general belief that the entire situation had spiralled out of control. A task force recently proposed some dramatic changes in New Jersey's system, including a new payroll tax to subsidize insurance purchases and shifting the care of Medicaid recipients to HMOs. But politicians in New Jersey are nervous about imposing additional taxes on a tax-conscious public.

The New Jersey experience illustrates the problems facing us in medical care today. Cost and coverage are both problems. There have been numerous proposals to modify or, in some cases, dramatically change our health care system. All proposals must be evaluated in terms of their theoretical effectiveness in meeting the goals of reducing long-term costs and increasing coverage. They also must be judged in terms of their ability to fit into the American political system.

The Search for Reform

The Canadian Health Care System

In recent years, there has been considerable interest in the Canadian health care system. It provides universal care for residents of Canada and recent surveys indicate that 81 percent of the population is either "very" satisfied or "quite" satisfied with the system. It also apparently has been able to control costs. In 1960, Canada spent slightly more as a percentage of GNP on the health sector (5.5 versus 5.3 percent), but by 1987 the United States was spending 11.2 percent while Canada's expenditures were 8.6 percent. Have they achieved the best of all possible worlds?[36]

The Canadian health system is funded jointly by the federal government and the ten provinces. The provinces can tailor their programs within a basic framework that guarantees individuals virtually free care at the point of access to the system. The provincial governments exert considerable control over payments and policies for hospitals and fees for physicians.

Each year the provincial governments provide a global budget, fixed in advance, for hospitals. These budgets are prepared in two parts. In the first part, the government estimates the funding necessary to maintain the same level of services as provided the previous year. In the second part, the government evaluates requests for funding for additional services. All capital expenditures must be approved by the provincial government as well, even when the hospitals can obtain funding from private sources. Through these budget and capital spending controls, the provincial governments exert substantial control over hospital operations.

Physicians operate on a fee-for-service basis, but the fee schedules are negotiated between representatives of the physicians and the provincial governments. Typically, negotiations concern average percentage increases for fees, with the relative fee schedules for different types of physicians being negotiated among the doctors. Because payment is on a fee-for-service basis, actual payments may differ from expected payments, but these can be adjusted in subsequent periods.

The Canadian health system has many admirable features. First, expenses can be lower because of reduced costs for billing and processing insurance claims. One estimate is that costs in the United States could be approximately 8 percent lower if paperwork could be reduced along the Canadian model. Second, the system has generally operated in an egalitarian manner. Unlike in the United States, hospitals that cater to rich and poor clienteles cannot easily be differentiated. Third, there have been effective controls on expenditures. A detailed study noted that the control system for hospitals had been more effective in controlling real expenditures than in controlling prices.[37] Bilateral bargaining between health workers and the government has led to an upward drift in costs.

There also have been some difficulties with the system. The strains of controlling costs and providing access have led to complaints of long waits for services, insufficient equipment, and, in some cases, denial of care. Nevertheless, satisfaction still remains high among the public. Physicians, however, have had complaints against the system. In 1984, the federal government passed legislation that prevented physicians from charging extra fees above the negotiated schedules. This law led to a bitter twenty-five-day strike in Ontario in which doctors urged that all but emergency care be terminated. The physicians lost the battle and are restricted from charging fees above the posted schedules.

Part of the cost-control program has been to limit high-tech equipment and treatment. While not all equipment purchases may be worthwhile, there are obviously some difficulties when doctors and hospitals in Canada view the capital expenditures of their neighbors to the south. In some cases, the contrast is dramatic. In 1990, there were more magnetic resonance imagers (MRIs) in Palo Alto than in the entire province of British Columbia. Unlike the United States, where competition between hospitals largely drives equipment acquisition, in Canada the provinces must assess the value and cost of new equipment purchases.

Could the Canadian system be transferred to the United States? There are a number of important reasons why it would be impossible to adapt the Canadian model. Two of the most basic reasons are political. With traditional American views of the virtues of the private sector, it would be nearly unthinkable to effectively nationalize an industry running at over 14 percent of GNP. It is hard to imagine physicians and hospital workers, as public servants, being furloughed when Congress and the president fail to agree on a budget. The United States has enough difficulties paying top-level federal workers (largely because Congress ties its pay raises to pay increases for those workers) without bringing vast numbers of additional workers directly under public control.

The other political factor is that a Canadian-style system would eliminate large segments of the insurance sector and health administration industries that have arisen over time in our health system. Not only would this change cause massive dislocations, but the lobby groups would create perhaps the worst of all possible worlds: overlapping and duplicative public and private payment systems.

Some other difficulties with adopting a Canadian-style system would plague other reform efforts as well. How will our legal system respond when care begins to be rationed and long waits develop for services? It is not difficult to envision a rash of lawsuits allegedly protecting the claims of aggrieved parties. The legal system has already become heavily involved in assessing the adequacy of funding for Medicaid. How will it react when federal or state policy decides to limit spending for exorbitantly expensive treatments that affect only a small segment of the population? Will a liberal Supreme Court in the (very) distant future deem that cost–benefit tests for medical care run afoul of the equal protection clause of the Constitution?

Our free and volatile press will keep these issues in front of the public eye. How will the public and their representatives in government react when the government blocks treatment for a child or an attractive young adult? Or what will the reaction be when the wealthy obtain access to care denied the middle class—as they inevitably will? These questions transcend the Canadian model and must be faced in other reform efforts as well.

Raw and Managed Competition

When markets appear to fail, there is an irresistible urge among economists and free-marketeers to claim that the markets would work if only given a chance. In the medical care area, some economists point to insurance as the culprit. If we somehow reduced excessive insurance coverage, the market would be improved. Ending the tax deductibility of insurance premiums and forcing more coinsurance would reinstall consumers as effective shoppers, bring discipline to the health care industry, and eliminate the need for regulation. This prescription is for raw competition.

Raw competition arouses strong passions in its opponents. Health economist Uwe Reinhardt criticized fellow economist William Baumol for recommending that Medicare "increase cost sharing borne by the aged at the point of service, although the aged already pay for the first day of a hospital stay, 20 percent of approved physician fees (and whatever extra charges the physician may bill the patient), and virtually all prescription drugs. For the poor aged, these out-of-pocket expenses amount to an average of 20 percent of disposable income. 'Such enhanced user sharing arrangements,' Baumol suggested, 'would provide a greater incentive for patients to shop around, to provide demand-side pressures that impede excessive charges, and would also help to curb unnecessary use of medical facilities.' Baumol's testimony, endorsed in writing by 10 prominent economists—several Nobel Laureates among them—suggests a remarkable faith in the ability of frail, elderly persons struck by illness to function as vigilant, rational health care shoppers, capable of disciplining wayward doctors and hospitals."[38]

Passions aside, there are a number of reasons why raw competition cannot work. First, the gains from coinsurance and cost sharing inevitably will be limited. At best, these measures can eliminate frivolous trips to physicians and some unnecessary procedures. But they will have no effect on costly interventions involving high-tech medicine that will inevitably exceed the caps on coinsurance. Second, there is strong resistance among the population to excess exposure to medical risks. As Reinhardt pointed out, substantial coinsurance and cost-sharing already exist, and it is difficult to imagine extending this exposure. Indeed, the ill-fated catastrophic health insurance law moved precisely in the opposite direction.

One example can illustrate the passion to be insured. When a large group of the elderly covered under Medicare transferred their coverage to HMOs, one in three still kept their Medigap insurance policies. The Medigap policies were expensive—over $600 per year—and totally unnecessary because the HMO covered all expenses. When the elderly who kept their Medigap policies were interviewed, they explained their seemingly irrational decision. They were worried, they claimed, that they might not like the HMO and, after several years, would want to leave the system. But then there might be some difficulties in obtaining Medigap insurance. In other words, they were willing to pay over $600 a year to insure against the possibility that they would want to leave the HMO, might not find comparable Medigap coverage, and would become ill. This is a true passion for insurance.

Finally, there is very little basis in economic theory for insisting on excessive coinsurance. As Richard Zeckhauser, an early student of this topic wrote: "But in a world of uncertainty, methods of charging which bring about efficient levels of expenditure will prevent effective risk-spreading. In such a world you will be damned if you do not introduce a risk spreading procedure, but you will be damned in another way if you do."[39] In other words, if you force too much coinsurance, the ill will bear too much risk, but without full coinsurance they will demand too much care. There are no magic solutions to this problem outside the give and take of the political system.

Alain Enthoven and Richard Kronick have proposed an innovative reform of the health care system based on the idea of managed competition.[40] They first make it clear that "raw," or unmanaged, competition will not work in the health care industry. "In a free market, health plans could pursue profits or survival by using numerous competitive strategies that would destroy efficiency and fairness and that individual consumers would be powerless to counteract: risk selection, market segmentation, product differentiation, discontinuities in coverage, refusals of insurance for some people, biased information, and anticompetitive behavior."[41] The goal of their plan is to develop a system that has the virtues of competition but that avoids these excesses.

The Enthoven-Kronick plan contains a number of key elements, some of which are common to other recent proposals. First, they build on the present system of employer-sponsored health care by requiring employers to offer and pay 80 percent of a basic health insurance plan that meets certain minimum criteria to all full-time employees. All part-time employees must pay an 8 percent payroll tax. A similar tax would be levied on all self-employed individuals.

To assist small businesses, subsidies would be available for financing the cost of insurance. Economists believe that payroll taxes are borne by workers and thus real wages would fall for part-time workers who currently are not provided insurance.

A second important element in the plan is limits on the amount of insurance that can be excluded from employees' taxable income. Enthoven and Kronick peg this amount at 80 percent of the cost of a qualified plan in the worker's geographical region. The worker is responsible for the remainder of the cost and thus will have an incentive to examine and evaluate alternative plans. The federal government would provide some subsidies to assist individuals and families near the poverty line with a portion of these payments.

The heart of their proposal, and its most novel feature, is the idea of "sponsors." Sponsors are organizations that serve as intermediaries between the health care providers and the individuals requiring care. They would include employers, existing government agencies, and newly created public sponsors for those who do not have insurance through employers. Enthoven and Kronick envision vigorous competition that will be enforced through these sponsors as they seek the best bargains in coverage and quality for their clients. The sponsors will also serve as monitors of the quality of programs and help create data on the effectiveness of treatments and procedures.

Competition among health care providers, enforced through sponsors, ideally will result in a range of treatment options. Enthoven and Kronick believe that the competitive standard for qualified plans, and thus the limits for tax deductibility, will be set by managed care plans such as HMOs and PPOs. Workers who buy more expensive insurance plans effectively will have to pay taxes on the income. Other plans may exist, but they will be more expensive to consumers. In their plan, raw competition will be restrained in a number of ways. There will be rules for continuity of coverage and annual enrollment periods to prevent problems with dismissals of high-risk individuals and denial of coverage. Qualified plans would also have strict limits on deductibles and total overall limits for coinsurance.

One difficult issue in any private system is the presence of different risk pools in the population. Consider, for example, an industry in the mid-1980s with a high proportion of male homosexuals. With the outbreak of the AIDS epidemic, any private insurance premiums for employees in this industry would have skyrocketed. Any sponsors would have had to raise fees, and thus the risks would not have been spread through a large segment of the population. This same process occurs less dramatically in the normal course of business throughout industries and regions in the country when there are any differences in the pool of employees. It is not clear that our political or legal system will tolerate sharp differentials in rates.

The ability of corporations and insurance firms to separate high-risk from low-risk members of the society poses fundamental challenges to systems based on competetion by volunteering organizations of sponsors. Under the U.S. pension law ERISA (Employee Retirement Income Security Act), states are prohibited from regulating or taxing corporations that self-insure and use insurance companies only to process claims. Nearly 70 percent of all large corporations choose this option. These large corporations can screen their employees, eliminate high-risk individuals, and leave them for others to insure. The New Jersey Uncompensated Care Trust fund has also been challenged as a violation of ERISA.

Moreover, in a dramatic case in 1991, a federal appeals court ruled that ERISA prevented states from intervening when self-insured companies sharply reduce their insurance coverage *after* individuals become afflicted with AIDS. In the case in question, an employee with AIDS found his insurance coverage reduced from a maximum of $1 million to $5,000. The court ruled that the states could not prevent this practice.

These problems with adverse selection and the fragmentation of risk-pools led M.I.T. economist Peter Diamond to propose a radical reorientation of the insurance market.[42] Diamond would have a federal agency organize the population into groups into which individuals would be assigned. Insurance companies would then bid for the right to serve these groups. Since individuals would be assigned to the groups, there would be little scope to fragment the insurance market. The government agency would then be responsible for monitoring the performance of the insurance companies. Unlike the Enthoven-Kronick plan, there is no natural affiliation (such as employee and employer) between the individual and the organization providing the service.

The Enthoven and Kronick proposal has a number of good features. By promoting competition, it would force some reductions in cost and lead to new ways of providing health care. It would provide nearly universal coverage (subsidies to individuals could be adjusted to provide varying degrees of coverage) and thus end the implicit subsidy to the uninsured, who currently rely on emergency care and charity. It also would build on our employer-based system of health insurance. These elements are all essential for any reform plan. We want to promote cost-consciousness by consumers and providers and universal coverage without deviating too far from our basic institutional structure.

It is not clear, however, how this plan would control the long-run growth of costs through new technology. Enthoven and Kronick envision that sponsors would evaluate technology and only move in cost-effective directions. But the average consumer in a basic, qualified plan would still have every incentive to demand that the plan include high-tech, high-cost treatments. Because coinsurance ultimately is limited, expensive treatments in rare situations would still be sought by individuals. Over time, of course, as use of these technologies and treatments becomes more common, costs for the basic plan will rise and employees will pay additional costs. But it is difficult to imagine that a far-sighted process of consumer awareness would prevent the introduction of new technologies. Competition in the 1980s in health care—not terribly different from that imagined by Enthoven and Kronick—did not stop the march of technology.

Regulatory Strategies

While competition may reduce inefficiencies, it is not sufficient to stop the upward march of expenditures. Henry Aaron recently offered a plan that directs itself to this issue.[43] Like the Enthoven and Kronick plan, it would require employers to provide insurance or pay an equivalent fee, and it also has a backup plan for those not covered directly through employment coverage. Insurance plans initially would be based on risk groups and experience ratings but would eventually move to community experience standards. But Aaron's plan differs in creating a small number (one, if possible) of financial agents that would be responsible for cost control.

Aaron's system, based on ideas proposed in New York, would have the financial agents directly negotiate with hospitals and doctors for services. They would be the single intermediary between health providers and the rest of the economy. Private insurance coverage would still exist, but payments from the insurance would be capped and the remainder of the bills would be paid by the agent. This arrangement would place the agent in direct control of acute care, which accounts for a large fraction of all medical costs.

Aaron did not specify precisely how the agents would control costs. Would they use a method based on the prospective payment system or place global limits on hospital budgets, as in Canada? Would physicians be paid on a fee-for-service basis with fees negotiated centrally, as in Canada, or would capitation (per-patient) arrangements be required?

As experience in other countries has shown, centralizing the payment for services would also lead to centralization of the providers. Physicians would become unionized and collective bargaining would globally determine fees and working conditions. This restructuring of the system would be truly radical.

The finance agent (or agents) would be in a position to influence the adoption of technologies through their payment mechanisms. One policy would be to adopt a two-part payment system for hospitals, as in Canada. The first part would adjust funds to maintain current service levels, while the second part would fund new procedures and technologies. By controlling funding for the second part, and perhaps capital expenditures, the agents can control the pace of adoption of new treatments and technology.

Yet Aaron's system implicitly calls for a radical restructuring of the entire medical profession and payment practices. Is there another way of achieving effective cost control while departing less rapidly from current norms?

Another possibility is to expand the direct and indirect regulatory powers of the federal government through Medicare and Medicaid. The federal government is already the single largest payer in the system and contributes over 40 percent to hospital budgets. There is also extensive regulation through the prospective payment system and extensive involvement in detailed relative fee schedules for physicians.

The first necessary change would be to control the adoption of new procedures and technologies through changes in the prospective payment system. Under the current system, there is no control over the procedures that hospitals use. If all hospitals adopt a new expensive technology, its use will become reflected in the cost base for reimbursement. The Health Care Financing Corporation could combine prospective payment with capital acquisition controls. Reimbursement would then be based on a two-part decomposition into existing and new procedures, as in the Canadian plan. Over time, this system might evolve into global budgets for hospitals, but it would require that Medicare and non-Medicare patients be treated equally.

Under any system, it will be essential to prevent elderly patients from receiving second-class treatment. To avoid this, hospitals that receive any Medicare funds would be prevented from acquiring equipment that would not be covered under Medicare. Since few hospitals could afford to lose Medicare compensation, this regulatory tool should prove to be effective. It is also a familiar regulatory mechanism; for example, colleges whose students receive any federal funds are restricted in a number of ways. These nondiscriminatory rules also would begin to eliminate the distinctions between Medicare and non-Medicare patients and pave the way for global budgeting.

Similar controls need to be extended to physicians. The new Medicare fee schedules will eventually place limits on total charges for physicians treating Medicare patients. It is thus a short step to placing fee caps for all other patients on doctors who treat any Medicare patients. The regulations suggested here are not very different from those currently in effect. By bringing all doctors who treat the elderly into the fee system, costs can be more readily controlled. The new Medicare fee system already includes "volume performance standards," or expenditure caps. These caps can be adjusted by legislation over time.

The proposed hospital and physician regulations allow a safety valve. Some doctors, hospitals, and patients may entirely opt out of the system and be free to practice unfettered capitalism. On balance, this development is healthy and should ease some pressures on the system. In an open world economy, it is also inevitable. The great majority of individuals, however, will be subject to the regulatory scheme.

The Health Care Financing Administration still would have to make difficult decisions about technology and treatment. This process will not be made any easier by inevitable micromanaging by congressional subcommittees. Over time, these decisions may become easier. If entrepreneurs and medical researchers envision possible restrictions on the use of their products, fewer resources will flow into this area and fewer new products will result. Costly medical miracles will become less frequent. Some may find this prospect antithetical to the American spirit, but it is the only realistic way to stem the rise in health costs.

Politicians have been fairly cautious in proposing remedies. Prior to the 1992 election, the Bush administration outlined a series of initiatives in the spirit of managed competition. Included in this package were generous vouchers and tax credits so that the poor could buy insurance. In addition, the package included a series of reforms for the insurance industry that included requiring insurance companies to provide continued coverage for prior clients and similar limitations designed to prevent the fragmentation of risk pools. There were also incentives for small businesses to collectively form larger risk pools. Sources of financing for the plans were not mentioned. The Congressional Budget Office reviewed the proposals and felt that they would significantly improve coverage but have little impact on cost control.

Democrats have been more divided on reform initiatives. Some have been pushing for a Canadian style health plan or other single payer strategies. Others have been pursuing alternative approaches to managed competition. One popular approach has been the "play or pay" programs in which firms must either purchase insurance for their workers (play) or contribute to a general fund (pay) that would provide coverage for other individuals in the society.

President Bill Clinton made health care reform a centerpiece of his 1992 campaign. He avoided, however, endorsing any specific plan. Toward the end of his campaign, he appeared to advocate a combination of managed competition and with centralized controls on total private and public spending. Reconciling these two diverse strategies will be a difficult challenge.

We should be realistic about the benefits of any additional health initiatives. The dismal health statistics of poor inner-city residents have much more to do with lifestyle than medicine. Drugs, AIDS, uncontrolled gang violence, and unstable family structures are the real culprits—not the lack of high- or even low-tech medicine. National health initiatives possibly can do two things. First, they can equalize the playing field a bit so that everyone has the opportunity to see a doctor regularly. Most Americans feel this is a basic right of citizenship. Second, national initiatives may be able to reduce costs to some extent. Other countries have coped somewhat better with cost control. But real progress on cost control will require limiting technology and options for some people. It remains to be seen how our political system will cope with these limitations.

Concluding Comments

After the dizzying complexity of health care reform proposals, it is important to return to basic principles. Market forces and politics interact in particularly complex ways. Here are the essentials of the story.

1. The market for medical care is replete with market failures that prevent laissez-faire from being an acceptable policy. The reason for the market failure is the pervasive uncertainty and asymmetry of information that prevails in the health market and that, in turn, prevents insurance markets from functioning completely.

2. Although insurance is crucial in coping with uncertainty, insurance helps to create additional market failures. Insurance insulates consumers from the true costs of many treatments and procedures. In turn, this protection biases technological progress in medicine toward high-cost drugs and innovations. Medical care is the only sector of the economy for which technological progress is a mixed blessing.

3. Federal and state governments have become dominant players in the market for health. Government involvement brings with it the entire range of political concerns and obsessions that make it particularly difficult to control costs. We have long abandoned the idea that medical care should be unregulated. With the involvement of government, political considerations become critical to the regulatory dynamic. Courts require that health care providers use state-of-the-art technology to treat patients, even if this policy conflicts with efforts to control costs. Innovative attempts to extend care to a wider range of the poor are vetoed by the federal government because they conflict with other regulations designed to prevent discrimination against the disabled.

4. Plans to reform the health system must face market and political failure directly. The best plans recognize these limitations. Reforms based on markets or managed competition recognize that competition can only take place within relatively large units or groups in the economy. Individuals cannot be left alone in the medical marketplace. Alternative reform proposals based less on markets and more on regulation must come to grips with rationing of care and controlling the introduction of new technology.

Further Reading

Medical care is such a complex area that it pays to step back and reflect on the basic issues, such as the relationship (sometimes tenuous) between health and medicine. Victor Fuchs has the most balanced and sensible overview of the big picture. His book *Who Shall*

Live? (New York: Basic Books, 1974) is probably the best single introduction to these issues. Henry Aaron also has a broad view of medical science, particularly on the role of insurance and the provision of medicine. See his essay in Henry Aaron, ed., *Setting National Priorities* (Washington, D.C.: Brookings Institution, 1990).

The politics of medicine is fascinating and complex. Both Democrats and Republicans have made proposals. Physicians, hospitals, insurance companies, organized labor, and all their lobbyists are keenly interested in these proposals. Julie Kosterlitz provides a keen political overview of this debate in "A Sick System" (*National Journal*, Feb. 15, 1992, pp. 376–395). She describes all the variations of pay or play and voucher plans for the poor and introduces who the lobbyists are for the various interest groups.

For more advanced reading and the latest debates on ongoing issues, I recommend two journals: *Journal of Health, Politics, Policy and Law* and *Milbank Quarterly*. The *New England Journal of Medicine* also devotes a number of its pages to debates about national health care.

Notes

1. Kenneth Arrow, "Uncertainty and the Welfare Economics of Medical Care," *American Economic Review* 53 (1963): 941–73.
2. Arrow, "Uncertainty," 966.
3. Henry Aaron and William B. Schwartz, "Rationing Health Care: The Choice Before Us," *Science* 24 (Jan. 26, 1990): 418–422.
4. Ron Winslow, "Hospitals Rush to Transplant Organs," *Wall Street Journal* (Aug. 29, 1989): p. B1.
5. See the overview in George Sweezey, "The Market for Physicians' Services: Theoretical Implications and an Empirical Test of the Target Income Hypothesis," *Southern Economic Journal* 48 (1982): 594–613.
6. Congressional Budget Office, "Projections of National Health Expenditures" (Washington, D.C.: Congressional Budget Office, October 1992), p. xi.
7. Victor Fuchs, "The Health Sector's Share of the Gross National Product," *Science* 247 (Feb. 3, 1990): 536.
8. "National Health Expenditures," *Health Care Financing Review* 8 (u) (1987): 1–36.
9. William B. Schwartz, "The Inevitable Failure of Current Cost-Containment Strategies," *Journal of the American Medical Association* 257 (Jan. 9, 1987): 220–24.

10. Fuchs, "Health Sector's Share," 536.
11. Jerome Avorn, "Medicine: The Life and Death of Oliver Shay," in *Our Aging Society,* ed. Alan Pifer and Lydia Bronte, (New York: W. W. Norton, 1986).
12. Victor Fuchs, *Who Shall Live?* (New York: Basic Books, 1974), 52–53.
13. Louise Verbrugge, "Longer Life but Worsening Health?" *Milbank Memorial Fund Quarterly* 62 (Summer 1984): 475—519.
14. "To Find a Way to Age in Health," *Insight* (Apr. 10, 1989): 8–15.
15. Avorn, "Medicine," 285.
16. James F. Fries, "The Compression of Morbidity: Near or Far?" *Milbank Quarterly* 67 (1989): 206–32.
17. "To Find a Way,"
18. H. E. Frech, III, and Paul D. Ginsburg, "Competition Among Health Insurers, Revisited," *Journal of Health Politics, Policy and Law* 13 (1988): 279–91.
19. Aaron and Schwartz, "Rationing Health Care."
20. Louise B. Russell, *Medicare's New Hospital Payment System: Is It Working?* (Washington, D.C.: Brookings Institution, 1989).
21. Russell, *Medicare's New Hospital Payment System,*
22. Congressional Budget Office, *Physician Payment Reform Under Medicare* (Washington, D.C.: Congressional Budget Office, April 1990).
23. Schwartz, "Inevitable Failure."
24. "A Two-Edged Sword," *Wall Street Journal* (Nov. 13, 1989): 21.
25. Aaron and Schwartz, "Rationing Health Care."
26. John Goddeeris, "Medical Insurance, Technological Change, and Welfare," *Economic Inquiry* 22 (1984): 55–67.
27. John Goddeeris and Burton Weisbrod, "What We Don't Know About Why Health Expenditures Have Soared: Interactions of Insurance and Technology," *The Mount Sinai Journal of Medicine* 52 (Nov. 1985): 685–91.
28. Dr. Alper "Inside the Medicare Dictatorship," *Wall Street Journal* (Jan. 10, 1990): A12.
29. Lawrence G. Goldberg and Warren Greenberg, "Health Insurance Without Provider Influence: The Limits of Cost Containment," *Journal of Health Politics, Policy, and Law* 13 (1980): 293–302.
30. Daniel Callahan, *Setting Limits* (New York: Simon and Schuster, 1987), 143–44.
31. Henry Aaron and William B. Schwartz, *The Painful Presumption: Rationing Hospital Care,* (Washington, D.C.: Brookings Institution, 1984). More recently, there have been attempts to introduce managed competition into the British health service. This trend has created considerable political controversy.
32. Henry Aaron and William B. Schwartz, "The Achilles Heel of Health

Care Rationing," *New York Times* (July 9, 1990) A19.

33. Henry Aaron, "A Prescription for Health Care," in *Setting National Priorities*, ed. Henry Aaron (Washington, D.C.: Brookings Institution, 1990).

34. Not all preventive care will necessarily be less expensive than treatments after a condition has occurred.

35. Aaron, "A Prescription for Health Care," 266.

36. See the survey by John N. Inglehart, "Canada's Health System," *New England Journal of Medicine* 315 (July 17, Sept. 18, Dec. 18, 1986): 202–08, 778–83, 1623–28.

37. Allan Detsky et. al., "The Effectiveness of a Regulatory Strategy in Containing Hospital Costs," *New England Journal of Medicine* 309 (July 21, 1983): 151–58.

38. Uwe Reinhardt, "Comments," *Health Care Financing Review* (Suppl. 1989): 101.

39. Richard Zeckhauser, "Medical Insurance: A Case Study of the Tradeoff Between Risk Spreading and Appropriate Incentives," *Journal of Economic Theory* 2 (1970): 10–26.

40. Alain Enthoven and Richard Kronick, "A Consumer-Choice Health Plan for the 1990s," *New England Journal of Medicine* 320 (Jan. 5, Jan. 12, 1989): 29–37, 94–107.

41. Enthoven and Kronick, "Consumer-Choice Health Plan," 34.

42. Peter Diamond, "Organizing the Insurance Market," *Econometrica* (Nov. 1992): 1233–54.

43. Aaron, "A Prescription for Health Care."

3

Providing for an Aging Society

Hotel Keepers and Pythons

Mathematics teachers like to tell the following story. Imagine a very large hotel with 10,000 rooms, all filled to capacity. On a cold and stormy night, a traveler arrives at the hotel. The hotel keeper apologizes but tells the traveler that all the rooms are booked and no accommodations are available. The weary traveler moves on to another hotel.

Now consider a very large hotel with an infinite number of rooms. The weary traveler arrives, and this time he is greeted by a beaming hotel keeper. "All our rooms are filled," says the hotel keeper, "but there is no problem. I'll just move the guest in room 1 to room 2, the guest in room 2 to room 3, the guest in room 3 to room 4, the guest in room 4 to room 5, and so forth. You can have room 1." The weary traveler thanks his hosts and carries his bags to the room. Life is much easier for a hotel keeper with an infinite number of rooms.

This mathematical tale of the powers of infinity also provides a good introduction to a pay-as-you-go social security system. Consider a hypothetical society with a constant population rate and continual technological change that smoothly increases per-capita income. At some point in time, this society starts a pay-as-you-go social security

63

system. The young generation is taxed at a fixed rate to pay for the retirement of the old. When the current young generation becomes elderly, it is supported in its old age by taxes (levied at the same rate) on the new young generation. Even though the tax rate remains the same, the living standards of the retired generations continue to rise because the income of the younger generation providing the support also continues to increase. As long as new generations continue to be born (the infinity assumption) this process can continue forever.

The young generation that started the system by levying taxes on itself does not suffer. They will be supported in their old age by the next generation. The initial elderly generation does gain a surprising windfall. They receive benefits in their old age without having paid any taxes when they were young.

The idea of giving a windfall to the elderly generation in the 1930s must have seemed like a wonderful idea. Here was a clear case of market failure. The elderly at that time were very poor, and pension schemes were not well developed in the economy. Insurance and annuity markets were not easily available to make provisions for old age. Furthermore, this generation was hard hit by the Great Depression. The economics of infinity provided a convenient mechanism to provide the elderly with a needed windfall—pay them now, and charge the young forever so that no bills ever catch up.

The constant population assumption played a critical role in this story. A constant population means that new individuals enter society at the same rate that the elderly leave. Thus, the proportion of the elderly to the working population (the "support ratio") remains the same over time. It then becomes possible to keep the tax rate levied on the younger generation the same throughout time. The standard of living of the elderly rises over time not because of tax rate changes but because the level of output increases with GNP.

Can anything go wrong with this story? Unfortunately, the answer is yes. If one generation produces too many children, the system will come under stress. If a baby boom is followed by a return to normal fertility levels, a pay-as-you-go social security system will not be able to maintain constant tax rates on the workers. Indeed, as the baby boomers enter the labor force, tax rates to support the elderly can be decreased because there are more workers to support the elderly population. The problem comes when the baby boomers retire. Now the support ratio turns unfavorable: there are relatively fewer workers to support the elderly than before. Maintaining the traditional standard of living for the elderly will require that higher taxes be levied on the younger generation.

Of course, this is precisely what happened in the United States. The crude birth rate in the decade of the Great Depression reached a low of 18.3 per thousand. By 1950–1955, the birth rate had soared to about 25 per thousand. By the late 1970s, the birth rate had fallen to 15 per thousand.[1]

Behind these numbers detailing the baby boom is the dramatic economic tale of the United States as it emerged from World War II. During the war, a young generation was sent to fight in Europe and the East. At home, goods were rationed, and increasing numbers of women were drawn into the labor force, often in factory jobs. The war revitalized the economy following the dreary decade of the 1930s, with its limited economic opportunity.

When the war was over, the soldiers returned home. Fears of a postwar depression disappeared as pent-up demand for consumer goods led to an inflationary surge. Suburbs began to be developed in the city and pioneers such as Robert Levitt provided new housing away from the confines of the city. Television began to penetrate the country. Tired of fighting European and Asian wars, the country sought peace, prosperity, and normalcy in the suburbs. This drive for normalcy led in many directions, including virulent anticommunism. But above all, it led to large families and a rapid growth in the population.

The key number in a social security system is the support ratio, the number of retired individuals divided by the number of the population of working age. Here is how the support ratio has changed over time and how it is currently projected to change:

Year	Ratio of 64 and older to population between 24–64
1950	.138
1990	.210
2030	.378
2060	.412

These numbers are startling. In 1950, more than seven individuals of working age were available to support those over sixty-four. By 1990, the number had decreased to slightly below five. By the year 2060, every five workers will have to support more than two elderly individuals.

These effects are not all from the baby boom, because by 2060 most of those born in 1950–1955 will no longer be alive. Falling birth rates in more recent years and increased life expectancies also account for these startling statistics. But the baby boom bulge is clearly important. Its effects are like a python swallowing a goat—it is clearly visible as it works its way through the system.

In addition to the additional financial burden, the baby boom generation may experience other difficulties. Richard Easterlin, in his book *Birth and Fortune*, argues that life will be more difficult for those born in a baby boom generation than in a "baby bust" generation. Intense intragenerational conflict among the large numbers of individuals in any age group takes its toll. According to Easterlin, who has studied the social dynamics of large generations, the boomers are more likely to:

1. Experience depressed employment prospects and wage growth when they are young.
2. Hesitate to marry and have more illegitimate births.
3. Feel pressure to postpone having children.
4. Find women forced into the job market, even though they have small children.
5. Experience marital stress and high divorce rates.
6. Feel under intense psychological stress.[2]

But there are some mitigating factors. The number of the baby boomers dictates the content of popular culture. When the boomers were young, the Beatles and Rolling Stones dominated the airwaves, they threw generational parties (Woodstock), and combined their political protests and marches with recreational drugs and sex. As they age, the Beatles still can be seen as cartoon characters on children's programs ("Sesame Street"), "oldie" stations now dominate the airways, and television executives develop programs that document their life transitions ("Thirty Something").

The Structure and Financing of Social Security

If the world were predictable and social affairs were conducted in tidy fashion, it would be easy to structure a retirement program. But people marry, divorce, have children, remarry, become disabled, and, in general, behave rather untidily. Markets do not and cannot exist to handle all these contingencies. And many people fail to save enough for themselves and their families in old age.

The Social Security system in the United States is much more than a retirement or pension system. It is a system of *social insurance* that attempts to insulate individuals and their families from some of the vagaries of life and provides a basic retirement pension. It attempts to insulate individuals from the first of our market failures, uncertainty. The complexity of the Social Security system—as well as some of its most controversial features—stems from the aspiration to provide social insurance along with retirement.

Social Security was started in 1935 during the depths of the Great Depression. From the system's beginning, benefits were paid based on earnings in industries covered by Social Security and not on the amount of taxes an individual worker paid into the system. Consequently, the first generation of retirees under the system received much more in benefits than they paid in taxes. This windfall is a natural feature of the initiation of a pay-as-you-go system.

In 1939, before any benefits were paid out, the system was liberalized to allow payments to the spouse and dependent children of a retired individual covered by Social Security as well as to widows or widowers and dependent children of a deceased worker. In 1956, the system was extended to include disabled workers over 50, and by 1960 all disabled workers were covered. The Social Security system thus provides old age, survivor, and disability benefits; hence, the initials OASDI are used to describe it.

Each of the components of OASDI is quite complex. Workers who have earned enough credits in employment covered by Social Security (now over 92 percent of the civilian work force), can receive retirement payments at the age of 65 and actuarily reduced payments beginning at 62. In addition, the spouse of a covered worker receives 50 percent of the benefits, as do all dependent children up to the age of 18, or 22 if they are in full-time schooling. An overall family limit places a cap on total family payments. A divorced spouse is also eligible for 50 percent benefits, but only after having been married for a minimum ten years.

The survivors component of Social Security pays benefits to dependent children of deceased covered workers. The spouse of a deceased worker also receives a lump sum payment and is eligible for additional payments if he or she provides care for the dependent children. The payments to the children continue regardless of the income or marital status of the surviving spouse. Widows or widowers, upon reaching the age of 60, can collect benefits based on the deceased worker's earnings—a type of deferred insurance policy. These benefits normally would not be available if a widow or widower remarries, but an exception is made for individuals over 60, who may remarry without losing benefits.

Disability payments are provided for workers who suffer from an illness that results in an inability to work for a minimum of a year or could be the cause of death. Spouses and dependent children of a disabled worker also receive benefits at a 50 percent rate, as in the basic retirement program. Children who become disabled before the age of 22 can receive benefits when a worker retires or dies. Disabled widows can receive benefits starting at the age of 50.

All three components of this complex system (retirement, survivor, and disability) are funded by payroll taxes that are paid into the OASDI trust fund. If one of the programs runs a deficit and another a surplus, there is routine borrowing between the programs. Thus, for all practical purposes, retirement benefits, survivor insurance, and disability payments are all part of the same system.

The Social Security Administration also runs the Supplemental Security Income (SSI) program, which provides a basic minimum level of support to the aged, blind, and disabled. The SSI program is meant to provide a basic level of support to those individuals who qualify. The program is "means tested"—that is, payments are restricted to those who have minimal income and assets. Unlike OASDI, funds for SSI come from general revenues.

The last major part of the Social Security system is Medicare. Medicare includes both hospital insurance (HI) and supplementary medical insurance (SMI), also known as Part A and Part B, respectively. The hospital insurance component is funded through payroll taxes. When OASDI, which is also financed by payroll taxes, is considered along with hospital insurance (HI), we use the acronym OASDHI. SMI is funded both through general revenue and payments from participants in the program. Medicare hospital benefits are automatically provided to workers and their married partners upon reaching the age of 65. They are also automatically enrolled in SMI but can disenroll if they choose. Widows or widowers of deceased covered workers are also enrolled in Medicare.

It is clear from this overview that the Social Security system is much more than a simple retirement system. Many complex provisions are interwoven in the basic retirement, survivor, and disability components of the programs. Almost all raise important policy issues. For example, is the treatment of a divorced spouse fair, on the one hand, to those married less than ten years and, on the other hand, to the unmarried? Should benefits be paid to the spouse and dependent children of retired workers with no comparable benefits paid to single workers? Should payments for disability be part of the Social Security system, or should there be a separate means-tested program for the disabled, funded from general revenues? These are just some of the micro policy issues that arise with our Social Security system. Before turning to analyze these and other micro issues, two additional important issues must be addressed to provide appropriate background to the discussion: the basic structure of payments under Social Security and the overall projected finances of the system.

A worker's retirement benefits from Social Security are based on accumulating sufficient credits in employment covered by the Social Security system. Once a worker accumulates enough credits, the worker is entitled to a full pension at the age of 65 or an actuarily adjusted pension beginning at 62. Workers who accumulate enough credits are "fully insured" and they and their families are eligible for the full range of social insurance benefits as well.

The key principle of Social Security is that retirement and other payments are geared to a worker's wages in covered employment, not the payroll tax contributions that the individual worker has made. Using the terminology of pensions, Social Security is a "defined benefit" as opposed to a "defined contribution" plan. Payments are made according to set formulas and not based on the contributions of any individual. Until 1984, all benefits received from Social Security were free from taxation. But after 1984, half of the benefits become taxable once a taxpayer's total income reaches a certain level.

The formula used to pay benefits is highly progressive— that is, it favors workers with low wages relative to those with high incomes. The easiest way to understand this principle is to compare the "replacement" rate for low, average, and high wage earners. The replacement rate is the fraction of a worker's wage earnings that are paid in Social Security benefits. In 1990, a low wage earner reaching the age of 65 would have a replacement rate of 69.7 percent; for average and high wage earners, the replacement rates are 42.3 and 24.7 percent respectively.[3] Thus, it is clear that the benefit system is designed to redistribute income to low wage workers away from higher wage workers.

The procedure for calculating benefits that generates this redistribution is relatively complex. The key concept in calculating a worker's benefits is the primary insurance amount (PIA). Almost all benefits paid under Social Security are related to this amount. For any worker, the PIA is based on the worker's average indexed earnings from employment covered by Social Security. In calculating average wages, past wages are inflated by the extent to which total wages in the economy have increased. For example, if average wages in 1970 were one-half of wages in 1990, when the average is calculated, a worker's 1970 wages would be doubled before averaging. This procedure essentially indexes workers' retirement benefits for the behavior of past wages in the economy and provides a basic benefit to workers that is related to the current wage level in the economy when they retire. The PIA is derived directly from a worker's average indexed earnings. For example, in 1988, the PIA was calculated as the sum of 90 percent of the first $319 of average monthly earnings, 32 percent of the amount between $319 and $1,922, and 15 percent above $1,922.[4] The formula is clearly redistributive, as smaller percentages are applied to the higher ranges of earnings. The ranges themselves are adjusted for average wage growth in the economy.

After the PIA has been calculated for a worker, this amount is adjusted for changes in prices in the economy. Thus, the benefits are kept constant in real terms. By using changes in wages in the economy to calculate the PIA and then adjusting benefits for inflation, workers are given retirement benefits that are adjusted for wage growth until they retire and then preserved in real terms. If, as in some recent years, prices grow faster than wages (that is real wages of workers fall), retirees on Social Security will improve their position relative to current workers.

One of the reasons that the Social Security system comes under frequent examination is continued concern about its finances. The system faced difficulties in 1977 that were temporarily patched, but by 1983 the system faced both a short-term cash flow problem and a long-term solvency problem. The crisis was a political hot potato. The Republicans were keenly aware of their vulnerability to charges that they wanted to cut benefits. They had proposed benefit cuts in the previous year but had changed their position in the face of a public outcry and a lack of cooperation from Democrats in the House of Representatives. The Democrats alone were not going to propose tax increases and then find themselves subject to the charge that they were the tax and spend party.

The solution to the problem was to appoint a "wise man," or expert, to head a commission to provide cover for the politicians. Alan Greenspan, former Chairman of the Council of Economic Advisors and later Chairman of the Federal Reserve, stepped up to take the task. The Greenspan Commission proposed a number of changes that were adopted and that solved the short-term cash flow problem and made some contribution to the long-run solvency problem. The changes made in 1983 included taxing some benefits, increasing payroll tax rates and taxes on the self-employed, increasing the retirement age from 65 to 67 with a gradual phase-in into the next century, and extending mandatory coverage to some groups currently outside the system. But from today's vantage point, the Greenspan Commission did not act aggressively enough to insure the long-run solvency of the system.

To understand the issue of long-run solvency, it is best to begin with the basic financing mechanism of Social Security. The OASDHI system (retirement, survivors, disability, and hospital insurance) is financed by payroll taxes levied on workers and firms. In 1990, the combined tax rate on workers and firms was 15.3 percent. The payroll tax applies for all earnings up to a limit of $51,300 and is adjusted for wage growth. For 1991 and beyond, Congress extended the wage base for the hospital insurance component of the tax to incomes up to $125,000.

The short-term financial picture for Social Security is very good. Payroll taxes currently collected far exceed benefits that must be paid. In the early 1990s, this surplus in the Social Security system is projected to grow to over $200 billion. Yet, the huge benefit payments that will be necessary when the baby boomers retire and must be supported by a smaller cohort make the long-run financial picture quite poor.

Aaron, Bosworth, and Burtless have calculated the payroll tax rates necessary to keep the entire system solvent.[5] Two issues arise in any calculation of this sort. First, what demographic and economic assumptions should be used to project future costs and revenues for the system? For their basic case, Aaron and his coauthors employed the intermediate assumptions (II-B) used by the Social Security Administration. The second issue concerns the timing of tax rate changes. In order to maintain solvency, should tax rates be changed only when the system reaches bankruptcy, or should rates be changed to maintain long-run balance between costs and revenues? Aaron and coauthors adopt the latter strategy, which leads to more frequent but less drastic changes in rates. In their estimates, they increase rates whenever the present value of future costs exceeds the present value of resources (future receipts plus any initial balance) by more than 5 percent. ("Present value" takes into account that a dollar in the future is worth less than a dollar today because interest can be earned on today's money.)

Excluding the Medicare hospital insurance component and adopting the intermediate assumptions, the picture does not look too bad. The combined employer and employee rates for OASDI in 1990 are 12.4 percent. Aaron and coauthors estimate that there would only have to be modest increases to maintain solvency, with the combined rates rising to 14.7 percent.

However, the intermediate (II-B) assumptions are very optimistic about the growth in productivity. Total factor productivity—the best economic measure of how much all resources can produce—grows at a rate of 1.4 percent under these assumptions. This figure is higher than the average productivity growth between 1950 and 1985, which was 1.0 percent, and substantially higher than the meagre .4 percent growth in total factor productivity during the 1973 to 1985 period. With lower productivity growth it becomes more difficult to support workers after they retire. Retiree benefits are designed to stay constant in real terms under Social Security while workers' wages rise at the rate of productivity growth. It is therefore harder to balance the system when there is slow productivity growth. Payroll tax rates must increase to maintain solvency in the system. If future productivity stays at the low rate of 0.4 percent a year, payroll tax rates will have to increase an additional 4 percentage points.[6]

When Medicare is included, the story is dismal. The factors documented in the last chapter—the skyrocketing costs of medical care and the rapid aging of the population—make the outlook bleak. Using the intermediate assumptions, the combined employer and employee tax rate for OASDHI will have to rise from 15.3 to 22.2 percent by the year 2060. Under pessimistic productivity assumptions, the rate for Social Security including hospital insurance will exceed 26 percent. To put this in perspective, these increases mean that employers and employees would each find their payroll tax rates rising from 7.65 percent to 13 percent, and the self-employed would pay at 26 percent. And this amount is before any federal or state income taxes, from which payroll taxes are not deductible.

Moreover, the assumptions about the deficit in the hospital fund are also very sensitive to precise demographic and productivity assumptions. The difference between the pessimistic and intermediate assumptions for hospital insurance, translates into a 6.5 percentage point increase in the tax rate.[7] Some of this gap is due to assumptions about reduced productivity, which we have already discussed. But Medicare financing is very sensitive to demographic assumptions, including future fertility rates and life expectancies. Under the intermediate assumptions, the aged as a proportion of the working population are projected to be 40.6 percent in 2035, whereas the estimate rises to 50 percent under the pessimistic assumptions. The proportion of the population over 85 relative to the working population is even more sensitive: the proportions are 12.1 percent versus 17.0 percent for the two cases.

John Holahan and John Palmer argue that the pessimistic assumptions may be more plausible.[8] They note that the intermediate assumptions assume an increase in fertility rates above the current level. Moreover, the intermediate assumptions also predict a much less rapid decline in the death rate than has occurred during the last twenty years. In addition, the assumptions about health care costs built into the intermediate assumptions are quite optimistic about the success of future cost reduction strategies.

Projections far into the future are obviously risky and uncertain. Before we digest forecasts of the year 2050 from our vantage point in 1993, we should pause and ask ourselves if sixty years earlier (in the early 1930s during the Great Depression) we would have been successful in projecting economic and demographic trends today. Nonetheless, these exercises do throw up warning flags. We have designed a social insurance system that, under our best guesses, will require payroll tax rates of between 22 and 30 percent. If federal and state income taxes remain in the same range, with average marginal tax rates of 30 percent, a typical wage earner would face marginal tax rates of between 52 and 60 percent.

Is this situation within the realm of possibility? European countries have sharply higher tax rates than the United States and a burden of taxation close to this range. But it is likely that pressures will arise to change the social insurance system to reduce its burden on future taxpayers. As the burden grows and taxpayers face higher rates, questions concerning the structure of the system constantly will be raised. This reasoning leads to two questions. How solid is support today for the Social Security system? And will a system that has enjoyed strong support continue to be perceived as fair in a more costly future?

Perceptions and Politics of Social Security

Since the 1970s, there have been waves of concern about Social Security. Most of these concerns centered around its financial stability. For example, one poll in 1982 found that 89 percent of adults between the ages of 25 to 34 had "only a little confidence" or "no confidence" that Social Security would have the funds to pay their retirement benefits.[9] Yet, despite this lack of confidence, there does not appear to be any decline in public willingness to pay for continued benefits.

Fay Lomax Cook polled large numbers of Americans of all ages concerning their attitudes to social programs, including Social Security. Medicare, Social Security, and Supplementary Security Income (SSI), programs that principally provide benefits to the elderly, had extremely high levels of support among the public. For example, over 96 percent of those surveyed stated that benefits should either be increased or maintained for those on Social Security. Support for these programs was considerably higher than for a group of programs that primarily served the nonelderly: unemployment insurance, aid to families with dependent children (AFDC), and food stamps. For example, 25 percent of those surveyed felt that food stamp benefits should be decreased.

Cook found that support for the Social Security program was widely based in the population. Differences in political affiliation, sex, and political ideology explained little in terms of differences in underlying support for the system. Perhaps most interesting is that young people were almost equally as satisfied with the system as the elderly. Eighty-one percent of the 18–34 year age group was satisfied with paying taxes for Social Security compared to a similar 88 percent of those over 65 years of age. These satisfied young adults are the same ones who expressed great doubts about receiving financial benefits in their own retirement.

What explains the high degree of support for Social Security? Cook was able to ask those surveyed a wide range of questions concerning both the nature of the program and the perceived characteristics of the system. She found only two factors that appeared to explain the support. Those expressing the strongest support were more likely to believe that "society benefits from the program" and that the elderly had "no alternative sources of income."

The belief that "society benefits from the program" is hard to interpret as other than generalized approval for the Social Security system. The belief that the elderly had "no alternative sources of income" is at variance with the views of the congressmen who Cook also interviewed. The congressmen were more aware that the status of the elderly had improved in recent years and that as a group they were on par with other groups. Many congressmen expressed more concern about children in poverty and worried, privately, that funds devoted to the elderly might be better spent on the nonelderly poor. Cook speculated that support for Social Security might decline if public perceptions of the economic status of the elderly began to more closely resemble reality.

In a historical analysis of Social Security, Martha Derthick probes why Social Security, which is now a vast social program, has had such popular support and has grown with relatively little controversy.[10] She gave essentially two answers to this question. First, policy making within the Social Security system was constricted, and decisions were made by a small group who shared common values and beliefs about the desirability of the system. Second, the policy choices embedded in the system helped to build its popular support.

Derthick argued that policy making in Social Security was dominated by a relatively small set of individuals in the Social Security Administration, key congressional committees, advisory committees, and outside experts. For the most part, these people believed in the continued expansion of the system and its basic philosophy. Largely because the Social Security system is highly complex, it was not easy for outside parties to develop the skill to influence the system. The leadership was also pragmatic and willing to take a long view in designing policies to expand the system.

But perhaps most interesting are the features of the system itself that helped to build public support. According to Derthick, "the central themes are ambiguity, inconsistency, obscurity and paradox—qualities that I believe go far towards explaining the overwhelming, seemingly unqualified acceptance of social security."[11]

As an example, consider the tension between providing a true social safety network for the elderly and also ensuring a system that delivers a fair rate of return on taxes paid—what Derthick calls the balance between "adequacy and equity." When Social Security was conceived, there was to be a link between total benefits and total lifetime contributions, a clear bow to equity. But before any benefits were paid out, the formula was changed to emphasize average earnings, not cumulative contributions—a move in the direction of adequacy.

Critics of Social Security such as Milton Friedman claimed that the program had confused objects. "It falls between two stools. It gives too much attention to 'need' to be justified as return for taxes paid, and it gives too much attention to taxes paid to be justified as adequately linked to need."[12] In the early years of the Social Security, this criticism was especially apt. The system covered a much smaller proportion of workers than today, and those not covered received no benefits at all from the system. Retirement benefits were based on average wages, so that recent entrants to the system, as well as low wage workers, were paid a much higher rate of return on their contributions than other recipients.

The executives of the program eventually wished to provide universal coverage and a social safety net, but they did not want to design a program just for the poor. "A program for the poor is a poor program," was their motto, which was based on keen political insight.[13] The idea was to build a middle class program that had support from the majority of the people. Only such a program truly would be politically secure. Using the payroll tax helped to provide this broad foundation. Although the benefits paid out were not directly related to contributions, in an important sense middle class workers thought that they were making a contribution for their own security.

Program supporters strongly objected to any means tests that would direct benefits primarily to the poor. Such a policy would change the popular perception of the system so that it would be viewed as a poverty program. At the same time, supporters also objected to viewing the system as a private insurance system providing an annuity to be claimed at a certain age. The image they promoted was the somewhat vague and inclusive idea of social insurance in which the middle class provided for its own in an uncertain world. One was required to contribute in order to share in this insurance, and the benefits paid were a mixture of an earned entitlement and insurance against adversity. This image helped build support for the system.

The debate about means testing continues today. In the face of proposals for increased premiums for Medicare in 1990 deficit reduction plans, some called for means testing benefits for the elderly: "We can no longer afford to treat the wealthy dowager living with an inheritance the same as we treat the little old lady on a fixed income in a cold water flat. But Congress is still clinging to that outmoded idea."[14] But attempts to introduce means testing quickly raise fears that the programs will be downgraded to welfare programs. Congressmen in the 1990s will vividly recall the furor created when they charged higher premiums for the wealthy in the catastrophic health plan. Universal treatment buys more political support.

Another factor that helped to build the popularity of Social Security was the high rate of return on contributions paid to those in the beginning phases of the system. This result is a natural feature of the start-up phase of any pay-as-you-go system. Over time, of course, this attraction fades and clearly cannot be a factor among—at least—the young today.

Payroll taxes for Social Security are paid in equal parts by workers and employers. Most economists believe that the burden of the tax falls almost entirely on workers; that is, their wages fall by the amount that the tax is levied on the employees. Yet, most workers do not recognize this fact and therefore do not perceive the full burden of the system. Indirectly, this misperception lends support to the system.

The Social Security system creates the possibility of distributional conflicts because there are real winners and losers in the system. Relative to contributions, benefits are higher for the first generation of workers in the system, those who qualify for coverage late in their working careers, married couples with one earner, low wage earners, and many other groups. High wage earners, two career couples, and workers in subsequent generations fare less well. But Derthick emphasizes that distributional conflict traditionally has not played a major role in the history of Social Security. Her explanation is both that the system is complex and confusing, so that distributional issues are partially hidden, and that the relative losers in the system do not form a natural unified group for political mobilization.

Conflict has occurred in Social Security when the programs have expanded into new areas. Two examples of what Derthick calls "boundary issues" are the 1956 inclusion of disability insurance and the 1965 Medicare program. It took many years and many false starts before these programs finally found their way through Congress and into legislation. Part of the reason the expansion of the system generates conflict is that it begins to impinge on groups that were not previously affected by the system. For example, the medical community initially was quite suspicious that a disability insurance program would lead to indirect regulation of physicians and "socialized medicine." The same factors, of course, were even more important in the design of the Medicare program.

When new programs are proposed, some insiders fear the future costs of the program. For example, when disability insurance was first enacted in 1956, it only applied to workers over the age of 50. There were two reasons for this restriction. First, it was too costly to extend the program to all disabled individuals. Second, there was also enlightened discussion that physical rehabilitation was possible before the age of 50 and thus that disability insurance was not fully necessary.

Once a new program has been established, expansion of the program is just a matter of time and persistence. In spite of all the debate about the proper age for disability payments, four years later, in 1960, the age restriction was dropped. And, as we saw in the last chapter, the expansion of Medicare regulation ultimately may lead to the socialized medicine that the physicians feared.

Incentives and Fairness

Critics of the Social Security system have charged that it creates adverse economic incentives, particularly in terms of retirement decisions and savings, and is unfair to large segments of the population. As financial pressures intensify on the system, these charges deserve careful examination. This section focuses on the micro issues of retirement and fairness. The question of savings is taken up in the following section.

In recent years, the typical retirement age for male workers has drifted down from 65 to 62. There are "peaks" in the retirement profile—the largest fraction of workers now retires at 62, followed by a second peak at age 65. The downward trend in retirement ages has disturbed many observers because it reinforces the problems associated with the forthcoming retirement of the baby boomers. The specter of the elderly living longer but working less is frightening.

Social Security and pension plans designed along similar lines do play an important role in retirement decisions. Different factors, however, explain the peaks in retirement ages at 65 and 62. After 65, workers lose Social Security benefits in an actuarial sense if they continue to work. That is, the extra benefits they gain from postponing retirement are not sufficient to compensate for the shorter expected remaining period of their life. Workers thus face an additional tax if they postpone their retirement past 65.[15]

Workers covered under Social Security can retire at 62 and their benefits are reduced in an actuarily fair manner. Yet, the Social Security system does help concentrate retirement decisions at 62. Two different factors are operating. First, while there may be an actuarily fair reduction in benefits for the population as a whole, it is probably individuals with ill health and shorter expected life spans who choose to retire at 62. For them, retiring at the age of 62 is an actuarily favorable decision.

The second factor is that a large number of individuals would prefer to retire before the age of 62. However, their current assets may be low and because they cannot borrow against their future Social Security, they cannot afford to retire. They therefore wait until they are 62 to retire in order to collect their Social Security benefits. If they had a more liquid retirement vehicle, they would have retired earlier. Thus, on balance, Social Security probably deters retirement for this group while it probably encourages retirement for those who work to 65. Higher living standards coupled with a general distaste for most work probably will continue the historical trend toward early retirement.

Workers who retire at 65 face restrictions on their earnings if they choose to supplement their Social Security. After reaching a certain level of earnings, called the "exempt" amount, workers face a 50 percent tax on any additional earnings. Careful analysis has revealed that it does reduce hours of work for those subject to the tax, but the vast majority of the elderly are not affected by this provision.[16] Although the tax on earnings is a recurring political issue, its impact on total hours of work by the elderly is quite small.

Social Security does provide different benefit packages to different groups of individuals. First, there is a vintage effect. Table 3–1 shows the rate of return, taking into account benefits and taxes paid, for married workers with a nonworking spouse scheduled to retire in different years. For those retiring in 1970, the system delivered an 8.5 percent secure, real return. For those who will retire in the year 2025, the return falls to 2.2 percent.[17]

Perhaps even more dramatic are the differentials by marital status. Table 3–2 presents one calculation of the net transfers to different

Table 3–1
Rate of Return on Social Security

Year of Retirement	1970	1980	1995	2010	2025
Percent Return	8.5	5.9	3.6	2.5	2.2

Source: Adapted from Panel B (updated) from M. Hurd and J. Shoven, "The Distributional Impact of Social Security," in D. Wise, ed., *Pensions, Labor and Individual Choice* (Chicago: University of Chicago Press, 1985) and author's calculations. Reprinted from Michael Boskin, *Too Many Promises: The Uncertain Future of Social Security* (Homewood, Ill.: Dow Jones, 1986), 85.

Table 3–2
Marital Status and Social Security Net Transfers 1983
(Present Value of Benefits over Costs)

1982 Earnings Total	Single Male	Two-Earner Couple	One-Earner Couple
$15,000	−$21,321	$3,318	$28,218
$30,000	−$56,347	−$24,808	$14,375

Source: Adapted from A. Pellechio and G. Goodfellow, "Individual Gains and Losses from Social Security Before and After the 1983 Amendments," *Cato Journal*, Fall, 1983. Reprinted from Michael Boskin, *Too Many Promises: The Uncertain Future of Social Security* (Homewood, Ill.: Dow Jones, 1986), 88.

groups. These transfers are defined as the present value of Social Security benefits less contributions. While the magnitude of the entries in the table are sensitive to the interest rate used in the calculation, the basic pattern is very clear. Married couples with one worker fare the best, next come two-earner families and, finally, single workers fare the worst under the system. Moreover, higher earning families and individuals also fare less well than their lower earning counterparts. These results are not surprising given the structure of the system: a redistributive benefit formula, spouse and dependent benefits, and survivor benefits.

Many proposals have been made over the years to design a system that would be free of these apparent inequities. One interesting proposal was put forward by economist Michael Boskin before he became chairman of the Council of Economic Advisers under President

Bush.[18] Boskin essentially wanted to preserve the link between benefits and total contributions. In his system, an account would be kept for each worker of the total taxes paid into the system. He preferred, but did not insist, that husbands and wives share equally in any contributions to the account. Upon retirement, benefits would be paid based on a fixed rate of return on the total amount of the accumulated account.

What about workers who had low earnings or suffered illness or disability? Boskin advocated a two-tier system. The first tier was the actuarily fair system based on accumulated contributions. The second tier would be a social safety net or welfare system for those who, for whatever reason, did not have sufficient resources from prior contributions. Funding for the second tier would come directly from general revenue and would have to compete against other claims on the budget, from roads to defense.

Boskin argued that his system was fair in that it provided an equal return for Social Security contributions and did not discriminate against single workers or working couples. It was also fair in the sense that it provided a safety net for the poor and unfortunate in society. This general assistance, however, should compete against other priorities, as do programs for the nonelderly poor.

Supporters of the current Social Security system have fought against proposals such as Boskin's for years. Before any benefits were paid out by Social Security, the formula for benefits was changed from one based on total contributions to one based on average wages. Progressive benefit formulas, always part of the system, were designed in part to prevent the elderly, as much as possible, from having to rely on general assistance. Yet, the inequities highlighted in Table 3–2 do seem striking. Is there any way to provide a rationale, based on fairness, for the existing system?

The philosopher John Rawls coined the term "veil of ignorance" to describe a thought experiment in which individuals evaluate an ideal social structure before they know their precise position. Consider the Social Security system in this light. Suppose you did not know whether you would have high or low wages, remain single or have a large family, or be subject to illness, disability, or a premature death. It might appear fair, in this case, to design a system that provides true social insurance so that low-wage workers, widows, and large families would not suffer a penurious retirement. Nor would this system depend upon the vagaries of societal largess. The veil of ignorance requires people to judge fairness before knowing whether they will be married or single, rich or poor.

Many, but not all, provisions of Social Security would look fair behind a veil of ignorance. Deferred survivor benefits provided at the age of 60 to widows or widowers would not have an obvious rationale. The ten-year rule for eligibility after divorce also seems rather odd in this context. But other aspects of the system do make sense. Disability insurance naturally fits into this framework as do survivor and, perhaps, some dependent benefits.

One could object that individuals do not just experience low earnings or large families, they choose them. And, indeed, individuals do make important choices in their lives. The degree of redistribution within a society must be sensitive to this. If a program redistributed money to left-handed people, the baseball leagues would be full of southpaws. But social factors outside an individual's control also heavily influence behavior. Class, religion, and ability affect an individual's career and family path. Social insurance tries to account for these factors.

Some analysts have suggested dispensing with social insurance and moving gradually toward fully privatizing the Social Security system.[19] Under one version, individuals would be allowed a dollar-for-dollar tax credit against their payroll taxes for any contributions made into individual retirement accounts (IRAs). This system would allow individuals to tailor their retirement vehicles as they choose and invest in their preferred mix of assets.

But, as Henry Aaron has stressed, these schemes are inconsistent with maintaining any system of social insurance.[20] Because the benefits formula redistributes funds to low wage workers, high wage workers would be the first to opt out of the system. Payroll tax rates would then have to increase to pay existing benefit levels. As this process of adverse selection continued, the system would eventually become unable to support itself.

Should We Accumulate a Large Trust Fund?

One of the very first issues that confronted the Social Security system soon after the initial legislation passed in 1935 was the desirability of accumulating a large trust fund. In the early years, payroll taxes would have generated significantly more revenue than was required to be paid out in benefits. The result would have been a large accumulation of reserves.

Conservatives argued against accumulating a large trust fund. The main argument was political. They felt that with a large trust fund, Congress would behave irresponsibly and either liberalize benefits or fail to raise payroll taxes when necessary.[21] The debate was resolved by liberalizing Social Security benefits in 1939 by adding survivors' insurance and dependent benefits. With these extra benefits, the Social Security system did not accumulate a significant surplus.

Until the 1980s, the system continued to operate in a pay-as-you-go manner. Contributions from workers were paid directly to individuals collecting Social Security benefits. The trust funds contained only a prudent reserve—usually less than one year's worth of benefits—to meet unexpected financial shortfalls.

The Greenspan Commission, convened in 1983 to address both short-run cash flow and long-run solvency issues, made changes in payroll tax rates that ended the pay-as-you-go system. Although it was not discussed fully at that time, the increases in tax rates and other changes initiated by the Greenspan Commission led to a significant surplus accumulating in the trust fund. By the early 1990s, the yearly excess of taxes over benefits was in the range of $120 billion. These funds were invested in government securities that earned interest for the trust fund. The total holdings in the fund are predicted to rise into the trillions of dollars and, by 2020, to be approximately 30 percent of GNP.

In the late 1980s, the yearly surplus in the Social Security trust fund started to mask the increasing deficit in the rest of the government budget. For example, in 1988 the Congressional Budget Office projected the total federal deficit for 1994 to be $121 billion. However, excluding the Social Security surplus from the calculations raises the deficit to $248 billion.

Senator Daniel Patrick Moynihan, a member of the Greenspan Commission, decried the fact the Social Security system was being used to offset a growing deficit in the conventional budget. According to Moynihan, the purpose of the trust fund was to increase national savings to meet the needs of society when the baby boom generation retired. The trust funds purchase government securities. When it is time to run down the trust fund to finance the baby boomers' retirement, the trust fund must sell the securities back to the government. The government will have to raise revenue to finance the purchase of these securities. If the Social Security trust fund were saved and channelled into investment, GNP would be substantially increased, thus making it easier to raise the funds necessary to purchase the securities from the trust fund. It is essential that the proceeds in the trust fund be saved in order to have increased investment and higher future GNP.

But, as Moynihan pointed out, if the government runs a deficit on the rest of its account, it is not contributing to an increase in national savings. It is saving in one account through the trust fund but dissaving in another account through the deficit in the rest of the budget. Or, to put it more dramatically: we are robbing the Social Security trust fund to pay for irresponsible behavior in the rest of the budget. National savings are not being increased, and the GNP will not be higher in the future when the baby boomers retire.

Claiming that he was disgusted with the entire charade, Moynihan proposed a cut in payroll taxes and a return to a pay-as-you-go system. While this may have been a serious proposal, some suspected that it was simply a clever device that the former Harvard professor used to dramatize the issue. The proposal initially attracted considerable attention but eventually died in deficit reduction negotiations for the 1991 budget.

In their interesting book *Can America Afford to Grow Old?*, Henry Aaron, Barry Bosworth, and Gary Burtless addressed the question of whether the surplus in the Social Security system should be saved.[22] They first calculated the increases in payroll tax rates necessary to keep the system in actuarial balance, as described earlier in this chapter, while assuming that the Social Security surplus was not saved. They then asked what burden would be imposed on future workers by the forthcoming demographic changes. They measured the burden by the increase in the percent of net national product that must be paid in retirement benefits. For example, including retirement and hospital insurance, from 1990 to 2030 an extra 3.5 percent of net national product above current levels would be required to finance the programs.

They then looked at the consequences of saving the Social Security surplus. The additional saving would lead to higher levels of investment, wages, and net national product. Retirement benefits would also increase somewhat as wages increased. The net benefit to future workers from saving the Social Security surplus, they argued, would be the gain from total additional consumption available in the society minus any additional benefits paid to retirees. Aaron and his coauthors concluded that there would be substantial net benefits to future workers if the Social Security surplus were saved. The net benefits could offset the burden of a higher fraction of net national product devoted to payments to retirees. When hospital insurance and retirement payments are both included, this offset would be less than fully complete. Nonetheless, the message of their book is that increased savings is desirable now in order to raise the consumption of future workers who will have to finance higher retirement payments for the elderly.

David Cutler and his coauthors challenged this conclusion.[23] They first pointed out that the lower fertility rates after the baby boom generation have two implications. While there may be fewer workers to support retired individuals, there will also be fewer children to support. Both the old and the young will depend on the working generation for support. A good measure of this burden is the total dependency ratio, which measures the burden that the workers must bear to support both the old and the young. Because there will be fewer children, the dependency ratio will fall for the next several decades before beginning to rise in the year 2020.[24] Thus the burden on workers will decrease for a while before eventually increasing.

Cutler and his coauthors also point out that the labor force is expected to grow more slowly in the next several decades than in previous years. Under these conditions, fewer savings are needed to provide workers with the capital necessary for production. Everything else held equal, slower labor force growth dictates less saving.

Combining the effects of slower labor force growth with the initial improvement in the dependency ratio, Cutler and his coauthors conclude that demographic effects alone should lead to a decrease in savings, not an increase. Their conclusion is further reinforced by the fact that the populations of Western Europe and Japan will be aging more rapidly than in the United States and will have smaller investment needs. Because of these decreased investment needs, the United States will be able to borrow at more favorable terms in world markets. This effect also should lead to a decrease in U.S. savings.

Which authors are right on this confusing issue? Both teams make correct points but take limited perspectives. Aaron and his coauthors correctly note that we can raise the consumption of future workers who must bear a higher burden in terms of the proportion of GNP devoted to the elderly. Cutler and his coauthors are correct that slower labor force growth, by itself, should lead to less capital accumulation.

Neither group of authors, however, takes a complete look at the problem. Whether we should save or not depends on a comparison of the welfare of the current generation versus future generations. Increasing savings now means a decrease in current consumption and an increase in future consumption. Historically, our country has saved more for future generations, despite the fact that the future generations are, on average, much wealthier. Our decisions about savings naturally depend on our assessment of the future. We would be less inclined to save if we felt that productivity growth would resume at levels prior to 1973. As both groups of authors recognize, long-run trends in productivity are more important than any other single factor in determining ideal savings rates.

Up to this point, we have been looking at the problem from the point of view of individuals today, comparing the welfare of the current generation with future generations. But consider the problem from the perspective of workers in the middle of the twenty-first century.

We have already seen that combined employer and employee payroll tax rates will have to rise to between 22 and 26 percent to finance existing benefit levels. Some commentators have suggested that if we save the Social Security surpluses, these rates will be lower in the future. For example, Martin Feldstein, a former chairman of the Council on Economic Advisers, wrote that "an increased capital stock can substitute for future tax hikes . . . because a larger capital stock will mean a higher level of gross national product when the baby boomers retire."[25]

One of the surprising results of the study by Aaron and coauthors is that this claim is incorrect. Saving the Social Security surplus will not lead to lower tax rates in the future. The reason is straightforward. Increased savings will lead to higher wages in the future. Because retirement benefits are linked to wages, benefits will rise as well. The trust fund will earn interest, but the additional savings will depress interest rates. In the simulations conducted by Aaron and coauthors, all these effects balance out. The result is that tax rates are roughly the same whether or not the Social Security surplus is saved.[26]

The future generation of workers will face high tax rates whether we save for their future or not. How will they react to these higher tax rates?

Each year the Tax Foundation announces a "Tax Freedom Day," which is the first day in which the average taxpayer's earnings remain with the taxpayer and are not turned over in taxes to the local, state, and federal government. In 1990, Tax Freedom Day was May 5th, corresponding to the fact that the average tax burden was approximately 34 percent of income. The notion of a tax freedom day has a very powerful appeal. One of the most common reactions of any young person receiving a first paycheck is to be shocked at the difference between pre- and post-tax income.

What will be the political consequences of the sharp increase in payroll tax rates? No one can predict them. Important variables include the relative political power of workers versus the elderly, the structure of the political system, the costs in terms of the distortions arising from higher marginal tax rates, the evolution of attitudes about a reasonable tax burden, and similar factors.

One factor, however, surely will be irrelevant. The fact that the prior generation bequeathed a higher capital stock to the workers of the future will be taken for granted. Those workers will not ask what their consumption would have been without the additional capital accumulation. Instead they will ask what their consumption would be if they reduced current benefits for the elderly. The psychology of Tax Freedom Day will dictate the terms of the debate.

Suppose we assume that the workers of the future would successfully reduce benefits to retirees. What should be our action today? One response might be to reduce our savings. Enjoy the fruits of GNP now, for the young may not reciprocate in the future. Could this justify a return to a pay-as-you-go system?

Clearly, there are enough difficulties in store from financing existing programs for health and retirement. But there are now loud and growing demands for additional programs to meet the increasing needs of the elderly.

The Next Decision: Long-Term Care

Proponents of increases in social insurance have already outlined their next major project, insurance for long-term care for the disabled elderly. In the late 1980s, several bills were introduced in Congress that included long-term care as Medicare, Part C. After the dramatic demise of the catastrophic health insurance program, the momentum for these plans subsided. But the basic problems still exist and will remain on the political agenda.

As the population ages, the long-term care issue will continue to gain increased attention. At present, about 14 percent of the elderly are disabled, but that figure rises to 58 percent for those over 85. The cost of nursing home care averages $22,000 a year. However, only 21 percent of the disabled elderly are in nursing homes. The great majority of the remainder are taken care of at home, so-called home care.[27]

Expenses for care for the disabled elderly are already quite large and will grow sharply as the population ages. About $33 billion is now spent on nursing homes. Another $8.6 billion is spent on home care, which covers a larger number of individuals. There is also a vast amount of unpaid care, supplied by family and friends. In the future, these amounts will necessarily increase. As we saw in Chapter 2, gerontologists have different theories of aging. Those who see the compression of morbidity would not predict as large an increase in days of disability for the elderly as those who predict longer life but worsening health. Predictions of expenditures will necessarily be sensitive to which theories are more accurate.

Unlike other expenditures on health care, only a tiny fraction (about 1 percent) of expenditures on care for the elderly disabled is paid for by private insurance. The bulk of the expenditures are paid for in roughly equal proportions by the elderly themselves or Medicaid. Medicare only pays limited amounts for stays in skilled nursing facilities following hospitalization. Medicaid does pay for long-term care but, unlike Medicare, it is a means tested program that requires the elderly to first deplete or "spend-down" their assets before they can qualify. It is also part of the welfare system and thus carries a stigma.

Policy analysts have pointed to a number of problems with the current system.[28] First, a disability is often unpredictable but very costly when it occurs. Second, the current public burden, through Medicaid, is large and will grow. Third, the reliance on Medicaid has the potential to create a two-tier system, one catering to the rich and another to the poor. Finally, current private and public policies create a bias toward nursing home care as opposed to home care, despite the apparent preference of the elderly for home care.

Some aspects of long-term care for the elderly facilitate private sector solutions, but other troubling aspects make private sector solutions somewhat difficult. In principle, care of the disabled is an insurable event. Only a minority of the elderly are disabled at any point in time. The entire elderly class, however, is at risk for disabilities. Thus, potentially, there is a large base of individuals over whom independent risks can be spread. This is the classic prescription for successful insurance.

A second factor that would appear to aid private insurance efforts is the relative predictability of costs for nursing homes. Costs for nursing homes will most likely rise at the same rate as real wages. Labor is the primary input into the production of services, and there is little room for technical progress in delivering care. Assuming that real wages increase over time, costs for nursing home care will rise as well. But, unlike other medical costs, the use of increasingly expensive technology is not likely to be an important factor leading to rising and unpredictable costs.

Several very important factors have limited the growth of private insurance. First, if the elderly wait until they retire before purchasing insurance, it will be take a larger fraction of their paychecks than if they buy it at an earlier time in their life. At present, few workers give serious thought to this problem, and insurance firms have not been successful in marketing insurance to individuals in advance of their retirement.

A more important factor, however, is the great possibility for abuse of insurance, or the "moral hazard" problem. The availability of insurance naturally leads to increased use. In the case of long-term care, this trend is particularly serious because of the vast amount of home care and unpaid care that is currently provided. No matter how altruistic and caring an individual may be, it would be hard to resist the temptation to use an insurance plan to hire caretakers from the market to replace current unpaid care. Moreover, how do we draw the line between a truly disabled elderly person and an elderly person in moderately weak health?

This is the nightmare facing private insurance companies and the real source of unpredictability of future costs. Insurance executives are well aware of the possible failures of free markets. Companies that have offered policies have attempted to limit their use in a number of ways. The policies emphasize coverage for nursing home care as opposed to home care and often have prior hospitalization requirements before patients become eligible for payment. There are often large deductibles and waiting periods before benefits can be collected. For the policies that do pay for home care, reimbursement rates are typically only one-half the regular benefit.[29] All these provisions try to assure that the individuals claiming insurance payments are truly disabled.

The great debate is now between advocates of public financing programs that would expand Medicare and advocates of private financing schemes. Each strategy faces the same underlying moral hazard problem but also confronts some unique problems.

Advocates of public financing argue that long-term care should become part of the Medicare program and be removed from Medicaid. This step would end means testing for long-term care and instead place it on the same social insurance footing as Social Security and Medicare benefits. It would be financed through increases in the payroll tax. Costs would depend on the nature of the plan. A comprehensive plan with limited deductibles (or income-related deductibles) would be the most expensive, with some estimates ranging to an additional 3 percentage points on the payroll tax.[30] A more modest plan, which provided care only for those who would be disabled more than two years, would be much less costly.

Proposals to include long-term care for the disabled as part of Medicare face three significant difficulties. The first is the uncertainty about the demand for services under any public program. Even advocates of public financing admit that the moral hazard problems for long term care may be severe. Will government agencies be able to control the demands placed on the system if unpaid care starts to disappear? Costs for the program will be highly sensitive to the design and administration of the system. Can a time when payroll tax rates are increasing sharply for Social Security and Medicare be appropriate for another program of uncertain costs?

A second difficulty with publicly financed programs is their tendency to expand. The history of Social Security and Medicare quite clearly shows that once a new program is initiated, it develops constituencies, loses old political adversaries, and expands coverage. One should expect this to be the case with any long-term care program, even one that initially provided only limited coverage for care after a prolonged period of disability. Critics would first point to inequities in the system, advocates and bureaucrats would claim that "true costs" could be reduced if the program were expanded, and program coverage would be expanded quietly. With the underlying moral hazard problems, these extensions would be inevitable.

A recent example of the inexorable expansion of entitlement programs occurred in the deficit reduction agreement of 1990. In the midst of painful cuts, when President George Bush was reneging on his no taxes pledge, proponents of national health care increased mandated coverage for poor children up to the age of 18 under Medicaid. This increase was part of a deficit reduction package.

There are already pressures to change the Medicare program so that the elderly do not have to "spend down" their assets to qualify for long-term care. One part of the ill-fated catastrophic insurance bill did survive—a provision known as the "spousal impoverishment benefit" that allows the "at home" spouse to retain over $66,000 in assets and $1,600 a month in income while the partner is covered under long-term care by Medicaid.[31] Several states have been floating plans to allow individuals who purchase some long-term care insurance to be covered by Medicaid. These states are in cahoots with the insurance companies, who see this arrangement as a vehicle to increase their market for long-term insurance. Although Congress has resisted giving waivers to allow this program, one state found a technical loophole and was offering a similar program. The private sector has also responded. New books and legal advice are now available detailing how middle-class individuals can legally hide their income and wealth from Medicaid officials.

Defenders of traditional Medicaid programs are alarmed by this potential expansion of long-term care for the middle-class elderly under Medicaid. The elderly already account for 22 percent of spending under Medicaid, even though they only account for 5 percent of the recipients. The Medicaid system is already under considerable stress, as it covers only 40 percent of the poor and is driving states like Oregon to radical programs in rationing care. Powerful members of Congress are trying to prevent further inroads into Medicaid by the elderly, but the coalition of the elderly and the insurance companies is strong. This program provides another vivid example of the inherent tendency of entitlements to expand.

Finally, public programs will be heavily influenced by court rulings, which normally pay no attention to costs. An example from the early years of the Reagan administration is illustrative. By the late 1970s, many analysts were disturbed by the growing number of disability claims under Social Security. When the Reagan administration came into office, this area was viewed as one in which significant reforms and cost reductions could be made. A massive review of disability cases was conducted in the first years of the Reagan administration. However, their administrative capabilities were not sufficient for such a large task. Clear errors in classifying cases were made, and congressional hearings dramatizing these mistakes were conducted.[32]

Then the courts entered into the dispute through their appellate roles. In reviewing claims for disability, the Social Security Administration took the position that the current health status of the individual was what counted. If there had been an incorrect assessment in the past, it should be corrected by the current review. However, the Ninth Appellate Circuit Court in San Francisco ruled that the agency could not apply this standard. The court held that the agency had to demonstrate that there had been an improvement in an individual's condition before disability payments could cease. Even a sharp critic of the Social Security Administration's handling of the disability reviews felt the court had overstepped its authority. "Invoking the language of the Social Security Act—language that was not relevant to the crucial issue—the court held that medical evidence . . . [had to] comprise 'substantial evidence' of a change in condition."[33]

One need not be a strict devotee of the doctrine of original intent to recognize that courts may stretch legislation in ways that were not fully intended by legislators. When they make changes of this sort, factors such as fairness or due process are emphasized, not economics.

Advocates of private sector solutions face an immediate challenge: Where are the private sector plans now? A number of suggestions have been put forward to simplify the tax and regulatory structure to encourage private sector provision of long-term care plans. Eugene Steuerle has suggested tying insurance for long-term care to retirement decisions and pension plans as an additional feature. "People don't usually buy cancer insurance, or insurance against heart disease, but instead buy health insurance that may contain those components. It therefore seemed logical that if they were to buy long-term care insurance, it might best be sold as a component of the pension or health plans for which they were or would be eligible."[34]

Under this plan, an individual would check a box to purchase long-term care insurance as part of pension benefits, perhaps at the expense of some retirement income or other benefits. It could possibly become a standard component of a retirement package. This measure would allow insurers to reach a younger base of individuals to pay premiums. Existing tax laws would have to be clarified to allow this scheme. Steuerle advocated having benefits initially taxable but allowing individuals to claim verified medical deductions on their income tax.

There are two difficulties with this private sector solution. First, the insurance companies will still have to find ways to deal with moral hazard problems. They would have a new partner in policing claims—the Internal Revenue Service—but the difficulties still remain. Coverage is likely to be more limited and less universal than under a public plan. On the other hand, insurance firms are likely to be more aggressive in pursuing dubious claims than the government.

The second difficulty is that not all workers will be covered by pension plans, and some workers, as many as half, will rely solely on Social Security in their retirement. Steuerle, who helped author a Treasury study on health care, noted that Treasury staff considered allowing individuals to receive long-term benefits under Social Security, but at the expense of retirement benefits. This proposal failed to make it into the final Treasury report because of the political controversy surrounding Social Security.

Proponents of private sector solutions should honestly face the issue that coverage will not be universal under a private scheme. Some of the elderly, although a decreased number, will spend down their assets and receive benefits under Medicaid. This may create some tendency toward a two-class system of long-term care. But, to put it bluntly, we already have a multiclass system for working individuals and their families. Despite utopian dreams, some people lead more materially enriched lives than others. Why should we expect this inequality to be different in old age, particularly if there is a safety net provided by Medicaid?

Concluding Comments

When considering the challenges of meeting the needs of an aging society, it is important to return to the main themes of market and political failure.

1. The Social Security system can be thought of as an elaborate device to reduce pervasive uncertainty in individual lives. Social Security is a social insurance system that attempts to shelter individuals and families from low wages, large families, premature deaths, and disabilities.

2. No social insurance system can work perfectly. There will al-

ways be concerns about adverse incentives and explicitly political trade offs between adequacy and equity. All plans to reduce the vagaries of life must confront incentive issues. People do not simply have large families—they create them. Similarly, low incomes may be a misfortune or may be caused by lack of effort or initiative. Furthermore, there will always be a tension between taking care of the poor—adequacy—and providing a fair return on the investment of funds for retirement-equity. Plans that would means test Social Security (reduce benefits sharply for the more affluent) must confront the tension between adequacy and equity.

3. Just meeting current obligations under Social Security and Medicare will require a sharp increase in taxes. The combined payroll tax rate on employer and employees will have to increase by between 7 to 11 percentage points to meet current obligations under the system. This requirement will create a large burden on future generations.

4. Proposals to provide long-term care for the elderly highlight the tensions that arise from the failure of markets and the tensions inherent in social insurance. Markets have not developed fully for long-term care for the elderly because of an asymmetry between the elderly and insurance companies. How can insurance companies distinguish between the desire for the elderly to live away from their families and true disabilities that force them into nursing homes? The same lack of information plagues any government insurance system. Moreover, the tendency for government programs to expand over time suggests that the costs of government long-term care programs could spiral out of control.

Further Reading

Two excellent books published by The Brookings Institution provide insightful treatments of Social Security. Martha Derthick's *Policymaking for Social Security* (Washington, D.C.: Brookings Institution; 1979) not only presents an excellent history of the system but brings to life the key policy debates that often get lost in jargon. Almost all of the policy issues discussed today have been discussed in the past, and Derthick's book is an excellent starting point.

Data and numbers about Social Security can be hopelessly complex. *Can America Afford to Grow Old?* by Henry Aaron, Barry P. Bosworth, and Gary Burtless (Washington, D.C.: Brookings Institution, 1989) presents a clear (but alarming) picture of the finances for Social Security. One need not agree with all their policy conclusions to benefit from their book.

For more radical reform alternatives, try *Social Security, Prospects for Real Reform*, edited by Peter J. Ferrara (Washington, D.C.: Cato Institute, 1979). Most of the discussion is about replacing or sharply reducing the scope of Social Security through the use of individual retirement accounts. Another useful book on possible changes is *Too Many Promises: The Uncertain Future of Social Security* by Michael Boskin (Homewood, Ill.: Dow Jones, 1986).

On the long-term care issue, the liberal perspective is presented in *Caring for the Disabled Elderly* by Alice Rivlin and Joshua Weiner (Washington, D.C.: Brookings Institution, 1988). Eugene Steuerle writes regular columns for the weekly magazine *Tax Notes* that cover social issues as well as taxation. His more conservative perspective on long-term care can be found in "Treasury's Health Report: Financing Long-Term Care" (*Tax Notes*, June 18, 1990).

Notes

1. Richard Easterlin, *Birth and Fortune* (New York: Basic Books, 1990), app., table 1.1.
2. Easterlin, *Birth and Fortune*, 4.
3. Henry J. Aaron, Barry P. Bosworth, and Gary Burtless, *Can America Afford to Grow Old?* (Washington, D.C.: Brookings Institution, 1989), 28.
4. Aaron et al., *Can America Afford*, 29.
5. Aaron et al., *Can America Afford*, 46.
6. Aaron et al., *Can America Afford*, 91.
7. John Holahan and John Palmer, "Medicare's Fiscal Problems: An Imperative for Reform," *Journal of Health Politics, Policy, and Law* (Spring 1988): 56.
8. Holahan and Palmer, "Medicare's Fiscal Problems," 57.
9. Fay Lomax Cook, "Congress and the Public: Convergent and Divergent Opinions on Social Security," in *Social Security and the Budget*, ed. Henry Aaron. Proceedings of the First Conference of the National Academy of Social Insurance. (Lanham, Md.: University Press of America, 1990).
10. Martha Derthick, *Policymaking for Social Security*, (Washington, D.C.: Brookings Institution, 1979).
11. Derthick, *Policymaking*, 8.

12. Cited in Derthick, *Policymaking,* 213.
13. Derthick, *Policymaking,* 217.
14. Jack Meyer, president of New Directions for Policy, quoted in Jason DeParte, "Furor on Medicare Cuts Offers Political Lesson," *New York Times* (Oct. 13, 1990): A11.
15. For a discussion of these points, see Robert Moffitt, "The Econometrics of Kinked Budget Constraints," *Journal of Economic Perspectives* (Spring 1990): 119–39.
16. Moffitt, "Econometrics."
17. Tables 3.1 and 3.2 are adopted from Michael Boskin, *Too Many Promises: The Uncertain Future of Social Security* (Homewood, Ill.: Dow Jones, 1986).
18. A high-level presidential appointee would never have made such a proposal. See Boskin, *Too Many Promises,* Chapter 8, for a discussion.
19. See, for example, Peter J. Ferrara, "Social Security and the Super IRA: A Populist Proposal," in *Social Security: Prospects for Real Reform,* ed. Peter J. Ferrara, (Washington, D.C.: Cato Institute, 1985).
20. Henry J. Aaron, "Social Security: The Labrea Tar Pits of Public Policy," *National Tax Journal* (Sept. 1990): 363–69.
21. Derthick, *Policymaking,* 234–35.
22. Aaron et al., *Can America Afford.*
23. David M. Cutler, James M. Poterba, Louise M. Sheiner, and Lawrence H. Summers, "An Aging Society: Opportunity or Challenge?" *Brookings Papers on Economic Activity 1* (1990): 1–74.
24. Cutler et al. used the reciprocal of the ratio defined in the text.
25. Martin Feldstein, "Social Security Can Build a National Trust," *Wall Street Journal* (Apr. 25, 1990): 14.
26. These results are sensitive to the degree of international capital mobility. If increased domestic savings flow abroad, domestic wages and benefits will not increase as much and tax rates will be lower.
27. Alice M. Rivlin and Joshua M. Weiner, *Caring for the Disabled Elderly* (Washington, D.C.: The Brookings Institution, 1988).
28. These are discussed in Rivlin, *Caring for the Disabled Elderly.*
29. *Financing Health and Long Term Care* (Washington, D.C.: U.S. Department of the Treasury, 1990), 39.
30. Rivlin, *Caring for the Disabled Elderly,* 229.
31. For an interesting discussion of this issue, see Julie Kosterlitz, *National Journal,* (Nov. 9, 1991): 2728–32.
32. Martha Derthick, *Agency Under Stress* (Washington, D.C.: Brookings Institution, 1990), chap. 1.
33. Derthick, *Agency Under Stress,* 138–39.
34. Eugene Steuerle, "Treasury's Health Report: Financing Long-Term Care," *Tax Notes* (June 18, 1990): 1515.

PART II

Regulation with Missing Markets

A short story about the California Energy Commission illustrates some of the characteristics of regulation of economic activity: suspicion of markets, a proliferation of experts, and the importance of raw politics.

The California Energy Commission was started in the 1970s with the first appointments made by Governor Jerry Brown. At the time, it seemed like a far-sighted and inspired idea. The Organization of Petroleum-Exporting Countries (OPEC) cartel had raised oil prices to unprecedented heights, gasoline shortages had occurred at times, and the country was preoccupied with its energy future. The California Energy Commission was given responsibility for forecasting energy use in California and, more importantly, approving new power plants in the state. The commission would determine California's energy future.

By the early 1980s, however, the market for energy had changed. The state was awash in power. A recession, conservation, plus the loss of power of OPEC had changed the balance between supply and demand. The state of Washington had to cancel two major nuclear projects—and litigation continues today from investors in these projects. The change in the energy market created a problem for the

California Energy Commission: no one wanted to build plants. The primary rationale for the commission, approving new energy plants, seemed to disappear.

But, like all great bureaucracies, the California Energy Commission survived. There were two secrets to its success. First, its finances were provided by a small surcharge on energy bills. Since it was not directly part of the state budget, there was no incentive for the governor or legislature to cut the budget. After all, cutting the commission would not give them any extra funds and it was a source of extra political patronage appointments. Second, the California Energy Commission slowly reoriented its mission away from siting power plants.

The commission joined the bandwagon of conservationists and critics of the utility companies who claimed that the energy market was inefficient. There were several sources of this inefficiency. Consumers, they said, were not conserving enough energy in their homes. Because of this alleged failure, the commission could prescribe new building codes that incorporated sufficient conservation. The other source of inefficiency was in the energy market's relationship to the environment. Numerous experts came before the commission and argued that energy prices failed to reflect all the environmental effects of energy use. They started with air pollution, but as the decade progressed, global warming and ozone depletion were added to their list.

The response to these warnings was to promote and subsidize clean, renewable sources of energy, such as solar power, biomass, and windmills. Unsuspecting visitors to several valleys in California can be excused if they feel they have ventured into an alien civilization. Huge windmills cover these breezy valleys and are an impressive sight. In promoting this industry, the commission developed close ties with producers of these alternative energy sources.

The commission and its staff believed that these alternative sources of power would be fully justified once all the negative, external effects of conventional power were taken into account. Studies were untaken by the staff of the commission and utilities in California to determine what were the appropriate subsidies to these alternative sources of energy taking into account the adverse environmental effects of conventional energy sources.[1] Unfortunately, the commission had an unpleasant surprise. Even taking into account the environmental effects, the alternative sources were not justified on economic grounds.

But the suspiciousness of markets among the commission and its staff and the political connections of the alternative energy source lobbies were too great to let alternative energy sources disappear. The solution was to have "technological set-asides" for alternative energy sources built into state law. It was affirmative action for solar power and windmills.

Note

1. Paul Joskov provides a critical discussion of the methods that have been used by states to address environmental concerns in the production of electricity. See Paul Joskow, "Weighing Environmental Externalities: Let's Do It Right!," *The Electricity Journal* (May 1992): 53–67.

4

The New Wave
of Environmental Regulation

If the events of 1990 are any indication, the decade of the 1990s will
become a laboratory for environmental issues, debates, and regulation. Here are just a few of the significant environmental events of the
early 1990s:

- The Congress and the president reached agreement on sweeping
  amendments to the Clean Air Act, the first major change since
  1977.
- California voters defeated a complex environmental ballot initiative, labeled "Big Green" by its supporters, that would have made
  sharp changes in pesticide use, greenhouse gas emissions, timber
  preservation, and regulation of activities of the oil and gas industries.
- The nations of the world gathered for a series of conferences on
  global warming and the greenhouse effect, and a United Nations
  task force analyzed the issues. The United States's positions were
  more cautious than those of other nations. The Bush administration generally advocated more study on issues such as global
  warming and was reluctant to make binding commitments in international forums for specific reductions in emissions.
- The Environmental Protection Agency (EPA) issued a report from

101

an advisory committee stating that the agency should start to refo-
cus its efforts and move away from traditional issues such as water
quality and oil spills to concentrate on global environmental issues
such as the loss of biological diversity and destruction of wetlands
and forests.

• Political candidates, sensing that Cold War threats would no
longer motivate voters, have placed global environmental issues on
their agenda.

The environment is a clear case in which markets fail. As noted in
Chapter 1, the different types of market failure are an inability to deal
with uncertainty, missing markets, and the need to provide public
goods. The environment is a classic case of problem two: missing
markets. No price is attached to industrial emissions or auto exhausts
that create pollution or social "bads." Economists have long recognized market failures in the environment and have debated, mostly
among themselves, alternative solutions. As the environment became
a political topic, experts of all types emerged to debate the issues.
Some experts brought sense and clarity to the debates; others brought
alarmism and pseudoscience.

Since economists have long recognized market failure in the environment, it is surprising that economists have not been successful in
influencing the public debate. This chapter discusses a number of reasons for this failure, but perhaps the most important is that it is difficult to establish markets where none exist. For example, how can a
market for auto emissions be established?

In recent years, the nature of the environmental debate has
changed so as to render cold, economic analysis even more difficult.
First, many of the new issues center around scientific controversy. Are
global temperatures rising and, if so, what is the role of our industrial
activities in this process? Do pesticides really pose significant cancer
risks, and how should we measure and assess them? In both these
areas, there is considerable scientific uncertainty that complicates any
economic analysis. Second, the preoccupation with species preservation, biological diversity, and wilderness preservation stretches conventional economic analysis. How do we put a value on preserving an
Arctic wilderness area that will not be visited by 99 percent of the
population in their lifetime when the same population expresses a
concern for its preservation?

This chapter focuses on the areas of controversy in traditional environmental regulations and in the new environmental topics that have come to the public agenda. The first section addresses air pollution. It surveys past strategies to obtain clean air and then examines the new amendments to the Clean Air Act. Some of these amendments are very costly and bring uncertain benefits. The new amendments also permit a market to develop in which public utilities can "trade" emissions. How successful will market-based environmental solutions be?

The next two sections highlight issues in which scientific uncertainty is important—global warming and pesticide regulation. What is the proper set of actions to take if global temperatures may rise a few degrees in the next century or if some chemicals in strong doses may cause cancer?

The last part of this chapter tackles the issue of biological diversity and species protection. Is there a scientific basis for preserving species or is it more akin to a religious preference? How should we value the demands to protect species?

The Quest for Clean Air

How We Regulate Air Pollution

The Environmental Protection Agency (EPA) was formed in 1970. This date also marked the key amendments to the Clean Air Act that form the basic core of our policy today. Our regulatory structure for air pollution is complex and confusing, as might be expected if one imagines the task of controlling air pollution throughout the diverse regions and industrial structures in the United States. Add to this task the political realities of protecting jobs and industries in the face of regulation and the complexity multiplies.

Before 1970, air pollution was regulated mostly by states and municipalities. At times, private law suits were brought against polluting parties. But all these approaches were limited in that they failed to come to grips with the public nature of air quality. Thousands of neighbors might be affected by a polluting plant, but how would the neighbors effectively organize to deal with the problem? Even state and municipal regulation would encounter difficulties as pollutants crossed political boundaries. Federal air pollution efforts began in 1955, but not until 1970 did the government make a comprehensive and systematic attempt to control air pollution on a national basis.

The structure of the Clean Air Act of 1970 can be best thought of as setting specific goals for air quality and prescribing certain means for achieving these goals.[1] The goals consisted of National Ambient Air Quality Standards (NAAQS) for common air pollutants that represented maximum permissible concentrations. Standards were set for particulate matter, sulfur dioxide, carbon monoxide, nitrogen oxide, ozone, and lead.

In setting the standards, EPA was directed to "provide an adequate margin of safety . . . to protect the public . . . from any known or anticipated adverse effects associated with such air pollutants in the ambient air."[2] The standards implicitly are based on the idea of a threshold below which pollutants cause no effects. That is, concentrations of pollutants below this level are assumed to cause no harm. Unfortunately, there is no scientific support for the threshold concept.

The law also directed that environmental standards be uniform across the country and not be relaxed for areas in which the costs of meeting the quality standards are exceptionally high. Issuing uniform standards also raises another question: what about the areas that already have concentrations below the standards? Should they be allowed to let their air quality deteriorate? Although the original law did not directly address this issue, a court case in the mid-1970s dictated that the EPA could not allow deterioration. In 1977, Congress took these court decisions into account in amending the Clean Air Act to create PSD—"prevention of significant deterioration"—areas. The Congress also created special rules to prevent any reduction of visibility in scenic areas such as national parks, even if there were no effects on health.

The means by which the Clean Air Act specified that the goals should be met are especially complex. First, specific uniform national standards for emissions of cars and trucks were built into law. The idea was to prevent states from enacting separate rules and standards that would make life difficult for car manufacturers. However, in recent years, some states, including California and New York, have put forward their own stricter standards.

Rules for regulating stationary sources of pollution (i.e., plants and factories) differ depending on whether they are for new or existing sources. All new sources have to meet "new source performance standards" (NSPS), EPA-promulgated standards that are supposed to embody state-of-the-art technology and affordability. In areas of the country that consistently fail to meet the goals set in the NAAQS, even stricter standards are required. Furthermore, in PSD areas, where the air quality is already high, other stricter standards apply.

All these regulations only apply to new sources of pollution, which are governed by the same federal standards. In contrast, regulation of existing sources is left to the states. Each state was asked to formulate plans to achieve the goals of the Clean Air Act by regulating existing sources. Monitoring and enforcement powers are also delegated to the states.

Paul Portney argues that having states control regulations for existing sources was politically important. No one notices if a plant does not locate in an area because of the costs of meeting pollution control regulations. But if a plant threatens to close because of regulations, an outcome that would result in layoffs for workers and reduced business for suppliers, the political system must respond. Some give and take is necessary on the local level, and the existing rules effectively allow the states to manage this political conflict.

The structure of the Clean Air Act differs significantly from the way an economist would design an ideal plan to clean the air. In the first place, an economist would seek to obtain at least some balance between the costs of cleaning up the air and the benefits of cleaner air. This approach would mean that the standards would be set not just to minimize health risks but also to take into account the costs of complying with the standards. Standards would probably vary by region of the country as a reflection of differences in compliance costs.

Perhaps more important, an economist would criticize the sharp distinctions made between new and existing sources of air pollution in the law. Both new and old sources pollute. It is by no means obvious that the same overall pollution targets could not be met more efficiently by pursuing a more vigorous program for existing sources. Policies should aim to achieve pollution reduction at the least cost. This goal requires allowing cost-efficient trade-offs between new and existing sources and among existing sources. The same basic principles apply to auto emission standards. Placing some of the burden on car owners through exhaust inspections may be more cost effective than mandates to car manufacturers.

But economists do not make policy, politicians do, and perhaps their solutions have some hidden virtues. It may be easier, for example, to enlist public support for air pollution standards when they are set at a uniform national level. This policy might prevent constant in-fighting among states and regions to relax standards. Perhaps only a national government has enough power to successfully regulate large automobile companies. There is a clear political rationale for distinguishing between new and existing sources of pollution. New sources do not protest as much. Despite this political virtue, the distinction between new and existing sources remains an economic liability. Stringent controls on new plants or new cars can lead firms and individuals to delay the introduction of new technology and exacerbate the pollution problem. Fortunately, the new clean air amendments allow more scope for meeting air pollution reductions through more cost-effective solutions.

How well has the Clean Air Act worked in practice? This question can be addressed in a number of different ways. First, except for ozone, the average concentrations of air pollutants are significantly below the NAAQS. These averages do, however, mask the fact that some regions of the country have persistent violations, especially for ozone. The Los Angeles basin is the prime example of a persistent failure to meet standards. Paul Portney provides a balanced summary: "The fairly steady improvements in urban air quality . . . have eliminated many of the more immediate or acute threats to health associated with air pollution. It is highly unlikely, for instance, that the United States will ever again experience episodes involving the criteria pollutants serious enough to trigger significant premature mortality like that which occurred in Donora, Pennsylvania in 1948, when a temperature inversion trapped a thick blanket of smoke over the city for an extended period. Yet ambient concentrations are clearly high enough in some areas during certain periods that even healthy individuals experience considerable discomfort and adverse health effects."[3]

On an international scale, U.S. cities have relatively clean air. (I urge the skeptical reader to visit Bangkok, Mexico City, or Taiwan.) EPA data on emissions of pollutants also indicates considerable improvement over time. Overall, air quality has improved, but problem spots still remain.

While air quality has improved over time, was it due to the Clean Air Act or to other actions taken by state and local governments and private industry? This question turns out to be very difficult to answer. One fact is quite striking. During the period 1966–1970 (before the Clean Air Act), air quality improved at a more rapid rate than it did after the passage of the act. Other, more detailed studies that have tried to link emissions of particular industries to their investment in pollution control equipment mandated under the law found only small effects from the mandates.[4]

The important question to ask is the counterfactual: what would air quality be today if the Clean Air Act had not been passed? With the economic growth since 1970 and the rapid increase in the number of cars, could state and local governments have continued the improvements in air quality that were evident before passage of the act? This is the question we ultimately would like to answer and one for which a sharp, convincing answer has not been forthcoming.

Costs and Benefits

Even if the Clean Air Act were effective in reducing air pollution, a further question is whether the benefits from improved air quality exceed the costs of the cleanup. This question is naturally difficult because it requires us to evaluate and place dollar values on improved health and reduced risk of death, changes in production stemming from improved air quality, and increases in visibility. Attempts have been made to assess the overall benefits and costs of the entire Clean Air Act.[5] Rather than review these difficult and somewhat conjectural exercises, it is more valuable to examine a recent cost–benefit analysis of the 1990 amendments to the Clean Air Act.

Before the 1990 amendments to the Clean Air Act were passed, Paul Portney brought his considerable knowledge of the economics of air pollution to estimate costs and benefits of the key provisions of the legislation that eventually became law.[6] These amendments were quite significant. Once they were fully phased in they would effectively double the total spending of society on air pollution control to about $60 billion a year.

There were three essential components to the 1990 amendments. The first was a plan for electric utilities to reduce sulfur dioxide emissions by 10 million tons from their 1980 levels and then have these emissions capped at lower levels. These emission reductions were designed to curb acid rain. The second component focused on urban air pollution and contained a variety of measures including: controls on volatile organic compounds (VOCS) emitted from stationary sources ranging from chemical plants to dry cleaners; emissions controls for cars and light trucks; and initiatives to require cleaner-burning fuels. The final provision dealt with controlling a class of "hazardous air pollutants" in order to reduce deaths from cancer.

Only for the amendments dealing with acid rain do the costs incurred by society even begin to approach the benefits. And the benefits from the acid rain provisions have little to do with stopping acid rain. Let's look at the 1990 amendments in more detail.

The acid rain provisions require utilities to reduce emissions of sulfur dioxide. For years, governors in the northeast states and our northern neighbors in Canada have expressed anguish over the effects of acid rain on their lakes, forests, and agricultural productivity. Many distinguished scientists have joined the states in blaming the acid rain on emissions from utilities. Some scientists demurred and felt the problem was more complex. In 1980 the federal government launched a massive ten-year study that, at the time, was viewed by environmentalists as a delaying tactic to forestall action.

As Portney reports, the conclusions from the study were unexpected. Surveys revealed that fewer lakes were acidified than previously had been believed and that agricultural crop damage was minimal. The extent to which any of the problems that did occur were due to utility emissions was unclear. There was some damage to forest tops in the northeast, but nationwide damage estimates were not available. In general, the scientific study downplayed both the damage from acid rain and the role of utility emissions in causing any damage.

This case is not the only recent instance in which further scientific research has dispelled common environmental beliefs. After engaging in massive asbestos removal programs throughout U.S. schools, scientists learned that threats to health were greater during the process of removing asbestos than when it remained in place.

Fortunately for the cost–benefit analysis of the acid rain provisions and for taxpayers, there are some benefits from the plan to reduce utility emissions. Concentrations of airborne sulfate particles will also be reduced, and this reduction potentially can have important effects on health and visibility. Portney estimated that the overall benefits from the emissions reductions would be in the range of $2–9 billion annually.

The costs of reducing utility emissions have been studied extensively, and estimates place them in the neighborhood of $4 billion a year. The costs would be several billion dollars higher without the emissions trading program that was part of the legislation. (This program is discussed in detail later.) Taken as a whole, the benefits for the emission reductions appear reasonable in relation to the costs.

This relationship is not the case with the other two initiatives. Portney estimates that the urban air pollution amendments will add approximately $20 billion a year in costs. Estimates for benefits were in the range of $4–12 billion, and the higher numbers in this range were clearly speculative. Clearly, the costs of the urban air initiatives far exceed any reasonable estimate of benefits.

A similar situation prevails for the amendments on hazardous air pollutants. Prior legislation had required the EPA to examine and regulate cancer-causing hazardous air pollutants. The EPA had only taken action on seven chemicals over a twenty-year period. The new amendments require the "best available technology" for approximately 190 chemicals and compounds. Portney's estimates of the costs put them in the range of $6–10 billion a year.

What are the benefits from controlling these pollutants? The best estimates are that 500 cancers a year could be avoided that, at worst, could lead to 500 deaths. Economists have used a wide variety of methods to estimate the dollar value of a human life. Although non-economists often find this effort shocking, there must be some way to balance the expenditures necessary to save lives with the number of lives saved. We implicitly make these judgments in the types of cars we buy, the jobs we take, the sports we enjoy, and the public facilities that we build. For example, additional safeguards could be incorporated into our roads and highways that would reduce the number of deaths. These safeguards, however, would raise the cost of the highways. In deciding not to incorporate additional safeguards, an implicit value is being placed on human life. Typical estimates of the statistical value of a life range from $1–5 million. Using $3 million as a mid-range estimate, saving 500 deaths a year should be valued at approximately $1.5 billion a year. Again, this falls far short of the $6–10 billion in costs.

Why have we recently undertaken these costly environmental actions when the benefits often fall far short of the costs? Portney suggests two reasons. First, the public and Congress simply do not have the information about benefits necessary to evaluate proposed legislation. Moreover, they may also overestimate the risks to health and cancer. When information is sparse, environmental activists can more easily obtain their goals by exaggerating the benefits. Second, some individuals place a higher value on reducing environmental risks than others. They also may be the activists pushing for legislation. But ultimately, it should be the attitudes of the general public that matter in these decisions, not simply the preferences of the environmentalists.

Pursuing Least-Cost Strategies

Because benefits from air pollution reduction are hard to quantify, many environmentalists are skeptical of using straight cost–benefit analysis to decide on basic policies. Some economists might share in this skepticism. But most economists would unite in seeking regulatory solutions that would achieve environmental goals at the least possible cost.

It is natural for economists to suggest using some variant of the price system to achieve these goals. In the environmental area, economists have typically recommended using emission taxes or allowing trading in permits to pollute. Ideally, firms seeking to maximize their profits would respond efficiently to these market incentives.

Setting taxes or prices for pollution has been controversial and only has been used in practice to a limited extent in Europe. There are two primary objections to setting prices for pollution: one economic and the other philosophical. The primary economic problem is that it is difficult for regulators to have enough information to set the price correctly. If the price is set too low, there will not be sufficient pollution reduction; too high a price will induce more reduction than had been deemed desirable. If the net benefits from pollution reductions are highly sensitive to the amount of actual reduction, these uncertainties pose serious economic problems.

The philosophical objections to using pollution taxes stem from the belief that this practice places polluting activities on par with other market activities.[7] Many environmentalists take sharp issue with this implicit moral equivalence. They argue that society should scorn polluters and that we must change overall attitudes toward pollution and our environment. Using pollution taxes impedes this change in attitudes by treating pollution as just another normal activity in the market. In some parts of the country, voluntary recycling activities have taken on an ethical dimension, and these activities would be less frequent if individuals had not changed their attitudes. Changing moral attitudes can be efficient. Prices for pollution could undermine these attitudes.

In the United States, regulators have been more willing to experiment with markets in which firms can trade emission permits. Markets for emission trading allow firms to meet environmental goals in a least-cost fashion. Suppose we have two firms each currently emitting ten units of pollutants and a goal of total emissions of sixteen units. We could simply mandate that each firm reduce emissions by two units. But if one firm could reduce pollution more cheaply than the other, it would be socially efficient for the firm with the lower cost to engage in more pollution reduction. Regulators only need to require that each firm hold two credits for reducing emissions. The low-cost firm could, in this case, gain four credits from reducing pollution and then sell two credits to the high-cost firm.

In general, firms would compare the price of buying an emission credit in the market with earning one by reducing its pollution. If the costs of a unit reduction are below the current market price, firms will engage in pollution reduction and sell the credit or keep it if it is needed. Firms whose costs are higher will buy credits from the market. This process will eventually result in an efficient, least-cost outcome.

Since 1975 the EPA has experimented with allowing some emissions trading. One initial impetus for this policy arose from the problems that occurred in areas that failed to meet air quality standards. It was politically impossible to prohibit new firms from locating in these areas. Instead, the EPA developed an offset program in which new firms could enter the area provided they obtained reductions in pollution from existing firms. Other programs included the "bubble" and "netting" plans. Under the bubble plan, existing sources in nonattainment areas can avoid strict technology requirements on each source of pollution as long as the firm's total package of emissions meets the new standards. Netting allows an existing plant to expand or be modified without having to meet new source performance standards as long as the total emissions from the plant meet certain threshold requirements.

There have been several reviews of marketable permit plans.[8] Both the bubble and netting plans were the most successful in reducing costs. Trading activity in the air pollution plans occurred primarily within single firms or plants, and there was only limited activity between firms.

In practice, there were a number of recurring difficulties in implementing marketable permit plans. The first problem concerned the appropriate baseline. Suppose a baseline level of reduction was set for each plant, but some plants were already operating below the baseline. Should they be allowed to earn and sell emission credits without taking any actions to reduce their pollution further? In this case, it would be possible for air quality to deteriorate. Firms operating below the baseline would have a surplus of credits to sell to other firms that could create more pollution. The EPA initially allowed a firm to earn credits if it were already operating below the baseline. Eventually, however, the regulations were changed to require the use of the minimum of actual or allowable emissions.[9]

The second major practical issue concerned "shutdown credits." Suppose a plant was closed. Could the owners be entitled to sell the credits now that emissions were zero? Environmentalists objected to this policy on several grounds. First, the goals set by the states usually assumed that shutdowns would occur naturally. If firms could sell shutdown credits, these air quality gains would be sacrificed. Second, plant shutdowns often have adverse effect on communities. Somehow it did not seem fair to allow firms to profit from this activity. In practice, the states that regulated these policies took a dim view of shutdown credits and tended to prohibit their use.

With the 1990 amendments to the Clean Air Act, we are about to embark on a major new experiment in emissions trading. The acid rain legislation mandates, among other things, significant reductions in sulfur dioxide by electric utilities. The objective is to cut emissions of sulfur dioxide in half by the beginning of the next century. In order to ease the costs of meeting these goals, the legislation permits emissions trading among utilities.

The proposal by the Bush administration to allow emissions trading was the key to solving the seemingly intractable politics of acid rain. The prior policy was a mess. Utilities were required to reduce sulfur dioxide emissions but were prevented from buying low-sulfur coal to meet these goals. The reason for this prohibition was the political power of the congressmen representing high-sulfur coal mining areas. Instead of using low-sulfur coal, utilities were forced to install costly "scrubbers" that reduced sulfur dioxide emissions. With this byzantine system, further reductions in emissions were not likely. The emissions trading system helped break the political logjam.[10]

A smoothly functioning market in emissions credits, however, is by no means guaranteed. Utilities are extensively regulated by the states. If public utility commissions adopt policies that are unfavorable to emissions trading, the markets could dry up. Regulators may want utilities to bank credits for fear that the market will dry up in the future. Or regulators could prevent credits from being sold to utilities in other states in efforts to insure that economic progress continues in their own state. They could also treat purchases of equipment for pollution reduction activities more favorably than purchases of credits in rate-setting hearings. All these actions could hurt the development of the market for credits.

Ideally, regulators will make policies that encourage the growth of a true market. While we may have set goals for sulfur dioxide reduction too high according to a cost–benefit calculation, we still want to keep these costs as low as possible. Trading among privately consenting utilities should not affect public morality very much. Most individuals have no idea about the complex world of public utilities. There is little danger that the emissions trading system would undercut a growing environmental consciousness.

Another large experiment in market-based pollution control will take place in southern California in the 1990s. The stubborn air quality problems in this region have posed a dilemma for the community. Strong measures are needed to clean up the air, but measures that are too strong could cripple economic growth. A partial solution to this dilemma was to create a market for pollution in order to meet air quality goals at least cost.

As currently envisioned, the market for emissions credit will be among the 2,700 largest firms in the Los Angeles basin. A government agency will monitor sales of pollution credits and provide latest price information. Some environmentalists wanted to exclude utilities from the plan (since they were already coming under stringent regulations) and to limit shutdown credits. But with concerns about companies leaving California, regulators have taken a flexible stand toward market solutions in order to reduce costs.

Another approach consistent with economic efficiency is to tax activities that generate pollution. Pollution taxes also have one other important feature: they raise revenue. Pollution taxes are efficient because all polluters face the same rate of tax. While it is often difficult to tax the pollution directly (for example, a direct tax on car emissions), it is much easier to levy taxes that indirectly affect emissions. Gasoline taxes discourage driving and indirectly reduce emissions.

Gasoline taxes traditionally have been used to finance highway improvements and related infrastructure. Proceeds from state and federal gasoline taxes have often gone into specific trust funds for these purposes and were not easily available for other uses. Because automobiles are the main source of air pollution in many areas, it perhaps is time to rethink the potential for higher gasoline taxes as a mechanism to reduce air pollution. Typical state plus federal gasoline taxes are currently about 30 cents per gallon, far below the levels in Europe. Doubling of this tax could be justified strictly on environmental grounds. The proceeds from this tax should not remain in highway trust funds but should be used as a general source of state and federal revenues.

Gasoline taxes, however, are not very popular politically. Surveys indicate that people object as strongly to increases in gasoline taxes as they do to increases in personal income taxes. Selling higher gasoline taxes to the public would be a challenge for politicians. But perhaps the business community (other than the auto industry) could see that higher gasoline taxes are a much cheaper way to buy pollution control than other forms of regulation. Revenues from higher gasoline taxes could be used for income tax rebates to offset public concern about higher taxes. While this program may not be politically popular now, perhaps contemplation of the other alternatives may make it seem more attractive in the future.

The Global Warming Controversy

Maybe it is the revenge of J. Peter Oppenheimer. When President Truman exploded the atomic bomb, it was against the wishes of many of the scientists who had developed the weapon. Oppenheimer, one of the key scientists, later lost his security clearance in the tense anticommunist period after the end of the war. To many observers, his security clearance was revoked because he held unpopular political views. The advancement of scientific objectivity in public has never recovered from these episodes. Many of today's scientists hold one alliance to science and another to their political values. Public scientific discourse has suffered accordingly.

One outrageous political event masquerading as science occurred in the summer of 1988. It was an uncharacteristically hot summer and farmers were very worried about prospects of drought. Temperatures in the 1980s were significantly higher than they had been in the 1970s. James Hansen, a climatologist and presidential science advisor, had a convenient explanation in congressional testimony for the heat wave. He was "99 percent" confident that the heat wave was due to global warming trends. This testimony, which was conveniently timed for the evening news, insured that the public could add global warming to the list of world problems.

Global warming may be an important environmental problem, and Hansen clearly was successful in bringing it to public consciousness. But tying the heat wave of the 1980s to the gradual trends in global temperature was only political theater and bore little resemblance to science.

According to available historical records, average mean global temperatures have increased by about 0.5° C since the 1880s.[11] Even this figure is only an estimate because records from different regions of the earth are highly incomplete. Indeed, some scientists have suggested that a substantial fraction of the measured increase results from the fact that our instruments lie close to areas undergoing urbanization. This "urban heat island effect" could lead to incorrect assessments of true average global temperatures.

Even if we take the historical data at face value, it is clear that mean global temperatures fluctuate widely around a slowly increasing trend. Temperatures in the late 1930s, for example, exceeded those in almost all subsequent years until the 1980s. These long swings in climate and the apparent randomness in our historical mean global temperature cast doubt on claims that attribute the heat wave of the 1980s to a gradual global warming trend.[12]

If the apparent global warming trend were just a natural change in the world's climate, it would not be a major public policy issue. But proponents of global warming theory argue that modern industrial growth has caused the increase in temperatures. Furthermore, according to advocates of this theory, without any change in the nature of world economic activity, global temperatures will continue to increase from anywhere between 1.5 to 4.5° C by the end of the next century. This rise would be an unprecedented change in the climate over a relatively short period of time.

Scientists have long recognized that atmospheric gases can play an important role in determining climate. So-called greenhouse gases are those gases that allow solar radiation to enter the atmosphere but absorb a significant amount of outgoing radiation. The primary greenhouse gases include: carbon dioxide, methane, nitrous oxides, and chlorofluorocarbons (CFCs). Carbon dioxide is the single most important greenhouse gas because it is a byproduct of all our combustion of fossil fuels. CFCs are highly potent greenhouse gases, but today they are used much less extensively than before. Their use is being curtailed worldwide because of the potential damage to the ozone layer. Much less is known about the causes and consequences of methane and nitrous oxide production.

There is a general scientific consensus about the properties of greenhouse gases and their increased atmospheric concentrations over time. However, there is much less consensus about the effects of increased concentrations of these gases on global climate patterns. Climatologists have developed highly sophisticated computer models to assess the effects of increased concentrations of greenhouse gases on future climate patterns. These models have to take into account a myriad of factors and must attempt to trace all the complicated interactions between ocean currents, sea ice, winds, and soil properties.

William Nordhaus provides a convenient summary of this research. Assuming that carbon dioxide concentrations double between now and the year 2100, the models indicate that global warming will be between 1.5 and 4.5° C.[13] This increase is large relative to the 0.5° average increase over the last 100 years. But, as economists have sorely discovered, in all mathematical computer models, the outputs are only as reliable as the inputs. These models all rely on particular theories and incomplete data. A current scientific consensus in this inherently difficult area later could be viewed as a fad.

It is very difficult to verify these global climate models. Our historical experience is quite limited. There is no natural laboratory in which to conduct experiments. In fact, the situation is roughly akin to that faced by economic model builders. With all due respect to those economists who provide us with predictions, how many of us would take their forecasts seriously for the year 2100?

More recent scientific work has also called into question the link between greenhouse gases and global warming. In late 1991, two Danish scientists published an article in the prestigious journal *Science* that established very close correlations between the length of cycles of sunspot activity and global temperature levels. During longer sunspot cycles the earth tends to cool and during shorter cycles, such as we have witnessed recently, the temperature of the earth tends to increase. This theory accounts for global temperatures much more accurately than measures of concentrations of greenhouse gases. Recall that temperatures in the 1930s were much higher than in all but recent years. If the sunspot theory is correct, it would severely undercut the models predicting global warming.

Other scientists contend that the link between global temperature and greenhouse gases is a classic example of reverse causation—higher global temperatures lead to higher concentrations of greenhouse gases. The source of this link, according to these scientists, is through the oceans. The oceans absorb different amounts of carbon dioxide depending on global temperatures and establish the link between greenhouse gases and global temperatures. Contrary to impressions conveyed by the popular press in the United States and Europe, there is considerable scientific uncertainty about the mechanisms of global warming.

But maybe we are being too cavalier. Even if there is some uncertainty about the future, shouldn't we be concerned about a potentially major change in the climate that could cause great economic dislocations?

Very little work has been done to assess the economic impacts of global warming if it occurs. Nordhaus estimated that with a doubling of carbon dioxide concentrations and a 3° C increase in mean global temperatures by the end of the next century, the costs to the United States would be only one-fourth of 1 percent of GNP, a relatively small amount.

A number of factors, Nordhaus contends, would reduce the economic effects of global warming for the United States.[14] These include:

1. Technology changes have allowed manufacturing and service industries to operate anywhere in the United States. Air conditioning led to the development of the sunbelt and the vast migration of people to the south and west. About 87 percent of American industry is insensitive to weather.
2. In their retirement, recreation, and migration decisions, individuals have shown a distinct preference for warmer climates. Technological developments, such as snow-creating machines, can offset some potential recreational losses in other areas.
3. Agriculture, forest sectors, and coastal lands will be the most sensitive to climate changes. But studies have shown that modest increases in carbon dioxide concentrations could improve agricultural productivity. Losses and expenses may occur in other areas, but these are relatively minor relative to the scale of the U.S. economy. Initially, scientists worried about massive increases in sea levels because of melting of the icecaps. But more recent research suggests that moderate global warming

could increase snowfall in the Antarctica; this finding has led to sharp reductions in projected increases in average sea levels.

4. Global warming, if it occurs, will come gradually over the next 100 years. The remarkable technological developments of the last 100 years suggest an immense human ability to adapt to changes in the environment. There is no reason to believe that we will be confronting tomorrow's problems with today's technology.

There is somewhat more potential for economic damage in developing countries, especially those dependent on coastal products. But, again, increased carbon dioxide concentrations may improve agricultural productivity. We also must recall that we are discussing developments in the next century, by which time one would hope that today's developing countries would have economic profiles not too dissimilar to today's developed countries.

William Cline has argued that individuals today would be willing to pay a high price to keep their environment constant.[15] He suggested, for example, that today's inhabitants of Washington, D.C., would have to receive extensive compensation for having the average high temperature rise significantly in the summer. Perhaps he is right, although the current miserable summer weather of the former swamp inside the Beltway has not stopped a massive in-migration. More seriously, arguments about current desires to keep the climate unchanged must take into account that it is future generations who may face higher temperatures and that these temperatures would gradually phase in over a number of years.

Suppose we decide that there is a reasonable probability of a 3° C increase in temperatures and that, contrary to current economic thinking, there would be substantial economic costs of this warming. How expensive would it be to stop the trend and significantly reduce carbon dioxide emissions?

Because fossil fuel products are so ubiquitous, one might expect small reductions in carbon dioxide emissions to be relatively cheap but larger reductions very expensive. This expectation is precisely the result of economic estimates by Nordhaus. A 16 percent reduction in greenhouse gases would cost only $6 billion a year; a 50 percent reduction would jump to $200 billion a year, nearly 1 percent of global GNP; a 90 percent reduction would cost nearly a trillion dollars a year—roughly the size of the entire U.S. federal budget.

Nordhaus combines his estimates of the cost of global warming (roughly one-quarter of 1 percent of GNP) with the costs of reducing greenhouse gases to arrive at the level of reduction suggested by cost–benefit analysis. According to his calculations, policies that lead to a 13 percent reduction in greenhouse gases are warranted: the total cost of this policy would be about $5 billion a year.

No one would be enthusiastic about proposals to make relatively small reductions in greenhouse gases along the lines suggested by Nordhaus. Many economists would wonder whether the small reduction in expected global temperatures would be worth any costs incurred today. Small changes could be accommodated easily by technological change.

Environmentalists would be even less enthusiastic. From their perspective, the risk of unpredictable global catastrophes increases with the rise of average global temperatures.[16] The frequency of these dramatic events may rise discontinuously with the average temperature. Environmentalists might also be concerned with the effects on existing species and habitats, which would be drastically changed; they would not put much stock in typical cost–benefit calculations. Finally, larger changes would require more dramatic human adaptation as well.

Thomas Schelling has outlined some of the difficult political issues facing the world community if it wants to take action against global warming. Perhaps the most basic point is that any solution must be truly global. Carbon emissions are increasing most rapidly in the poorest countries in the world. By the middle of next century, these nations will account for over half of the total world carbon emissions. China, India, and Eastern Europe will be major contributors to the problem.[17]

But developing countries and those with massive populations are not going to be willing to spend large sums to stop carbon dioxide emissions. China and India have more pressing problems, and Eastern Europe has to make up for years of regress under central planning.

The ivory tower economist's solution to achieving an efficient reduction in carbon emissions would be to have a tax on carbon dioxide or a carbon-dioxide-equivalent tax on other greenhouse gases. The principle behind a worldwide tax is similar to the rationale for sulfur dioxide emissions trading by electric utilities under the Clean Air Act. If every producer in every country faced the same tax, they would all take appropriate cost-effective actions to reduce emissions. This would achieve the desired reduction in the least costly manner.

While a market solution may work within the limited electric utility market in the United States, it is sheer fantasy to believe that it could work globally. First, the poorest countries in the world would face relatively steep penalties from the tax. They would never agree to a uniform world tax. Second, among the developed countries there are vast differences in carbon dioxide production. France, for example, with its efficient nuclear power industry, produces relatively little carbon dioxide, while the United States would be at the other end of the spectrum. These initial differences in usage would make it difficult to agree on any uniform tax.

As Schelling stressed, a worldwide tax levied at a sufficient level to make a major difference in emissions would raise vast sums of revenue. Who would decide how to allocate these revenues? Presumably, some of these revenues would be rebated to developing countries. But it is unrealistic to believe that governments of countries around the world, always in a bind for cash, would willingly turn over large sums of money to other countries.

Rather than a single uniform tax on carbon emissions, some have suggested that taxes only be applied to the extent that a given country exceeds its quota of greenhouse gas emissions. This proposal also has a number of difficulties. The first problem is how to decide upon quotas for individual countries, all of whom have a strong incentive to overstate their current emissions (to raise their quota) and also to overstate their costs of reduction. Uniform quotas would be unacceptable to already efficient countries like France; nonuniform quotas would be difficult to rationalize. The dynamic problems would also be formidable. If a country successfully met its quota, it likely would be penalized in the next round with even tougher standards. Thus, there would be strong incentives not to take actions that would lead to reductions below existing quota levels. Finally, it would be hard to set quotas objectively for poor, developing countries, even if tight quotas on them would be both feasible and effective.

Schelling believes that the best arrangements the world community could undertake to achieve a reduction of carbon emissions would be multilateral negotiations, led and financed primarily by the developed countries. These agreements would set provisional goals for carbon emission reductions, promote technology transfers to developing countries, and continually explore scientific knowledge of the global warming problem. The process would have to work on a trial-and-error basis, and goals and quotas would have to be revised as new information became available. This arrangement could provide a framework if scientific knowledge eventually dictates that more drastic action to stop global warming is required.

The administration of President George Bush received considerable criticism for its approach to global warming. The Bush administration took a cautious, pragmatic policy stance. Before throwing vast sums of money into any program, they argued, we should try to resolve some of the scientific uncertainties concerning the global warming process and also learn much more about the costs of alternative policies. To this end, the Bush administration allocated about a billion dollars for research on this problem.

At the same time, it may be possible to make progress on carbon emission in developing countries through general initiatives to promote energy efficiency and curb air pollution. China, India, and Eastern Europe are far from the technological frontier in this area. It would be perfectly appropriate—and initiatives are underway—for the World Bank and other international organizations to begin including environmental considerations in their aid and development packages.

A billion dollars in research and tying development aid to environmental concerns may not make the evening news. But these initiatives are probably the best responses that we can make today to a problem that may or may not appear and whose future costs could be minor.

Pesticides and Our Food Supply

In 1989, prominent celebrities and their friends in the media helped promote a report called *Intolerable Risk: Pesticides in our Children's Food* from the National Resources Defense Council (NRDC). The report predicted that 5,500 to 6,200 children would be stricken with cancer because of the consumption of fruits and vegetables— primarily tomatoes and apples. When the television show "60 Minutes" aired an alarming message, the public responded.

The apple industry was hit hard. The report and the "60 Minutes" broadcast highlighted a chemical called Alar that was used to improve the appearance of apples. The report claimed that this product was particularly dangerous and was used on apples throughout the country. There was an immediate reaction to the report, as school districts across the country began taking apples and apple products off their menus and parents began pouring apple juice down the drain.

The apple industry responded quickly by recommending that growers voluntarily stop using Alar and by gathering the scientific and regulatory community to challenge the scientific basis of the NRDC report. Apples became fashionable again as government agencies, such as the EPA and the Food and Drug Administration (FDA), and noted individuals such as Surgeon-General C. Everett Koop attacked the scientific basis of the report.

Although the NRDC claimed that their work was "peer-reviewed," it eventually came under scathing attack from prominent scientists. One major flaw was that the council assumed that all eight chemicals they examined were genotoxic. A genotoxic chemical causes genetic damage in humans and cancer. But most of the chemicals that they examined were not genotoxic. As Chris Wilkinson, a member of the EPA's Scientific Advisory Panel, stated: "This is a very serious flaw in their whole risk assessment procedure. . . . The effect of being exposed to a genotoxic material in early childhood is dramatically different from exposure to a nongenotoxic material. The difference is just enormous, hundreds of times the difference in exposure."[18]

Hollywood celebrities, fueled by their media reception, later campaigned actively in the losing cause of "Big Green," an all-encompassing environmental initiative in California that would have banned a large number of pesticides. Bruce Willis, Chevy Chase, and others joined Meryl Streep in the campaign. Meryl Streep was particularly concerned about pesticides. She was quoted in a food industry magazine about protecting her children: "It's for the little one that I'm doing it, because the other ones are—you know—cooked."[19]

Despite Streep's worries, her older children are likely to survive. But there are quite legitimate concerns about the use of pesticides. Our framework for regulating pesticides is both confusing and contradictory, and our entire scientific basis for evaluating cancer risks has also been challenged. But before examining these issues, it is useful to describe the modern use of pesticides.[20]

Essentially, three main types of pesticides are commonly used in food production today. Fungicides control molds and other plant diseases; insecticides control insects; and herbicides control weeds. Farmers use all three types to reduce their use of additional labor and to reduce waste and disease.

The most obvious benefits of pesticide use are greater abundance and, thus, lower prices for food products. Pesticides also can be used to prevent natural toxins. Myotoxins are molds that can invade food crops during all stages of production. These toxins, which are dangerous to humans, can be eliminated through pesticide use. A more controversial use of pesticides is to improve the appearance of fresh fruit and vegetables. Pesticides are used to avert the emergence of mildew and holes in fruit. Without their use consumers would probably have to pay more for produce that meets today's standards of appearance.

The nature of pesticides has changed over time. Over forty years ago, pesticides were toxic and had to be used in doses that left heavy residues on food. These residues caused health problems among consumers. Modern chemicals leave less residue on food but are more ecologically damaging and acutely toxic.

Farmers today are experimenting with other methods to combat pests. As they have discovered, genetic mutations among pests eventually can reduce the effectiveness of pesticides. There is currently strong interest in integrated pest management (IPM) approaches. IPM is a strategy in which various natural enemies of pests, pest-resistant crop varieties, and crop rotation are employed to reduce the need for chemicals. The emerging biotechnology industry clearly will play a role in control of pests in the future. To the extent that IPM develops, pesticide use can be reduced.

Genetic engineering is destined to bring even more controversy to this entire area. As an example, biotechnology firms have produced new genetic varieties of crops that are resistant to herbicides (weedkillers). The companies contend that this property will allow farmers to use smaller doses of less toxic herbicides. Some environmental groups argue, however, that herbicide-resistant crops will lead to increased herbicide use and consequently more residues and ground water contamination.

Concerns about pesticide use come from a variety of sources. Acutely toxic chemicals can cause severe health problems for farm workers. There is also the risk of falling into a pesticide trap as nature's pests adapt to existing pesticides and ever-stronger chemicals become required. Finally, there is the uncertainty over the long-run health risks from the use of pesticides. These risks make this political area highly charged.

The regulation of pesticides in the United States is complex because different government agencies are involved. States may set their own more stringent standards, and different concepts of risks and benefits are used in different contexts. The result is a bewildering maze to the uninitiated.

The most basic pesticide law is the Federal Insecticide, Fungicide, and Rodenticide Act, or FIFRA. Under FIFRA, no pesticide can be introduced into commerce in the United States unless it has been registered by the EPA. The criterion for registration is that "when used in accordance with widespread and commonly recognized practice [the pesticide] will not cause unreasonable effects on the environment." In turn, "unreasonable effects" are defined as "any unreasonable risk to man or the environment, taking into account the economic, social, and environmental costs and benefits of the use of any pesticide."[21]

Compared to most environmental regulations, this is remarkable language. Environmental and social benefits are to be weighed explicitly against costs. Moreover, the costs should be gauged in the context of actual practices, not worst-case scenarios.

Registration procedures for pesticides differ according to whether they are new products or pesticides that were in use before modern scientific standards and have to be reregistered. For new products, the burden of proof is on the manufacturer, and extensive testing must be undertaken. There are formal administrative hearings for each new product. For existing products that must be reregistered, the burden of proof shifts to the agency to demonstrate that the products pose an unreasonable risk. Until recently, the EPA had not begun reregistering old products, but this process is now underway. EPA was given nine years to complete this review.

When pesticides are used in foods, additional and complex regulations come into play.[22] The EPA establishes tolerances for pesticide residues on raw commodities under the Federal Food, Drug, and Cosmetic Act to protect the public health while taking into account the need for an "adequate, wholesome, and economical food supply." This portion of the act clearly mandates balancing costs and benefits.

A different portion of the act applies to processed foods under rules governing food additives. Such residues must be "safe," which is defined as a "reasonable certainty . . . that no harm" to consumers will result from the additive. In weighing these risks, benefits are not allowed to be considered. Moreover, this portion of the act also contains the infamous Delaney Clause, which prohibits the approval of any food additive that has been found to cause cancer—either benign or malignant tumors—in humans or animals.

Under a request from the EPA, the Board on Agriculture of the National Research Council was asked to examine these conflicting regulations. They decried the "dichotomous standards" applicable in agriculture. "A pesticide regulated on a risk/benefit basis at the time of registration and in setting for tolerances for residues in or on raw agricultural commodities becomes, solely because it concentrates in processed food, subject to the Delaney Clause's ostensible zero-risk standard."[23] They note that this double standard can have far-reaching effects. If any pesticide tends to concentrate residues in processed foods and runs afoul of the Delaney Clause, the EPA will also ban its use for raw commodities and prevent its reregistration under FIFRA for other use. This problem has the potential to be quite serious as older products are reviewed for reregistration. New toxicological data potentially can lead to the banning of many tried and true products. The EPA's data suggest that forty different compounds widely used in older pesticides may be involved.[24]

In their report, the National Research Council Board estimated the cancer risks associated with the use of common pesticides. Their total estimate from the use of all pesticides was that seventy years of exposure would lead to a lifetime cancer risk of about .006. This compares to the overall risk of .25 from all possible sources that individuals currently face. Fungicides comprised the largest portion (60 percent) of the risk. Reducing the use of fungicides would primarily affect potatoes and peanut crops.

Older pesticides appeared to generate a larger share of the risk than newer pesticides. Much of the risk was concentrated in a few compounds and there was much greater risk from raw than from processed food. Half of the dietary risk comes from products that have no processed form and thus are outside Delaney considerations.

The report recommended that a uniform standard be adopted for both raw and processed foods. Their suggestion was that a minimal risk standard be adopted in both cases. They suggested a level of one in a million for each product.

The EPA appears to be heading in a direction similar to that proposed by the committee. In October 1988, they announced that they would adopt a new policy that applied a uniform standard for new and old pesticides and allowed their use as long as the risk is less than one in a million. The EPA claims the strict application of the Delaney Clause can be avoided by invoking a *de minimus* doctrine. This doctrine holds that regulatory agencies need not apply a law literally if it would lead to a nonsensical result. If risks are lower than one in a million, the EPA would take no action. If the risks are higher for processed foods, the Delaney Clause binds and the pesticide would not be allowed. For pesticides used exclusively in raw foods, the existing benefit–cost policy would stand.

There are legal risks to this policy. In related cases, there have been Appeal Court verdicts against a similar policy by the FDA. The EPA had planned to apply this policy on a case-by-case basis, but lost an important recent case. There are also legislative risks. Bills have been introduced to prevent consideration of benefits when examining pesticides and to adopt a more stringent definition of "negligible risk."

All our regulatory apparatus is geared to examining artificial chemicals, with a particular emphasis on whether the chemicals cause cancer. But recent work in biochemistry, often associated with Dr. Bruce Ames at the University of California, Berkeley, suggests that natural food contains carcinogens that are much more potent than most artificial products. In one study, a nutritionist eliminated all foods that contained carcinogens from a lunch and was left only with a heart of palms salad.[25]

But before rushing to enjoy heart of palm salad, it is worthwhile reviewing the definition of carcinogens as the term is used in regulatory practice. Tests on animals are used to determine if a substance is a carcinogen. Typically, very high doses of substances are fed to animals, often the maximum amount they could tolerate without dying prematurely. Scientists then look for tumors in the animals. A substance will be classified as a carcinogen even if only one species is affected by a substance. Negative evidence concerning humans is not sufficient to overturn a finding of tumors in animals.[26] It is important to keep in mind that these findings in animals are not linked in any way to epidemiological studies in humans or, for that matter, rats and mice.

Defined in this way, carcinogens are ubiquitous in our food. Dr. Ames suggests that these carcinogens are "nature's pesticides." Without them, plants would be at the mercy of their enemies, ranging from bacteria to insects. "There are large numbers of mutagens (substances causing mutations) and carcinogens in every meal, all perfectly natural and traditional. Nature is not benign. It should be emphasized that no human diet can be entirely free of mutagens and carcinogens."[27] It has been estimated that humans typically eat 10,000 times more of nature's pesticides than artificial ones.

Ames's research has been controversial and has been criticized by other scientists. Some of the points of contention include Ames's estimates of the dietary exposure to natural pesticides, his estimates of natural carcinogens, and his limited selection of carcinogens to use in his analysis. Some criticisms of Ames's research have been technical, and others pertain to the broader generalizations that he and others have made from his work.

Nonetheless, this scientific work suggests that our policies need reviewing. First, if we are truly worried about carcinogens, we must rethink the dichotomy we have created in our regulatory apparatus between synthetic and natural compounds. There appears to be no scientific basis for this distinction. Second, if Ames is correct, even the one-in-a-million standard promulgated by the EPA seems preposterous given the larger doses in our foods. We must be more focused in our approach, concentrate on chemicals whose use and dose is likely to be a threat, and not waste valuable time routinely reregistering relatively harmless chemicals.

Owls, Snail Darters, and Exotic Habitat

Poll most individuals and ask them what they think are the most pressing environmental concerns that we face today. Chances are that they will mention oil spills and groundwater contamination as serious threats. They would most likely not mention species extinction or habitat alteration as serious problems.

Environmental experts, however, would reverse these priorities. In September 1990, the EPA issued a report of its Science Advisory Board entitled *Reducing Risk: Setting Priorities and Strategies for Environmental Protection*. The charge of the advisory board was to assess the thrust of EPA's past activities and suggest directions in which the agency could be most productive in the future. In the past, EPA has concentrated on traditional air and water pollution. For example, large grants were given to local communities for waste water treatment plants, and implementing the Clean Air Act was a major activity. The advisory board suggested a radical reorientation for the EPA.

To give the flavor of the report, the board classified risks to natural ecology and human welfare as high and low. As outlined in the report, here are two of their relatively high-risk problems:

> *Habitat alteration and destruction:* Humans are altering and destroying natural habitats in many places worldwide—for example, by causing the draining and degradation of wetlands, soil

erosion, and the deforestation of tropical and temperate rain forests.

Species extinction and overall loss of biological diversity: Many human activities are causing species extinction, depletion, and the overall loss of biological diversity, including the genetic diversity of the surviving species.[28]

Two other high-risk activities the report highlights are stratospheric ozone depletion and global warming. The relatively low-risk problems are:

Oil spills
Groundwater pollution
Radionuclides
Acid runoff to surface waters
Thermal pollution

Clearly the experts differ from the general public—or, for that matter, the head of the EPA, who immediately rushed to Alaska following the *Exxon Valdiz* oil spill. The report of the advisory board, however, was favorably received at the EPA and given extensive publicity. Should the EPA change its focus and start worrying about issues such as global warming, species extinction, and habitat alteration? As noted previously, the rush to action on global warming may not be justified either from a scientific or an economic point of view. The romantic appeal of protecting innocent species and pristine habitats may impede thoughtful environmental policy as well.

The spotted owl controversy is one of the latest episodes arising from our current policy to protect species under the Endangered Species Act adopted by Congress in 1973. Using the act as their justification, groups concerned to protect the spotted owl have squared off against those whose economic livelihoods depend on cutting down old-growth forest in northern California and the Pacific northwest. Earlier, efforts to save the snail darter stopped the Tennessee Valley Authority from completing the Tellico dam project. Some economic inconveniences may be justified if there are major benefits from protecting particular species, but upon closer examination, the benefits from species protection are surprisingly difficult to pin down.

The first type of benefits from species arises simply from their commercial and recreational value. Some of us eat fish, and others of us hunt deer or wild boar. In these cases there is an obvious direct economic value in terms of consumption and recreation. But these benefits only apply to a small variety of species and have very little connection to the problem of species extinction, except in situations in which overharvesting occurs. In these cases, economic analysis works reasonably well and, in some cases, could dictate extinction. This outcome would occur if the costs of preventing extinction exceeded the benefits.

The second type of benefit that is often mentioned is the medicinal value of different species. There are important examples of naturally occurring species that provide valuable medical treatments. But many observers have felt these benefits are quite low. The National Cancer Institute has had an extensive plant screening program in force since 1956, but has had very little economic success.[29] Again, traditional cost–benefit analysis would apply in this case and could dictate extinction of species.

The third type of benefit from species is their option value. Species may not be valuable now for commercial, recreational, or medicinal purposes, but they may become valuable in the future. Our tastes and scientific knowledge change, and species that might not be valuable now potentially could become valuable in the future. Economists have studied this option value problem. Their conclusion is that the option value is a valid additional reason to preserve species that should be added to benefits from normal use. But option values are not infinite and cannot by themselves rule out a policy of extinction.

This detached economic discussion misses the main objections of those who seriously argue for species preservation. To them, saving species is a moral issue. In their book *Extinction,* Paul and Anne Erlich honestly express their opinion. They ask rhetorically if we would really miss the snail darter. "Wasn't it preposterous to try to stop the Tellico dam, a multimillion-dollar construction project in Tennessee, because it would destroy an insignificant fish, unknown even to most ichthyologists?" They briefly review some arguments but then stress their most important point. "But there is, we think, a still stronger argument: *the line has to be drawn somewhere.*"[30]

The Erlichs argue that developers and projects always will threaten species. If we give into the developers here, what will stop them in the future? "There will always be developers, politicians, and just plain people to argue that short-range economic values must take precedence over other values. For they do not understand that *their own fates* are intertwined with the Snail Darters of our planet. They are unaware of how much they would indeed miss those little fishes."[31]

As part of their reverence for nature, the Erlichs and other environmentalists seem to treat humans as "unnatural." This is an ancient tradition starting with the myth of the Garden of Eden where humans upset a natural order. Species extinction that occurs through the natural Darwinian process appears to be morally acceptable, but human actions with the same result are not legitimate. The Erlichs are honest about the snail darter and admit that it has no special merit in and of itself. It is human arrogance that is on trial, a familiar theme of the religions of the world.

With their characteristic lack of moral fervor, economists have coined a term to describe the sentiments expressed by the Erlichs. Economists have coined the term "existence value" to highlight the fact that individuals value species or places just because they exist. But labelling an attitude does not define it, nor does it tell us how to weigh the feelings expressed by existence values against other values, both economic and noneconomic.

There is general agreement among economists that the free market will not necessarily produce the correct level of species protection or preservation of habitats. There generally are no markets in species. Inventive economists have developed some schemes, used in a few places, to create market-like settings by auctioning parts of streams or selling licences to kill sport animals. But outside of hunting or fishing environments, the private property relations necessary for efficient outcomes do not exist. Species protection and habitat preservation can be thought of as public goods—goods that all can enjoy but that no one is held responsible for.

Without markets, any sensible regulatory policy must be based on some notion of benefits (however elastic) and costs. Measuring benefits in the absence of markets is very difficult. Economists have developed several different approaches to estimating environmental benefits.

There are two basic methods of estimating benefits. The first relies on the revealed behavior of individuals, while the second relies on their stated preferences. One example of the revealed behavior approach is based on travel costs. Assume that individuals travel from all over the United States to watch a particular bird in its natural state. Because resources were spent in travelling to its habitat, we can estimate the value that people implicitly put on this bird by determining how much it cost for them to make the trip. Similarly, if a deluxe package tour that includes sightings of wild elephants costs $500 more than a routine safari, the additional value of seeing wild elephants is probably about $500. By determining how many people take the deluxe package, one can estimate the extra value of visiting the wild elephants.

Methods based on revealed behavior are probably reasonable for recreational opportunities and hunting and fishing. While fishermen may generally enjoy the outdoors, they are only really interested in those settings in which they can catch fish. Observing their travel costs to these locations is probably a reasonable method for evaluating the benefits of a site.

These methods fail miserably for existence value. Some people may enjoy knowing that there are strange creatures living near the North Pole without having even the faintest desire to visit them. Even more important, such people may be willing to pay money to insure that these creatures exist, perhaps through donations to an ecology group. Methods based on stated preferences may work in this case. Simply ask people: How much would you be willing to pay to save these creatures? Economists call this procedure the method of contingent valuation.

Obviously, asking the right type of questions is important, and economists have enlisted the aid of cognitive psychologists and survey experts to improve their techniques. Although this approach is probably a step in the right direction, it has some clear limits.

The main problem is that individual preferences are likely to be rather strange.[32] Suppose that twelve exotic elephants are living in Africa and six die suddenly. Has their total existence value increased or decreased? Or, consider a pristine wilderness area that has no particular natural beauty but is valued because it is impossible for humans to reach with conventional technology. Changes in technology now allow individuals to visit the wilderness area routinely. Its use value has increased, but its existence value has probably decreased. If existence value is as delicate as it seems, it will be difficult for any social scientist to measure it.

Existence values are also likely to be unstable. If people never visit an area or see a particular species, their enjoyment only comes from popular discussion and public discourse. But fads occur regularly in public opinion. An exotic wilderness that is fashionable now may be out of public consciousness tomorrow. And human emotions can be quite fickle.

Faced with these problems in measuring benefits, we might want to simply set aside a fixed sum of money for species or habitat preservation. But then we immediately face the classic economic problem of allocating the resources. Should we spread the resources relatively thin and try to reduce the probability of extinction a little for a wide range of species, or should we concentrate our resources on a few selected species or habitats? To make this decision requires a ranking of species or habitats based on some notion of their relative values. Evaluating benefits is inescapable.

The Endangered Species Act fails to meet any of these tests of reasonableness. Under the act, the Fish and Wildlife Service is given the responsibility of making a finding of whether a species is endangered. If so, the act requires that any proposed action that threatens the survival of an endangered species or its critical habitat must be altered or cancelled. No balancing is allowed under the act; species preservation takes precedence over all. The act was modified slightly in 1978 to allow for a cumbersome and difficult appeal process, but the basic thrust of the act is to protect endangered species at all costs.[33]

The Endangered Species Act has made snail darters and spotted owls household words, but what about the furbish lousewort? The discovery of this variety of snapdragon, long thought to be extinct, curtailed a hydroelectric facility in Maine. About the same time, a lawsuit over the snail darter reached the Supreme Court, which ruled that protection under the Act was absolute. After Congress amended the act in 1978, the review panel still did not approve the project. Finally Congress wrote in an exception into law to allow the building of the Tellico Dam.

A recent Inspector-General's report critical of the government's management of the Endangered Species Act indirectly highlights its inherent difficulties. The report identified 34 species that became extinct without any direct action by the Fish and Wildlife Service and also indicated that there were an additional 600 known and 3,000 probably endangered species.[34] The Fish and Wildlife Service did not challenge the conclusions of many of the findings of the report. Their main difficulty, they claimed, was the lack of resources to do the job. Before any actions can be taken, species must be officially listed as endangered. This process requires numerous studies that would cost a considerable amount of money. The Inspector-General estimated the costs for this work at $4.6 billion compared to the $8.5 million available today. But without any hard evidence of benefits, will taxpayers fund billions of dollars to protect species that they know nothing about?

The scientists and environmentalists who urged the EPA to change its directions toward more emphasis on preserving ecosystems sincerely believed that these systems are crucial to long-run economic and human health. They are, as some economists have dubbed them, "technological pessimists" with regard to our ability to use technology to compensate for ecological damage.[35] "Ecological systems like the atmosphere, oceans, and wetlands have a limited capacity for absorbing the environmental degradation caused by human activities. After that capacity is exceeded, it is only a matter of time before those ecosystems begin to deteriorate and human health and welfare begin to suffer."[36]

Scientists can be wrong. Many respected scientists have predicted that we would run out of natural resources and that our industrial system would collapse. The most dramatic of these predictions have been discredited by other scientists and economists who have recognized that technological progress and changes in consumer and producer behavior could avert a crisis and allow growth to continue.

But scientists also can be right. As the global warming controversy illustrates, scientific uncertainty and political agendas mix uncomfortably closely in public discourse these days. For the general public to be willing to fund the research, travels, and conferences of globetrotting scientists, they must be convinced that the enterprise is serious. Careful scientific assessment must be coupled with a careful balancing of costs and benefits to gain long-term public support. The religion of ecology may reign today, but it needs a scientific and economic basis to avoid degenerating in the future into a minor cult.

Concluding Comments

Tensions run high in discussions of environmental policy. In thinking through the issues, here are the key points to keep in mind.

1. Some type of regulatory structure is needed to manage environmental concerns because of missing markets. Without some regulatory structures, no price is attached to industrial emissions or to auto exhausts that create pollution. With no price associated with emissions, firms will not have any incentive to economize on emissions.

2. While it is often difficult to use cost–benefit analysis to determine the optimal level of pollution reduction, mechanisms are available to meet any desired level of reduction at least costs. Here is where market incentives can play a role. For example, the 1990 Clean Air Act allowed emissions trading among utilities. Establishing mar-

kets in emissions can allow firms to efficiently allocate reductions in pollution among themselves in a least-cost manner.

3. Regulations for air pollution have, to some extent, tried to balance costs and benefits. But in the new wave of environmental regulation, this balancing is often absent because of the emotional response to these areas. Regulation of pesticides and species preservation, in particular, have inflexible regulatory standards. Zero-tolerance standards for carcinogens and all-or-nothing regulation for species preservation prevent rational economic policy from being formulated in these areas. Discussions of global warming often proceed as though there were scientific unanimity rather than a wide range of divergent opinion.

Further Reading

For an excellent overview of traditional environmental regulation from an economic point of view, the best source is Paul Portney, ed., *Public Policies for Environmental Protection* (Washington, D.C.: Resources for the Future, 1990). Air and water pollution as well as toxic chemicals are treated in depth. Skepticism toward the economist's viewpoint is eloquently expressed by Steven Kelman in *What Price Incentives? Economists and the Environment* (Boston: Auburn House, 1981).

Two essays on the economics of global warming are especially worthwhile and accessible: Thomas C. Schelling, "Some Economics of Global Warming" (*American Economic Review*, Mar. 1992, pp. 1–14) and William D. Nordhaus, "Global Warming: Slowing the Greenhouse Express," in *Setting National Priorities*, ed. Henry Aaron (Washington, D.C.: Brookings Institution, 1980, pp. 185–211).

Finally, to understand the new wave of environmental regulation, it is best to review the documents from the EPA. See *Reducing Risk: Setting Priorities and Strategies for Environmental Protection* (Washington, D.C.: Environmental Protection Agency, 1990), which provides an overview of the reports from three scientific working groups.

Notes

1. For this description, I draw on the excellent account of Paul R. Portney, "Air Polution Policy," in *Public Policies for Environmental Protection*, Paul R. Portney ed. (Washington, D.C.: Resources for the Future,

1990): 27–96.

2. Portney, "Air Pollution Policy," 32.
3. Portney, "Air Pollution Policy," 45–46.
4. Portney, "Air Pollution Policy," 50–51.
5. Portney, "Air Pollution Policy," 69–70.
6. Paul R. Portney, "Policy Watch: Economics and the Clean Air Act," *Journal of Economic Perspective* 4 (Fall 1990): 173–82.
7. Steven Kelman, *What Price Incentives? Economists and the Environment*, (Boston: Auburn House, 1981).
8. See Robert W. Hahn, "Economic Prescriptions for Environmental Problems: How the Patient Followed the Doctor's Orders," *Journal of Economic Perspectives* 3 (Spring 1989): 95–114; and T. H. Tietenberg, "The Implementation and Effectiveness of Emissions Trading in the U.S." (Waterville, Maine: Department of Economics, Colby College, 1990).
9. Teitenberg, "Implementation and Effectiveness."
10. The final bill also contained some transition benefits to miners of high-sulfur coal to grease the political wheels.
11. My technical descriptions are drawn from William D. Nordhaus, "Global Warming: Slowing the Greenhouse Express," in *Setting National Priorities*, ed. Henry Aaron (Washington, D.C.: Brookings Institution, 1990), 185–211.
12. See Figure 6.1 in Nordhaus, "Global Warming," 191.
13. Nordhaus, "Global Warming," 188.
14. Nordhaus, "Global Warming," 192–94.
15. William R. Cline, "Comment on T.C. Schelling's 'Economic Response to Global Warming,'" in *Global Warming: Economic Policy Responses*, ed. R. Dornbusch and J. Poterba (Cambridge, Mass.: MIT Press, 1991).
16. This point was made by Thomas Schelling in an otherwise critical view of the greenhouse furor. See his, "Economic Response to Global Warming," in Dornbusch and Poterba, *Global Warming*.
17. Schelling, "Economic Response."
18. Quoted in Donna S. Shimskey, "Cracking Under Scrutiny," *Fruit Grower* (May 1989): 8.
19. Shimskey, "Cracking," 8.
20. Jennifer Dinsmore contributed to this section.
21. These quotes are taken from Michael Shapiro, "Toxic Substances Policy," in *Public Policies for Environmental Protection*, 212.
22. For an extensive discussion, see National Research Council, *Regulating Pesticides in Food. The Delaney Paradox* (Washington, D.C.: National Academy Press, 1987).
23. National Research Council, *Regulating Pesticides in Food*, 2.

24. "EPA Sets New Policy on Pesticide Cancer Risks," *Science* 242 (Oct. 1988): 366.
25. Does Nature Know Best? (Summit, N.J.: The American Council on Health Sciences, 1985), 8.
26. *Does Nature Know Best?*, 5.
27. *Does Nature Know Best?*, 22.
28. *Reducing Risk: Setting Priorities and Strategies for Environmental Protection*, (Washington, D.C.: Environmental Protection Agency, 1990): 13.
29. See, for example, Gardner Brown, Jr., "Valuation of Genetic Resources," Department of Economics, University of Washington, paper prepared for the Workshop on Conservation of Genetic Resources, 1985.
30. Paul Erlich and Anne Erlich, *Extinction* (New York: Random House, 1981), 10.
31. Erlich, *Extinction*, 11.
32. Raymond Kopp pointed out the "strangeness" of these preferences to me.
33. For an extensive discussion, see Winston Harrington, "The Endangered Species Act and the Search for Balance," *Natural Resources Journal* 21 (1981): 71–92.
34. See Phillip Sheron, "Agency's Flaws Linked to Extinction of Endangered Species," *New York Times* (Oct. 18, 1990): A18.
35. See Peter Passel, "Rebel Economists Add Ecological Costs to Price of Progress," *New York Times* (Nov. 27, 1990): B5.
36. *Reducing Risk*, 17.

5

Liability

If There Is a Crisis, Can We Solve It?

It was a typical night for the city council hearings. The council had decided it wanted to have a skateboard facility for its youth. A combination of outspoken skateboarders, their parents, and angry merchants who were tired of chasing the skateboarders off their property had all contracted with an architect to make a preliminary sketch of the facility and present a proposal for a full-scale building plan.

But that night the skateboard proposal hit a snag. The architect insisted that she would not provide a full-scale plan to the city unless they took full financial responsibility for any lawsuits that might arise against the architect for the design of the skateboard facility. The council members resisted this request. They knew that building a skateboard facility would expose the city to risks from major lawsuits if, as likely, some skateboarders were injured. If the architect also could be liable in some lawsuits, their own risk would be reduced. Of course, this risk was precisely why the architect insisted that the city indemnify her against any lawsuits.

Welcome to the world of liability. In all phases of life, we now plan our actions around threats of future lawsuits. In some cases, we can buy insurance against these lawsuits. Doctors, for example, will purchase malpractice insurance. But the costs of malpractice and other insurance have dramatically increased. There is strong anecdotal evidence that physicians are switching from certain areas of medicine in which the malpractice suits have soared. In some regions of the country, this tendency has led to a shortage of obstetricians and deteriorating health care, especially for the poor.

The threats of lawsuits and the cost or, in some cases, the inability to obtain insurance has dramatically affected the behavior of a number of industries. The United States has long been a leader in developing new drugs and treatments, but there has been a dearth of innovation in areas involving fertility and reproduction. It is revealing to note that it was the French, not the Americans, who introduced the first "morning-after" pill. And it probably will be threats of lawsuits, not prolife activists, that prevent its introduction into the United States.

Children are directly affected by these trends. Just a few years ago, parents faced long delays in obtaining vaccinations against whooping cough for their children. The reason was that the firm manufacturing the drug was facing some lawsuits arising from unexpected side effects of the vaccinations.

In some parts of the country, such lawsuits have affected citizens in their everyday life. Some little leagues have closed, cities have eliminated firework displays, and some sporting equipment has become unavailable. Prices of products now reflect large premiums for insurance, particularly in inherently risky areas such as private airplanes or medical services.

In the late 1980s, complaints from affected parties such as business and local and state governments grew sufficiently that some reforms were enacted. There is currently a debate over whether these reforms have changed the underlying trends or whether further reform is necessary. But to evaluate the need for further reforms, we need to step back and ask some basic questions. What are the social purposes served by civil lawsuits against products or professionals? What market failures, if any, drive this litigation? How did we reach the state today where litigation seems to be the driving force in our society, and is there any evidence of a decline of prior trends? Why has insurance disappeared for many cities and companies? And if we find the situation unsatisfactory, are there any reasonable alternatives?

The Theory of Tort Law

The branch of law that we are discussing is called tort law. "Tort" means a civil wrong, and lawsuits are brought under tort law to address these alleged wrongs. Tort law has evolved dramatically over the last twenty or thirty years, and the law today bears little resemblance to the law even in the early 1960s. But before discussing the evolution of tort law, we should think about what, in principle, we hope tort law can accomplish.

Imagine that your child became sick and doctors agreed that an operation was necessary to cure a rather routine problem. The surgeon performed the operation but your child failed to recover and became permanently disabled. You later discover that the surgeon had been at fault and that his lack of attentiveness in the operation had led to your child's permanent disability.

You are deeply distressed and outraged. You bring a lawsuit against the doctor and the hospital for a huge sum to compensate you both for your anguish and for the substantial sum required to care for the child and compensate for his loss of future earning power. In this case, the doctor was clearly negligent, so his insurance company quickly settles the matter. The doctor, in turn, loses his insurance and can no longer perform surgery.

In this example, your ability to bring a lawsuit had two consequences. First, it provided compensation for the damage done to your child. Without this compensation, you would have had to rely on much more limited private insurance or government welfare to partly compensate for the injury. Second, the ability to bring a lawsuit should deter future surgeons from being as careless in the operating room. Finally, although much harder to evaluate, the lawsuit provided a means of retribution or vengeance against the physician.

Vengeance aside, the two key elements in an ideal system of tort law would be deterrence and compensation. We would like providers of goods and services to be responsible and take the appropriate level of care in manufacturing the goods or delivering the services. In the event that the manufacturer of the good or the provider of the service failed to take adequate precautions, the victim should be provided some compensation. Holding the manufacturer or service provider responsible in this case, serves to deter inappropriate behavior. The payments in the lawsuit effectively provide insurance to the unlucky victim. Thus, the victim receives compensation.

This arrangement seems relatively simple at first. Hold producers of goods and services responsible for compensating victims of accidents when they fail to exercise the proper amount of care.[1] But upon further reflection, the apparent simplicity of the ideas disappears. Ponder the following questions in the following paragraphs.

1. What is the appropriate level of care? By spending more money and increasing the cost and price of a product, it is generally possible to make a product safer. Should we insist on ever-increasing levels of safety regardless of cost? Do the poor want the same level of safety as the rich, even if the cost of products is substantially higher?

We know that lighter automobiles are often more fuel-efficient than heavier ones, but they are also more vulnerable in the case of an accident. Suppose a car manufacturer produces two models of cars, a light economy car and a Cadillac-style car. If individuals are injured or die from accidents in the lighter vehicles and could have avoided or reduced the injuries in the heavier cars, should we hold the car manufacturer liable in lawsuits?

Or take the case of inherently risky activities such as skiing, skydiving, or racing off-terrain vehicles through the desert. Clearly the care taken by the individual will matter in these cases. Should the providers of these activities be held responsible for accidents, regardless of the actions on the part of the participants?

2. What parties should be liable in a lawsuit? Suppose you buy a faulty lawnmower from your local independent dealer and are severely injured when the lawnmower engine explodes. If you were limited to suing your local independent dealer, you would be unlikely to receive sufficient compensation because the dealer probably has limited insurance or other resources. In this case, it makes sense to be able to bring the lawsuit directly against the manufacturer. The manufacturer produced the faulty product and perhaps needs to be deterred from continuing to do so. The manufacturer also has more resources.

But consider an individual hit by a drunken driver with no insurance and few assets. After some investigation, it was discovered that the city had thought about changing the traffic design at the intersection where the accident occurred but had decided against it because the reduction in risk could not be valued anywhere close to the full cost of changing the intersection. A jury hearing the matter decided that the drunken driver was 99 percent at fault but that the city also bore 1 percent culpability in that they could have designed the intersection differently and thus might have slightly reduced the probability of an accident. The jury also recommended, and the judge concurred, that because the drunk had no assets, the city would be liable for the entire payment to the driver. This decision certainly provided compensation, but did it provide deterrence? And what would happen if municipalities became fully liable for all accidents in which they had only a minor role?

3. What standards of causation should we use in determining liability? If a drunk driver crashes into your car, you can easily determine that the drunk driver was the principle cause of your accident. But suppose that a chemical herbicide used during a war was well known to be toxic in large doses. After the war, a large number of soldiers complain of a wide variety of symptoms. How do we decide if the herbicide is the source of the problem or if the illnesses and complaints are the results of the other stresses of war? The lack of scientific proof did not limit a large class action suit against the government for its use of Agent Orange, despite lack of convincing scientific evidence that this chemical was the principal culprit.

Or, take the case of Benedictine, a drug for morning sickness that has been used for thirty years and has been declared "safe and effective" by the Food and Drug Administration. After giving birth to a child with deformities, the mother sued the manufacturer of Benedictine. After a three-week trial, a jury awarded damages to the mother, despite lack of scientific evidence that Benedictine caused the deformities. A rash of lawsuits in the 1980s eventually led to the withdrawal of this drug from the market, again despite a general scientific consensus that the drug was safe.[2] What standards of causation should we require before assessing damage claims?

4. If negligence is found, how large should be the damage claims? In the example of the incompetent surgeon, our instincts for vengeance lead us to agree that payment for the pain and suffering of the parents would be justified in addition to the payments to take care of the child. And perhaps vengeance is the appropriate response in this case.

But from the point of view of providing compensation or insurance against accidents, payments for pain and suffering should not be allowed. The easiest way to see this point is to think about buying insurance against the crib death of your new infant. You certainly would suffer terribly if your infant succumbed to crib death, yet you would not purchase an insurance policy against this event. All insurance does is allow you to transfer money across different periods of your life. You pay for the insurance during good times and receive compensation during bad times. There is no reason to purchase insurance against crib death unless, for some reason, you would need more money after the event. But this need is unlikely, as after the child's death your total expenses would probably decrease. Though pure pain and suffering or mental anguish may be terrible, insurance is not the answer.

Yet, if juries routinely award large sums for pain and suffering, the prices of goods and services will begin to reflect the increased insurance premiums and could become higher than consumers want to pay. In some cases, the additional premiums could be high enough to drive the products from the market. The prices of small airplanes are over $80,000 higher because of this premium. Cessna Aircraft had to withdraw some of its smaller planes from the market precisely because the increase in costs eliminated demand. Piper Aircraft went into bankruptcy in 1991 and sold its assets to a Canadian firm largely to avoid lawsuits in the United States. Virtually, the only small planes now made in the United States are essentially do-it-yourself craft that survive under a quirk in the law that allows airplanes to be flown without Federal Aviation Administration approval as long as they are not used for commercial purposes and are 51 percent built by the owner.[3]

After further thought, the principles of liability do not seem simple after all. But this complexity did not stop the courts from increasingly liberalizating tort law. These steps often were taken with the best of intentions—to increase deterrence and provide compensation for victims—but without foresight of all the complications that would result.

The Evolution of Tort Law

The modern tort system has changed rapidly since the 1950s. Prior to the 1950s, the law had reached a fairly stable equilibrium in which parties could be sued for negligence but sharp limits were set on the process.

A number of key concepts limited the extent of recovery of damages through the tort system. The first important idea was the notion of privity, which meant that you only could sue someone who directly affected you. This naturally limited the extent of lawsuits and the potential for compensation. A second key idea was the role of contributory negligence. If you were injured while using a product and contributed to the injury in any way, you would not be able to sue for damages. As an example, in 1964 under these standards a court ruled that a child who fell and was injured by a rotary lawnmower that had no guard could not sue for damages from the company. The "act of falling" the court held, was an independent act that contributed to the accident.[4] While this ruling may seem rather unfair today, it was an accurate reflection of the law at that time.

A third factor limiting liability was awareness on the part of the consumer that an accident could occur in the normal course of using a product. Thus producers of risky products had some protection as long as consumers were adequately forewarned about the possible consequences from using the product.

Beginning in the 1950s and continuing through to today, the courts have moved from these basic principles. The aim in most cases was to deter accidents more effectively and to provide more insurance or compensation through the liability system. The liability system, in this view, could serve as a decentralized mechanism for both guaranteeing safety and providing a more robust social safety network.

A core idea in this revolution of jurisprudence was to place increasing liability on the producers of services. The rationale was that producers of services were best positioned to make necessary investments in the safety of their products as well as provide the necessary compensation in the face of accidents. In general, the courts moved in the direction of "strict liability" for products. Producers increasingly were held liable for all accidents that occurred, sometimes even in the face of gross incompetence on the part of the consumer.

But to accomplish this goal, the law had to be changed to shift more liability to producers. The first component of the older system that fell was the doctrine of privity. A New Jersey Supreme Court case in the 1960s gives a flavor of the new jurisprudence. A new car was purchased from a dealer. Several days after the purchase of the car, the driver heard a loud noise, the car veered to the right, and then crashed. The driver sued both the dealer and the manufacturer of the car, claiming they had been negligent, although there was no proof of either a defect in the car or any negligence on the part of the dealer or manufacturer. The court held that the driver could sue the dealer and the manufacturer because there was an implied warranty inherent in sale. The court declared that "under modern marketing conditions when a manufacturer puts a new automobile in the stream of trade and promotes its purchase by the public, . . . [there is] an implied warranty."[5] This decision may seem quite appropriate today, but it—and similar decisions—indicated a new direction for contract law.

A second major change was to dispense with the idea that explicit disclaimers on the part of manufacturers or providers of services eliminated future liability. We have all purchased airline tickets or received parking receipts that had numerous disclaimers, often written in small print, on the back of the ticket. Prior to the revolution in tort law, these disclaimers were viewed as contracts that limited the right to sue for any damages. However, the courts increasingly began to view these warnings or disclaimers as mere paraphernalia of commerce and not serious contracts. Despite warnings or disclaimers, in principle a party could bring suit after an accident.

The next area of judicial innovation was the development of broader views on liability. First, the courts held that if a product had a defect that arose during the manufacturing process, the company would be held fully liable for any consequences of the defect—whether or not a warning or disclaimer was given. But the next step was much more radical. Couldn't there be products whose design was defective? The Chevrolet Corvair (which Ralph Nader made famous by inventing its slogan, "unsafe at any speed") was the first major case in which design defects were recognized. This move, of course, dramatically expanded the scope of liability. Lawyers no longer had to prove a particular defect in the product that caused an injury but could attack a whole class of products. This decision also gave a rationale for consolidating lawsuits and raising the stakes both for lawyers and clients.

But who was to judge whether a particular product design was defective? How can one decide whether a firm should have built a somewhat safer product at a much greater cost? Juries of lay people would have to decide these cases, usually in the face of expert witnesses on both sides of case. This task is daunting for juries. Judges naturally feel that they should give guidance on these issues. The California Supreme Court developed its own judicial test for a design defect. A jury in California must determine whether "the risk of danger inherent in the challenged design outweighs the benefits of such design." The jury is also to "consider, among other relevant factors, the gravity of the danger posed by the challenged design, the likelihood that such danger would occur, the mechanical feasibility of a safer alternative design, the financial cost of an improved design, and the adverse consequences to the product and to the consumer that would result from an alternative design."[6] This task would be daunting even for a team of skilled design engineers and economists.

Liability expanded in a number of different directions. The doctrine of "joint and several liability" became common, under which a party that was only partially responsible for an accident could be held responsible for the entire financial claim. Naturally, this doctrine is dreaded by large corporations and local governments. Another innovation was to use "market share" of a product to determine liability when it was impossible to determine what company had produced a product that injured a consumer. A famous example of this was a class action suit brought by daughters of women who had taken the drug DES; they alleged that the drug caused vaginal cancers. No one knew which company had manufactured the drug that any particular mother had taken, but the judge ruled that the products were so similar that liability could be assigned fairly on the basis of a firm's share of the entire market.

Environmental risks and risks caused by toxic products posed special difficulties for tort law. First, statutes of limitations had to be overturned because of long latency periods, often decades, before symptoms might emerge. Second, it is almost impossible to prove that a person became afflicted with cancer because of a particular disposal in a hazardous waste site; after all, cancers are extremely common among the population. Rather, it is necessary to produce epidemiological evidence that compares the incidence of cancer in a population relative to the expected incidence. But calculating this is inherently difficult because it is hard to control for all the potentially relevant factors and to make the proper statistical inference that any occurrence was unlikely to have happened by chance. Juries must make these interpretations based on conflicting scientific evidence in an era in which applied science has become highly politicized.

In thinking about these innovations in tort law, one cannot but admire the ingenuity with which the judges have placed additional burden on producers of goods and services and found new ways to provide compensation. In many cases, the logic of the new tort law seems irresistible taken on its own terms. Yet, the outcome of this process has in many areas been far from satisfactory. What went wrong with the theory?

Problems in the Tort System

Complaints against the tort system are numerous. It has been alleged to stifle innovation, prevent new products from coming to market, randomly destroy many businesses, limit the opportunities for high-risk recreational activities, and place U.S. businesses at a competitive disadvantage in the world market. Perhaps more importantly, the system has eliminated many types of medical care for the poor and cur-tailed the use of beneficial life-improving drugs. How could the good intentions of the tort system have led to such disastrous outcomes?

The new tort law was supposed to improve both deterrence and compensation. Unfortunately, in many cases it fails to do either.

Even if a corporation faces stiff penalties in the event of an acci-dent, there will be no effective deterrence unless the corporation can respond in some fashion. Is there, for example, an alternative design for a product that is safer without being more expensive than the cur-rent design? If so, the corporation likely will adopt it and trumpet it in its advertising. But if there is no obvious alternative design, the potential for stiff penalties only increases the financial burdens on a corporation and has no real deterrent effect.

A recent case in the Chicago appeals court provides an excellent example of this phenomenon.[7] A clerk in a department store was in-jured when a child played a prank and pushed the emergency stop button on an escalator. The store paid lost wages and medical bills under workers compensation, but the employee also sued Otis eleva-tor to recover damages for pain and suffering. The employee argued that Otis should have known better than to put a red emergency but-ton in plain sight where a child could push it. The jury awarded $43,000 to the plaintiff in the original trial. The appeals court noted that Otis had purposely put the emergency button within easy reach and with a highly visible marking precisely because people could find it quickly in case of emergencies. A verdict against Otis would not change its behavior; there is inevitably a trade-off between an easily accessible emergency button and the potential for accidents. Were it not for the appeals court, Otis would have faced increased liability.

But what is wrong with placing increased liability on producers even if we grant that their behavior may not change? In an accident, someone is hurt and should be compensated. Why not place the burden on wealthy corporations? Effectively, this would be a tax levied on purveyors of products that cause accidents. But instead of the tax being levied through the normal fiscal process, we levy it through the legal system.

The tax analogy is instructive because it brings to mind a basic principle of the economics of taxation. Stated simply the key principle is: tax me if you can find me. Economists have long known that high levels of taxation can discourage economic activities. In some cases, high rates of taxation eliminate the activity.

Modern liability law is often murky and uncertain, and it poses unknown risks and dangers to the corporation engaged in commerce. In areas in which the risks are evident or in which juries are liable to be sympathetic to claims—for example, in cases involving toxic wastes or birth defects—a corporation faces a significant probability of a major lawsuit. The G. D. Searle Company withdrew all its IUDs from the market after finding that it was spending over $350,000 to defend each lawsuit.[8]

Faced with substantial risks of large litigations, a corporation will tend to rely on old, tested products and will not innovate if the innovations expose it to risks. What better way to avoid a lawsuit than to not introduce a new product? These actions, of course, in the long run lead to less safety, not more.

Even if it produces a new product, a firm will have to raise its price to reflect its expected liability in the future. Everyone who buys the product will pay this additional tax. The benefits from the tax, however, will not be evenly distributed. In personal injury cases, high-wage earners who are injured collect more than low-wage earners. Benefits in lawsuits tend to be positively related to the wealth of victims. Thus, we have a classically unfair system of taxation: everyone pays the same tax, but the rich collect more benefits than the poor.

If a firm or municipality does not want to bear the risk of a lawsuit, it may turn to the insurance market to purchase some insurance against liability. One might think that insurance companies would welcome changes in tort law that expose companies to risks—after all, insurance companies exist to reduce risk. Unfortunately, the insurance markets cannot function easily in our current legal environment.

To write insurance, a company must have a good idea of the risk involved, whether it is insuring a large corporation, small firm, or municipality. With the rapid evolution and uncertainty of tort law, insurance companies have no idea what future courts will rule. Moreover, in cases involving hazardous wastes or drugs, the insurance companies may be liable for many years. The natural response for the insurance company is to try to limit its exposure. For example, typical insurance contracts in the environmental area specified payments only for sudden or accidental damage, such as dynamite exploding or a local dam bursting. Jackson Township in New Jersey had such a policy. Nonetheless, in a toxic waste case, the judge held that the insurance company must pay to help clean up problems from waste storage that clearly were not "sudden and accidental."[9] The response of the insurance companies was to withdraw all coverage. This move places the full burden on the municipalities and naturally deters a wide range of activities.

Insurance companies face additional problems. Not only does the legal system create additional risks, it creates them for certain classes of products—perhaps all the products in an industry—or certain classes of services provided by municipalities. If the courts start to find liability in these areas, it is likely to affect all similarly situated firms. An insurance company does not face independent risks in this case and cannot easily eliminate the risks through diversification.

In many of these areas, corporations or municipalities may know that they are less liable for lawsuits than others. These corporations or municipalities may find the price of insurance in the market too steep and decide to insure themselves. Of course, their withdrawal increases the likelihood of claims among those remaining in the pool, so insurance rates will rise. This increase, in turn, may prompt others to opt out and, in the extreme case, the market for insurance could collapse. This phenomenon is precisely the same as the adverse selection at work in the health insurance arena. It explains why corporations or municipalities may find it impossible to purchase insurance at any price. The market for insurance then disappears.

As an example, consider the case of tavern owners. They now face the risk of liability if one of their customers has an accident after too many drinks. But not all tavern owners are alike; some would cut off a customer from further alcohol before others. An insurance company would not be in a position to evaluate tavern owners. Thus adverse selection would quickly operate in this market and prevent any insurance from being offered to tavern owners.

The final problem in the tort-system is the large and unpredictable verdicts of juries. It must be hard, as a juror, to see a disabled plaintiff in court. The natural reaction must be: suppose this accident happened to me? This empathy and compassion disposes jurors to provide adequate compensation for the individual that will include generous allowances for pain and suffering.

But the jury system is far from ideal in these circumstances. First, there is a tendency to be more generous to a particular individual than toward an entire class of similarly situated individuals. Our sympathy is naturally increased in individual cases, and this inevitably leads to large awards. On the other hand, a plaintiff may face an unsympathetic jury and lose, even with a case that is factually similar to that of someone who recently won. There is a large element of randomness in jury verdicts.

As noted, the basis for awarding large sums for pain and suffering is tenuous. Because individuals would not want to insure themselves against pain and suffering, it is not clear why juries should award damages based for these afflictions. Moreover, how can a jury determine what is adequate compensation for pain and suffering when, by nature, these damages defy monetary measurement? Finally, how can a jury reasonably determine how much pain and suffering an individual has undergone? All this uncertainty leads to vast unpredictability in the liability system.

Has the Revolution Subsided?

The changes in tort law and the related insurance crisis have attracted much attention and critical comment. Could some of this critical comment have reached the bench and started a counterrevolution in liability law?

This is the thesis of Henderson and Eisenberg in an often-cited *UCLA Law Review* article.[10] They discuss what they term a quiet revolution in liability law. "This quiet revolution is a significant turn in the direction of judicial decision making away from extending the boundaries of products liability and toward placing significant limitations on plaintiffs' right to recover in tort for product-related industries . . . scholars are likely to trace the turn in judicial lawmaking to the early to mid-1980s."[11] This trend is important, they argue, because industry leaders and policy makers have been operating from false premises. "Industry leaders have characterized products liability lawyers and clients as a 'plague of locusts' who 'have brought a blood bath for U.S. business and are distorting our traditional values."[12]

Henderson and Eisenberg present their argument in two steps. First, they discuss anecdotal evidence that judges are ruling differently today than they were several years ago. But the most substantial part of their article is an analysis of data on federal and appellate district court opinions. Based on this data, they make the following claims:

1. Since the mid-1980s, more court decisions now favor defendants in product liability cases.
2. In the same period, more precedent-setting, or "breakthrough cases," began to favor defendants.
3. Again, beginning in the mid-1980s, the success rate in product liability cases began to fall relative to the success rate in other cases.
4. Finally, fewer product liability cases began to go to trial relative to other cases.

The authors interpret these findings, presented with simple graphs in their article, as evidence that the liability revolution in product law has been reversed.

In a careful analysis of Henderson and Eisenberg's data, Arthur Havenner finds no evidence of a reversal of the products liability revolution.[13] Havenner found a number of difficulties with their study. First, their own data show an upward trend in real per-capita recoveries by plaintiffs from the early 1980s to later in the decade. This statistic is the most important of all, for it measures the real claims paid. This figure is increasing, not decreasing. Second, Havenner also finds that the average or mean recovery rate by successful claimants has increased sharply. Thus, even with a slight decrease in the probability of success, the expected returns from litigation have increased.

Henderson and Eisenberg do look at expected returns, but they express these returns relative to the expected returns in other nonproduct liability cases. Because there has been a general increase in returns in nonproduct liability cases, the trend in product liability cases is disguised. Havenner notes that if the revolution in product liability preceded liberalization in other areas of the law, it would be natural for awards in the other areas to catch up and grow more quickly for a period of time.

But Havenner's main point is that looking at success rates in trials does not give an accurate picture of the underlying process. Havenner first notes that the per-capita trial rate has increased. "If the number of lawsuits is going up, it is possible for defendants to stop a higher percentage of cases before trial and still face more trials. An analogy may help. Wednesday you stepped on one cockroach and saw two live ones scuttling for cover; Thursday the count was two stepped on and three that got away. . . . If you look at percentages, you might conclude that your bug problem is abating. . . . If you look at absolute numbers, you are likely to phone the exterminator."[14]

But there is an even more basic problem with looking at success rates. Lawyers on both sides of the battle are canny; they know the state of the law and the probable outcome of litigation. Because litigation is very costly, there will be a general reluctance to litigate unless there is a decent chance of winning. Because both sides have similar incentives and share similar knowledge of the recent cases, we would expect according to the simplest model for the success rate to hover around 50 percent regardless of the state of the law. To put it another way, the cases brought to trial are not necessarily representative of the claims in the population. The mild decline in the "success" rate for plaintiffs may have resulted from an overconfidence on the part of their lawyers that no one could lose a product liability case. Data on "success" rates on trials tell us precious little about the underlying state of the law.

It is also not clear that trends in the law are moving toward plaintiffs. In late 1991, the California Supreme Court (known as a conservative court) ruled that a defendant can be liable for conduct that was a "substantial factor" in producing an outcome. The defendant did not have to be the direct cause of the accident but only contribute to it. The court rejected a much stronger "but for" test in which the defendant would not be held liable unless the harm would have not occurred "but for" the defendants actions. The case in question involved a child who had drowned in a lake after falling from a surfboard-like craft. In the trial, evidence was presented that the boat was tipped over by an older sibling and that the parents had not properly supervised the children. Nonetheless, the manufacturer of the pleasure craft was held responsible.[15]

Many state courts had previously adopted similar standards, but the California Supreme Court ruling is likely to be influential both in California and other states. The fact that this ruling comes from a conservative court demonstrates the dramatic changes in liability law that have occurred and continue to occur.

What Can Be Done?

In 1986, the Conference Board, an organization sponsored by large corporations, undertook a survey among Chief Executive Officers (CEOs) of the liability problem faced by the largest corporations. As might be expected, the CEOs felt that liability was a very serious problem and most claimed that liability matters occupied a significant part of their own time. The Conference Board also asked for suggestions for reform of the law. Here were the top seven desired reforms:

1. Replacement of strict liability with a fault-based system.
2. Curtailment or elimination of joint and several liability.
3. Caps on pain and suffering damages.
4. Caps on punitive damages.
5. Limitations on attorneys' contingency fees.
6. Limitations on the time span during which a suit may be filled.
7. Allowing use of state-of-the-art defenses.[16]

Several of these items are quite reasonable and changes have been made in these directions. Some states have curtailed joint and several liability, and there is extensive discussion of caps on pain and suffering damages. Limitations on punitive damages are more controversial because punitive damages supposedly punish egregious behavior. Cases involving limitations on punitive damages are now reaching the Supreme Court.

Limiting contingency fees for lawyers would be a fundamental change in the U.S. system. Clearly, contingency fees allow more adventurous lawyers to operate, but also allows defendants of limited means to find representation. In any case, the lobbying power of lawyers is too strong to think of limitations as a likely possibility.

The highest priority of the CEOs was to change the liability system from strict liability, under which corporations are held responsible for all accidents, to a doctrine based on fault or negligence. But there is no single doctrine of strict liability in the courts. Rather, a general trend in the law has been moving in that direction. Essentially, the CEOs are calling for a massive counterrevolution in liability law.

Other respected commentators have called for similar changes.[17] But law is made gradually in state courts across the country in a great diversity of cases. A massive revolution would require a major effort at codifying a new body of principles governing torts. This endeavor may be worthwhile, but it would not be a quick or easy task.

The executives would also like to see "state-of-the-art" defenses and shorter statues of limitations. State-of-the-art defenses absolve a corporation from liability if the product, at the time of the design, was using the appropriate technology. But critics have worried that this provision would prevent corporations from retrofitting older and less safe products when new technologies become available. Statutes of limitations may be reasonable in some areas, but they make less sense in cases of environmental contamination or toxic wastes, in which delays before detecting problems may be quite long.

Of course, common sense is needed in this arena, and judicial change may occur as the conservative federal judges appointed in the last decade begin to view the issues on appeal. But it would be a mistake to believe that liability will or should disappear.

Take the case of medical malpractice. According to Patricia Danzon, malpractice by physicians is a serious problem.[18] She quotes studies that found that one in twenty hospital admissions resulted in adverse outcomes caused by medical care and, of those, 17 percent resulted from clear negligence. Thus, a little less than one percent of all patients admitted to these hospitals suffered because of negligence. This is a large number of cases! Physicians are lax in disciplining their brethren, and thus there is no obvious alternative to malpractice suits to provide quality control.

Danzon points out, however, that the system is quite costly. Litigation and overhead costs absorb sixty cents of the dollar compared to twenty cents for normal third-party insurance. The malpractice system does not operate cheaply. Danzon also suggests some useful reforms. Placing caps on awards for specific afflictions, as some states have done, would discriminate against younger plaintiffs whose overall needs may be higher and also could be unconstitutional. Danzon suggests that states might develop payment schedules based on the specific damage as well as the age or occupation of the plaintiff. Juries' open-ended abilities to award pain and suffering damages also should be limited.

In the environmental area, Peter Huber, a noted scholar, is pessimistic about prospects for reform.[19] The key issues, he notes, are not strict liability versus negligence or product design or even pain and suffering damages but questions of causation and the existence of damages. For example, is there a pathology of cancer in a certain area and, if so, was it caused by a particular toxic chemical? The courts have not found an easy way to grapple with these issues. Huber suggests that we may have to resort to mechanisms such as the Superfund that effectively socialize payments to recipients and that are funded by industrywide taxation. But experience in this area, as with Black Lung disease, shows that the ability to restrict payments to potential claimants is quite limited.

One radical alternative would be to socialize all damage payments through the government. But this step would give up the deterrence value of the liability system. In its place, society would need a massive Consumer Protection Agency to oversee every business and municipality. Not many citizens would welcome this intrusive government behavior. A superagency is not a serious alternative to tort law.

There will be no dramatic counterrevolution in liability law. But a number of valuable reforms—such as payment schedules, caps on pain and suffering verdicts, a movement toward state-of-the-art defenses, and judicial common sense—need to be put into effect on a state-by-state basis. Federal legislation is also possible. In 1991 Congress considered a tort reform bill that included a number of useful changes in the law, including limits on deep-pocket awards for pain and suffering, high standards for punitive damages, and allowing FDA approval to absolve drug manufacturers from lawsuits.

But as we make these reforms, we will always be in conflict with a basic instinct in an affluent society: If someone is injured in an accident, shouldn't that person receive true compensation, not just welfare, for the misfortune, regardless of the precise circumstance of the accident? As long as this view is strongly held, the liability counterrevolution will be a lengthy process.

Finally, we should note the possible role of lawyers in promoting the liability explosion. Since 1970, there has been a massive expansion in the number of lawyers in our society. From 1870 to 1970, the number of lawyers was always less than 1.5 per thousand. But since 1970, the proportion of lawyers has doubled and now exceeds 3 per thousand.[20]

Lawyers, of course, do more than litigate liability cases. They lobby, write regulations, assist business in navigating our laws and regulations, and provide general counsel. However, total litigation has increased dramatically in our society. Lawsuits in federal courts were roughly 90,000 a year in 1960, now exceed 300,000 per year. Did the growth in lawyers cause the increase in regulations and lawsuits, or did the growing regulations, changing nature of the law, and the increased complexity of our society create the demand for lawyers?

Concluding Comments

The debate over liability and tort reforms fits directly into our framework of market and political failure. Here are the essential points to keep in mind:

1. Explicit markets for product safety and medical malpractice do not exist; hence, we have a classic case of problem number two: missing markets.

2. The idea behind tort law is straightforward: use the civil law system to provide compensation to victims of accidents and deter unsafe behavior. Ideally, the tort system operates as a "tax" on unsafe behavior, with the proceeds from the tax providing compensation to victims.

3. Although the principle of tort law is straightforward, its application is not. The result is a system that provides uneven compensation and does not produce true deterrence. As juries and judges have grappled with the issues of specifying causation, liability, and damages, the original vision of tort law has been transformed in ways that originally were not foreseen. Juries and judges feel compelled to rule in favor of unfortunate plaintiffs. In some cases, standards for causation and liability have become so extreme as to virtually close down entire industries.

4. State and federal legislation is needed to reform the worst abuses, but this process would be an uphill political battle. The trial lawyers have developed a tightly knit, effective lobbying network to protect their interests. They have been successful in blocking legislation in many state legislatures and in Congress.

Further Reading

A provocative introduction to the liability crisis with a distinct point of view is Peter Huber, *Liability*, (New York: Basic Books, 1988). Huber began his career as an engineer and then went to law school and clerked for Associate Justice Sandra Day O'Conner. He is also an excellent writer.

A more traditional academic collection of articles is Robert E. Litan and Clifford Winston, ed., *Liability, Perspectives and Policy* (Washington, D.C.: Brookings Institution, 1988). The articles by George Priest, Patricia Danzon, and Peter Huber are especially interesting. The editors' introduction provides a useful starting point for the debate. The book also is replete with references to an extensive literature on insurance and liability. Another excellent article that ties tort law to problems in the insurance industry is George Priest, "The Current Insurance Crisis and Modern Tort Law" (*Yale Law Review*, June 1987).

To really get the flavor of the debate, you need to read about some cases. Huber's book is full of anecdotes. The law section of the *Wall Street Journal* often carries stories about the latest developments in tort law.

Notes

1. Technically, this principle is known as a negligence standard. An alternative standard is strict liability, which holds the producer responsible for all accidents as long as consumers exercise proper due care. As long as the standards are chosen to minimize the total costs of accidents, either standard should lead to the same frequency of accidents. However, under the negligence standard, the consumer bears the risk for accidents that occur despite adequate precautions, while under strict liability, the firm bears the risk. As discussed later, the trend in the law has been toward strict liability but with increasingly lax standards of due care for consumers. For a discussion of this point, see George Priest, "Products Liability Law and the Accident Rate," in *Liability, Perspectives and Policy*, ed. Robert E. Litan and Clifford Winston. (Washington, D.C.: Brookings Institution, 1988). Actual legal practice, however, is not described well by either pure standard. On this point, see Ross Eckert and Rodney Smith, "Strict Liability for Products in Law and Economics," (mimeo, Claremont Men's College, June 1988).
2. For a further discussion of this case and others as well as a lively, though pointed, account of the liability controversy, see Peter Huber, *Liability* (New York: Basic Books, 1988).
3. "Liability Costs Drive Small-Plane Business Back Into Pilots' Barns," *Wall Street Journal* (Dec. 11, 1991): A1, AG.
4. See Priest, "Products Liability Law," 202.
5. Quoted in Huber, *Liability*, 28.
6. Quoted in Peter Shuck, "The New Ideology of Tort Law," *Public Interest* (June 1990): 102.
7. This account is taken from L. Gordon Crovitz, "Offenses Against the Rule of Law: This Year's Winners," *Wall Street Journal* (Dec. 26, 1990): 7.
8. See George Priest, "The Current Insurance Crisis and Modern Tort Law," *Yale Law Review* (June 1987): 1521–1590.

9. For a discussion of environmental law, see Peter Huber, "Environmental Hazards and Liability Law," in Litan and Winston, *Liability*.

10. James A. Henderson, Jr., and Theodore Eisenberg, "The Quiet Revolution in Products Liability: An Empirical Study of Legal Change," *UCLA Law Review* 37(1990): 479–553.

11. Henderson and Eisenberg, "Quiet Revolution," 480.

12. Henderson and Eisenberg, "Quiet Revolution," 481, quoting from a statement by the chairman of the Board of the National Association of Manufacturers.

13. Arthur Havenner, *Not Quite a Revolution in Products Liability*, (New York: Manhattan Institute, White Paper, 1990).

14. Havenner, "Not Quite a Revolution," 7.

15. "California Supreme Court Relaxes Standards on Negligence Liability," *Wall Street Journal* (Dec. 12, 1992).

16. The Impact of Product Liability (New York: The Conference Board, Research Report no. 908, 1988), Tab. 33.

17. See, for example, George Priest, "The Current Insurance Crisis."

18. Patricia Danzon, "Medical Malpractice Liability," in Litan and Winston, *Liability*.

19. Peter Huber, "Environmental Hazards and Liability Law," in Litan and Winston, *Liability*.

20. Jonathan Rauch, "The Parasite Economy," *National Journal* (Mar. 25, 1992): 980–85.

PART III

The Search for Governmental Structures

With the collapse of the Soviet empire, less need for military spending, and insatiable demands for domestic spending, it was natural that politicians looked toward national defense as a source of budget savings and additional resources. But there is a catch: military spending occurs in congressional districts and states, and no one wants their area to be affected. Moreover, in the early 1990s, slow growth and recession plagued the economy and there was a general fear of drastic cuts.

It was in this environment in early 1992 that the Congressional Budget Office (CBO) issued a report entitled "The Economic Effects of Reduced Defense Spending." The report looked at the general macroeconomic effects of a reduction in military spending on growth and unemployment. It also looked in more detail at the effects on three communities that depended on military spending.

This last part created political heat for the CBO. The specific areas they studied were the effects of closing Fort Ord in Monterey, California; the effect on the Bath Iron Works in southeastern Maine; and the effects of defense cutbacks in St. Louis, Missouri. These three disparate areas all had one thing in common: they were in the districts of Democrats in leadership positions. Fort Ord was in the district of

Congressman Leon Panetta, the Chairman of the House Budget Committee; St. Louis was the home base of Congressman Richard Gephardt, Majority Leader in the House of Representatives; and Maine was the home of Senator George Mitchell, Majority Leader in the Senate.

To put it mildly, the Democrats were not pleased by this notoriety and, I suspect, the phones lines were humming at the CBO. What was the source of this mischief? The preface to the study notes that it was conducted at the request of the Minority Leader of the Senate—Republican Senator Robert Dole.

This anecdote illustrates some of the political infighting that occurs even when there is a general sense that some action—in this case, a reduction in military spending—needs to be taken. Part III examines in more detail the issues and problems that arise from our need to take collective actions in our economic affairs and to insure that the public interest is served through our economic institutions and decision making.

Each of the subjects treated in Part III deals with a specific problem in taking collective actions. In international trade, the key problem is curbing special interests and harnessing diverse groups in our economy and abroad to support open markets and free trade. This tension between special and general interests is common in many areas of government but most pronounced in the debate about international trading arrangements.

Monetary policy and international finance raise difficult issues of delegation of authority and the responsibility to experts. While the details of domestic and international money and finance are clearly far beyond the expertise of most informed citizens, the decisions made in these areas determine the economic fortunes of ordinary citizens. How should institutions be designed so that the risks inherent in any decision properly reflect the concerns of the governed? How should policy makers be judged and evaluated? Should they be governed by strict rules or allowed discretion? These are some of the difficult issues that arise in the delegation of authority to experts.

Fiscal policy poses similar problems for collective decision making. With our persistent federal deficits, fiscal policy appears to reflect delegation run amok. How can special interests (represented by individual members of Congress and lobbyists) be channeled toward the general interest? Can rules or institutions that are designed to bind the hands of Congress (such as the Gramm-Rudman laws and proposed constitutional amendments to balance the budget) work effectively?

In all three areas—trade, monetary policy, and fiscal policy—we have had diverse experience with the problems of collective decision making. In the subsequent chapters, we study these experiences with an eye toward a design for institutions that would further our goals and promote sound decision making.

6

Is Free Trade
in the National Interest?

Challenges

The Uruguay round of trade talks under the auspices of the General Agreement on Tariffs and Trade (GATT) was in purgatory in the early 1990s. It did not quite die, despite dramatic stories of its collapse and dire predictions for the future of world trade. It was not quite alive either, as deadlocks continued on important issues and prevented all the parties from reaching agreement. The negotiations more closely resembled a boxing match with two overaged heavyweights staggering from exhaustion in the last several rounds. All the parties prayed for its end.

The talks did not make the front pages of most papers. Although foreign trade has become a major political issue in the United States, there has been very little interest in the recent GATT negotiations. Are the American people and newspapers failing to keep track of crucial world developments, or is the most recent round of GATT negotiations just another international boondoggle for negotiators?

Economists have a deserved reputation for favoring free trade. Surprisingly, however, there has been considerable controversy over whether the traditional international GATT process for achieving free trade has any useful future. Naturally, opponents of free trade would not be fond of the GATT process, but many economists and practical men and women of affairs who advocate free trade also find these international negotiations a mere sideshow. Nevertheless, many others still view the latest round of trade negotiations as critical for the world's economic development.

Trade and foreign economic relations are front-page news. The OPEC-engineered oil price increases of the 1970s with their concurrent stagflation forced the public to realize that the economic fortune of the United States was not solely determined within the borders of the fifty states. The large U.S. trade deficits in the 1980s both directly and indirectly brought even more attention to trade.

As Japanese consumer goods flooded U.S. markets, it was hard to recall the period in the 1950s when Americans scoffed at goods made in Japan. Certainly the automobile manufacturers and fabricators of computer chips were not scoffing as they forced the government to protect them against their Japanese competitors. While a "national malaise" may have died with Jimmy Carter's presidency, a "competitive malaise" set in. The biggest growth industry in the 1990s might be seminars for businesspeople with titles like "Can America Compete?"

While the trade deficit brought attention to foreign goods and products, it also indirectly forced attention on foreign economic power. When other countries ran trade surpluses with the United States, they accumulated dollars that were used to purchase U.S. assets. This result struck many populist Americans as doubly unfair. Not only were the Japanese selling goods in this country, thereby damaging the interests of U.S. workers, but they were turning around and using their profits to buy the United States. Van Gogh paintings disappeared into Japanese boardrooms. Even Rockefeller Center in the heart of Manhattan, the American symbol of ice skating at Christmas, came under Japanese control. What would be next, the statue off the south coast of Manhattan?

The academic and political environments both turned in the 1980s. The brightest young trade economists wrote on strategic trade policy that highlighted national interests and penned articles with titles such as "Is Free Trade Passé?"[1] This viewpoint was a major change in emphasis. While trade economists had long recognized some exceptions to the free trade principle, there was a general presumption in its favor. But the new theory emphasized that trade was likely to be intimately connected with market failure so that governments could, in principle, play a beneficial role by intervening in the process.

Members of Congress learned a new phrase. When asked if they supported free trade, they would reply, "No, I support *fair* trade." These comments were code words for aggressive tactics against our trading partners, especially the Japanese. Only a sequence of ideologically free trade presidential administrations in the 1980s prevented a drastic shift to protectionism.

The United States adopted its own standards for assessing fair trade in world markets, contrary to the rules of GATT, in the so-called "Super-301" legislation. Several countries ran afoul of this law, and others changed their trade practices in fear of unilateral U.S. retaliation.

By the end of the 1980s, other trade winds were blowing. The European countries launched an ambitious project of economic unification that was designed to lead to a single, unified market in Europe by 1992. This movement caused non-European firms and countries to fear that this great market would be effectively closed to them. At the same time, the United States also embarked on its own bilateral efforts, with free trade pacts first with Israel and then, more importantly, with Canada. Talks also progressed rapidly on a free trade pact with Mexico that would have profound effects on Mexico's near-term development.

With the Europe in 1992 proposals and the United States embarking on major free trade pacts, there was clearly movement toward trade liberalization. But these pacts were limited in scope, embracing at most a small number of countries. The spirit of GATT and the major postwar liberalization efforts did not favor bilateral pacts but tariff reductions that applied to all members of GATT. The thrust of GATT was toward multilateral reductions in trade barriers and universal access to markets, not preferential deals struck between countries. The rapid growth of free trade arrangements in the late 1980s and early 1990s was one of the reasons that the value of GATT negotiations came into question.

The GATT process had been valuable in the postwar era. From the Geneva round in 1947 through the 1980s, tariff rates (tax rates on imports) were reduced sharply. Indeed, by the 1980s, tariff levels were very low in developed countries. For example, average tariff levels in the early 1980s were approximately 4.9 percent in the United

States, 6.0 percent in the European Community, and 5.4 percent in Japan.[2]

International trade grew dramatically in the postwar era—at faster rates than world incomes. From 1953 to 1973, world incomes grew roughly 4.5 percent per year, while trade grew nearly 7.5 percent a year. Income and trade growth slowed following the OPEC shocks of 1973, but trade still grew at a faster rate than world income.[3]

While GATT was successful in reducing tariff rates among developed countries, in the 1970s countries began to restrict trade in a number of other ways through nontariff trade barriers. These barriers operate in a variety of ways, including restrictive health and safety regulations whose primary purpose is not public welfare but the welfare of producers competing with threatening imports, "local content" policies that discriminate in favor of domestic producers, and a host of other imaginative mechanisms for discriminating against imported goods.

Most important, however, were voluntary export restraints (VERs), which covered a wide range of important products. Japanese exports of automobiles to the United States and Europe are covered by VERs. In the United States, for example, the domestic automobile industry had sufficient political clout to get some measures taken against imported Japanese cars, which American consumers, much to the automakers' chagrin, were finding very attractive. The auto industry wanted restrictions on Japanese imports. Quotas against the Japanese were not legal under GATT, so the U.S. government persuaded the Japanese to "voluntarily" restrict their imports. With fewer Japanese cars coming into the U.S. market, the price of these cars rose, as did prices for domestic cars because domestic manufacturers faced reduced competition. The VERs are technically legal under GATT but clearly violate the spirit of the international agreements. The steel industry also managed to obtain protection against imports in a similar fashion.

Thus, as we move into the 1990s, the world trading system is deviating sharply from GATT principles. While tariffs in developed countries remain low, nontariff trade barriers have taken their place for many key commodities. Bilateral negotiations (or, in the case of Europe, limited multilateral negotiations) have replaced ambitious multilateral GATT negotiations. Countries have increasingly taken it into their own hands to negotiate the terms of access to their markets with their economic friends and enemies. Proponents of this process call it realistic progress; opponents fear it will lead to fragmentation of the world trading system.

This chapter examines these conflicting perspectives. It first explores the internationalist view, including the basic case for free trade, the GATT process, and the challenges facing the world trading system that may require truly multinational negotiations. We then turn to the nationalist perspective: the new theory of strategic trade policy and its potential applications, the wisdom of unilateral threats, and the selective pursuit of unilateral opportunities to create limited free trade areas. Finally, we explore several alternative institutional arrangements that may lead to more efficient political–economic arrangements for trade.

The Internationalist Perspective

The Case for Free Trade

The case for free trade goes back to the eighteenth-century economist Adam Smith, who argued against policies that protected domestic producers and inhibited the free flow of goods across borders. Smith's arguments met resistance then, and free trade ideas meet resistance now. Economists and practical people perhaps differ more on this issue than any other. Economists tend to view free trade as an indirect form of cooperation. Practical men and women of affairs often view trade as an extension of national warfare. While there may be several reasons for the divergence of these views (including a lack of understanding by the practical side of some basic economic principles), one of the reasons for disagreement may be that there are two different rationales for free trade, each with different policy implications.

Jagdish Bhagwati, the eminent trade economist at Columbia University, has distinguished between a *unilateral* and a *cosmopolitan* rationale for free trade. The unilateral case, which is the one most frequently advocated by economists, states that, with only a few exceptions, a country will be better off by unilaterally adopting a free trade policy regardless of the actions, protectionist or otherwise, of its trading partners.

The rationale for this view is based on the principle that if the world allows a country opportunities to trade, it cannot harm itself by taking advantage of those opportunities. Suppose that, before engaging in trade, an economy produces both apples and oranges and that apples are twice as expensive as oranges. In world markets, apples and oranges trade at the same price, which is assumed to equal the domestic price of oranges. Given this divergence in the relative price of apples and oranges between home and world markets, the country would be better off if it shifted some production from apples to oranges and then traded the additional oranges on world markets. A little reflection shows that this policy could allow a country to consume more apples and more oranges. Domestically, each apple costs two oranges in terms of production; internationally, each apple costs one orange. This difference between the relative prices of apples to oranges in domestic and world markets allows an economy to profit unilaterally from trade.[4]

There are two traditional qualifications to the advice to shift production toward oranges and allow unimpeded trade. The first qualification is that domestic externalities may affect the production or consumption of apples and oranges. For example, suppose orange production had a negative environmental impact. Then we would not necessarily want to expand orange production until we had taken care of this externality through appropriate taxes. The free trade economist would tell us to take care of our domestic externality first and then allow free trade.

The second traditional qualification to free trade is that a country may be large enough to have market power in certain commodities and may wish to take advantage of this power to change prices. Suppose our country was large and additional purchases of apples would change world prices. In this case, we may wish to limit our demands for apples to some degree in order to avoid raising their price. A small tariff or tax on apples may be appropriate in this case.

The unilateral view of free trade tells a country to take advantage of the differences in relative prices regardless of their source. Apples could be cheaper in world markets for a number of reasons. It simply may be that the agricultural conditions are more favorable for growing apples abroad than at home. Another possibility, however, is that foreign governments, for reasons of their own, may be subsidizing the production of apples. The unilateralist view advocates reducing domestic apple production in either case. If a foreign government is foolish enough to subsidize the production of apples, this policy only will benefit domestic consumers; it would be foolish not to take advantage of these opportunities.

Existing apple producers, however, would not be as sanguine

about the advantages of reducing production of apples. To the extent that they have resources invested into apple production, they would be hurt as apple prices fall following trade. If the apple producers are inefficient relative to other world producers, then it would be difficult, although not impossible, to make a strong political case for their protection. But if their disadvantage arises because of a foreign subsidy, their domestic political position would be much stronger. Whether it's the New England fishing industry facing competition from subsidized Russian ships or the aerospace industry facing subsidized European products, it does not seem fair to allow these industries to be hurt. Unilateral free trade in this case seems like unilateral disarmament.

The unilateralist free trader would insist, however, that we still should take advantage of the foreign subsidy. According to this view, what we produce is irrelevant. There is no special virtue in producing apples, oranges, or computer chips. If there are externalities—that is, some vices or virtues not accounted for by the price system—then they should be taken care of with appropriate taxes or controls. But, in the absence of externalities, the composition of our domestic production should be irrelevant. Moreover, with the gains from trade we could, in principle, compensate the industries that suffer losses.

While the economic arguments of the unilateral free trader, once suitably qualified, may be correct, they fail the ultimate political test. Countries are reluctant to let powerful industries collapse because of foreign subsidies. Not only do these policies seem unfair, they also, as Bhagwati points out, fail the "Darwinian test" of trade—that is, only the strongest survive. The strongest do not survive if there are pervasive subsidies by foreign governments.

The cosmopolitan or internationalist view of free trade is better equipped to cope with these political arguments. According to this view, the purpose of trade should be to promote the optimal allocation of resources throughout the world. A country that arbitrarily subsidizes one industry will not be promoting world efficiency. Subject to the caveats about externalities, world efficiency can only be achieved through extending free markets throughout the world. A properly functioning world price system, free from governmental interference, would bring world efficiency.

From the cosmopolitan point of view, a country should object if another country unfairly subsidizes a particular industry. The subsidy would distort world production and thereby prevent the world economy from reaching its full economic potential. At least with regard to foreign subsidies, domestic business and government interests are in line.

GATT is a creature of this cosmopolitan view. It is an international institution designed to promote world efficiency. How has it worked in the past, and is it still a useful vehicle for today's trade problems?

The Past and Future of GATT

After World War II, the plans for reconstruction initially called for three new organizations: the International Monetary Fund (IMF), the International Bank for Reconstruction and Development (the World Bank), and an International Trade Organization. The last organization never materialized because of sharp disagreements over its role. Nonetheless, a large number of countries felt that some tariff reductions were important, and they gathered in Geneva to agree on a set of mutual tariff reductions. This meeting was the beginning of GATT.

Major tariff reductions have been spread over seven completed rounds of negotiations; the Uruguay was the eighth trade round. The most important and productive rounds were the initial one in Geneva and the Kennedy round, which spanned the period 1964–1967. The preamble to GATT states that it is for "reciprocal and mutually advantageous arrangements directed to the substantial reduction of tariffs and other barriers to trade and the elimination of discriminatory treatment in international commerce."[5] This statement indicates the two basic themes of GATT: nondiscrimination in trade and mutual and reciprocal concessions.

The goal of nondiscrimination in trade is enforced by the Most Favored Nation clause in GATT. If a country reduces its tariffs in negotiations with other countries, the tariff reduction applies to all members of GATT. This arrangement gives all countries equal access to markets. Once goods enter a country, they are to be accorded "national treatment"—meaning that they are supposed to be treated on equal terms with domestically produced goods.

Tariff negotiations initially occur between individual countries in which they pursue "reciprocal and mutual" arrangements. Bhagwati describes this process as *first-difference* reciprocity—that is, countries negotiate on the margin, from existing levels of barriers, in their pursuit of concessions. During trade rounds, all the countries can observe the outcomes of negotiations among other countries and thus can insure that they are making good deals.

Two basic ideas lie behind international and multilateral trade negotiations. The first is to provide a counterweight to domestic political pressures for protection. The second is to prevent a fragmentation or "Balkanization" of trading patterns between countries. The GATT process assists in each of these goals.

There is a fundamental problem that every country faces in attempting to insure free trade. For many goods, especially consumer goods, the beneficiaries of free trade are the consumers in the country. The beneficiaries of protection are the domestic producers. Because there are typically large numbers of consumers and relatively few domestic producers, the benefits of free trade are spread widely, while the benefits of protection are highly concentrated. This disparity naturally leads to an asymmetrical political situation in which the producers find it easy to organize but individual consumers do not find it in their interest to try to counteract the lobbying efforts of producers. A typical case is the quotas on sugar imports into the United States that cost individual consumers only a few dollars a year but bring huge returns to domestic sugar manufacturers. The potential tyranny of special interests is one of the classic problems in collective action.

To counteract this asymmetry in the political arena, it is necessary to find other interests that would experience substantial benefits from opening trade. Export interests fit this bill. In international negotiations, exporters know that access to foreign markets can only be achieved when there is reciprocal access to domestic markets. Politicians can therefore harness the political resources of outward-looking exporters to combat pressures to protect domestic industries.

While international negotiations can lead to reduced trade barriers by pitting export and import interests against each other, they do not prevent countries from cutting deals among themselves to the exclusion of third parties. This practice can lead to efficient producers being cut out of markets and to a fragmentation of world trade. The result would be less efficient world production. Such deals also can allow large countries to bully smaller countries and gain asymmetric advantages for their own exporters.

GATT attempts to circumvent these tendencies through its Most Favored Nation clause. Once countries have completed a tariff negotiation, they must open their markets to all other members of GATT on equal terms. The Most Favored Nation provision thus attempts to prevent the Balkanization of world markets.

But GATT is not a perfect institution. From the standpoint of promoting universal free trade and open access, it has two major problems. First, historically there have been important exceptions to its principles. Second, many grey areas allow trade practices that clearly violate the spirit of GATT although not the letter of the treaty.

Four principal exceptions have found their way into GATT. These cover agriculture, developing countries, textiles, and custom unions. The developed countries have refused to dismantle their intricate schemes to protect their domestic agricultural industries. Until the 1980s, the United States shared this view, so progress in reducing trade barriers in agriculture through GATT was negligible. However, in the 1980s, the United States began to perceive that its national interest was to open agricultural markets worldwide because it believed its industries could compete favorably in free world markets.

The U.S. conversion to free trade in agriculture put it in direct conflict with the European Community, which had long protected agriculture through its Common Agricultural Policy. This policy raises prices for products in Europe sharply above world prices and then uses export subsidies to allow the products to compete in world markets. Although these policies are very costly to the European Community and raise food prices for their consumers, the political power of farmers, particularly in Germany and France, has prevented any change. In recent international negotiations, the United States joined with the Cairns group (a lobby of agricultural exporting countries) to push the European Community to commit to a policy of opening their markets. The refusal of the European Community to change their negotiating position directly led to the problems with the Uruguay round.

The developing countries also were largely exempted from GATT requirements of opening their markets. Instead, arrangements were made to allow them to maintain their tariffs and to have some preferential access to the markets of developing countries. At least through the 1950s and 1960s, the developing countries believed that the road to industrialization was through developing their own manufacturing industries and not through the promotion of agriculture. They adopted policies of "import substitution," or high tariffs, to promote their own manufacturing industries. Thus, while the developed countries protected agriculture—a natural export of most developing countries—the developing countries tried to build their own manufacturing industries behind tariff walls. By the 1970s, it became increasingly apparent that this strategy was not working. Nonetheless, tariffs remain high in most developing countries and access to the agricultural markets of developed countries remains blocked.

The trade agreements in the textile industry are an economist's nightmare. Textiles always have had protection throughout the postwar era. The latest agreement is the Multi-Fiber-Agreement. Essentially, this agreement specifies in detail the permissible levels of imports of textiles and clothing on a country-by-country basis. There is no pretense that the cheapest and most efficient producer will capture a market. Whoever has the historic quota of imports into a particular country can have that share of total imports.

Finally, GATT also compromises with Most Favored Nation status by allowing the formation of custom unions (agreements among nations that allow free trade and free movements of labor and capital) and free trade areas. These arrangements allow the preferential flow of goods, with reduced tariffs and other barriers, among the member countries. Although a custom union does promote free trade among its members, it violates the Most Favored Nation clause of GATT and its internationalist perspective. The provisions in the GATT treaty governing custom unions were interpreted liberally largely because the United States was sympathetic toward the general objectives (excluding agriculture) of the European Economic Community.[6] More recently, the United States has pursued this strategy with Israel, Canada, and Mexico.

GATT does allow countries to take limited actions to protect their domestic markets in the event of unfair trade or to provide temporary protection for an industry. If a country is dumping its goods—that is, selling at a price in the export market below its domestic price—a country is allowed to place a countervailing tariff to offset this practice. GATT also allows a country facing a sudden surge in imports to take temporary action to protect a domestic industry. In this case, the GATT rules effectively require some compensation for the exporting country. This compensation may take the form, for example, of tariff reductions in other markets. Ideally, the protection of the domestic industry should be in the form of a temporary tariff, and market access must remain equal for all members of GATT.

But in practice these escape clauses have not been sufficient to deter countries from finding other mechanisms to secure protection without violating the rule of GATT. Two of the most prominent devices are to invoke the antidumping provisions very liberally and to engage in voluntary export restraints (VERs).

Alan Oxley, an international trade negotiator, wrote that the European Economic Community (EEC) has developed its antidumping rules into a new "European specialty."[7] The EEC has been extremely aggressive in finding dumping. One notorious case is that of videocassette recorders from Hong Kong. Because there was essentially no domestic market in Hong Kong for videocassette recorders, dumping, defined as setting prices in foreign markets below those in domestic markets, could not literally exist. Yet, the EC brought dumping charges against Hong Kong and took action to protect their domestic markets. There is an extensive debate about whether the procedures used by the EEC to detect dumping are constructed so that findings of dumping are virtually inevitable.[8]

While the EEC may be the most aggressive group manipulating antidumping rules, other countries also can use the antidumping rules under GATT in unusual ways. The United States, for example, charged that Poland was dumping golf carts into the United States. Poland, of course, had no domestic markets for golf carts. Not only could dumping literally not exist, there were further problems in determining whether Poland was pricing below its costs. Because at that time Poland was a centralized economy operating within the Soviet bloc, there were no obvious prices with which to calculate appropriate costs. In the end, the United States used prices in Spain to determine whether Poland was dumping golf carts, under the theory that, if Poland were a capitalist country, its price structure would be similar to that of Spain.

Countries or groups of countries can invoke these unusual antidumping procedures because GATT allows the countries themselves to adopt procedures and make determinations about dumping. In addition to the EEC and the United States, Canada and Australia also pursue vigorous antidumping policies. Several Asian countries have proposed that GATT modify its antidumping rules to prevent what they perceive as unfair discrimination against their own products. But these changes are not likely to be agreed to by the EEC and the United States.

As already noted, voluntary export restraints are used by the United States against Japanese automobiles and, until recently, against imports of steel; they are used by the EEC to stem the flow of automobiles and videocassette recorders. VERs technically are not illegal under GATT, unlike a normal quota, because the exporting country voluntarily agrees to restrict exports. In the 1980s, VERs became the most important method of restricting trade and were applied to important products such as automobiles.

Initially, the U.S. automobile industry pressured the government to negotiate VERs with Japan. But the Japanese have learned to live comfortably with VERs, if not to embrace them. American consumers perceive Japanese imports to be of higher quality than American products, and, thus, when the number of imports was restricted, the resulting higher prices led to profits for the Japanese exporters. But the Japanese were not content with these higher prices on their existing models. They recognized that they could make even more profits by upgrading the quality of their products—packing more luxury features into their cars. The VERs, after all, applied to the number of imports, not their composition. The result was that Japanese imports moved up market and successfully challenged the upscale market in the domestic car industry.

In the summer of 1991, Japan and the EEC reached an agreement on limiting the number of Japanese cars sold in Europe until the year 2000. The Japanese agreed to limit their share of the market in the year 2000 to 16 percent, which is up from the current 11 percent. After the year 2000, the markets are supposed to be fully open. One of the difficult parts of these negotiations concerned Japanese cars manufactured in Europe. While imports of cars were to remain unchanged throughout the decade, production of Japanese cars in Europe would increase substantially. Nonetheless, there are limits to the extent to which the Japanese can increase production in Europe. It is clear from this agreement that voluntary export restraints can lead quickly to discussions of foreign direct investment.

In addition to renewed disputes about agriculture and methods to circumvent GATT rules, new areas were brought to the international negotiations. These new areas, which were advanced by the developed countries, were services, intellectual property, and trade-related investment measures.

As the composition of GNP in developed countries shifted from manufacturing toward services, services naturally became an important issue in international trade. Typical services that are important for international trade include air transport, shipping, financial services, and telecommunications. These industries historically have been highly regulated and protected. Attempts to open markets thus far have been in the nature of bilateral deals that allow access to markets on only limited terms.

The United States and the EEC would like to see open access for their own corporations and especially would like to be able to penetrate the relatively primitive, yet potentially highly profitable, markets in the developing countries. The developing countries have been highly suspicious of these initiatives. Having relatively little experience in these areas, the developing countries are leery of writing trade rules that would prevent them from eventually developing their own industries in these areas. Moreover, the developed countries also want protection in some areas. The United States, for example, has indicated that it would like to protect shipping and financial services.

Intellectual property rights are an area that has been aggressively pushed by United States firms in the pharmaceutical, recording, and information-related industries. From the point of view of these firms, the problem is simple. A pharmaceutical firm, for example, spends vast resources to develop a new drug or product. In order to earn a return on its investment, it must be able to sell the product above its production cost. In the United States and other developed countries, patent agreements allow the firm to pursue this strategy. But in many developing countries patent protection is ineffective and local firms copy the drugs, thereby preventing the firm from reaping monopoly profits from this market.

In other markets, lack of effective copyright protection allows bootleg production and distribution of books and records. Corporations, record producers, and authors in the developed countries all lose profits because of these activities. This loss naturally inhibits the growth of these industries in which the developed countries have a comparative advantage.

The developing countries are strongly opposed to initiatives to strengthen patent and copyright protections. It is not difficult to see why. If India allows firms to copy foreign drugs and produce them at low prices for the domestic market, its own citizens benefit. Essentially they are establishing a generic drug market, similar to that in the United States, but without the delay caused by patent protection. India also has exported some of these drugs to Africa. These markets clearly benefit India. Are there any costs? To the extent that profits of the companies that develop drugs are reduced, there may be less innovation and the flow of new products may be reduced. But the firms in the developing countries still will be innovating and competing, and the prospect of a slightly reduced flow of new drugs to the Indian market seems remote, particularly compared to the benefits of increased current domestic consumption.

In other areas of intellectual property, the motives may be less noble and more akin to pure piracy. Still, the concept of "property in ideas" is much less concrete than the concept of property as possession. What is a valid use of a new phrase, a new tune, or a new idea? Does the basic foundation of communication and language presuppose a form of reciprocity and freedom of use? Whether or not these philosophical considerations are taken seriously, they can be used as rationales for different policies in different countries.

At some point, however, even developing countries have an interest in protecting intellectual property rights. Computer firms in Taiwan have lobbied for strict enforcement of property rights in software. They have found that U.S. firms will not subcontract any work or enter into joint agreements as long as piracy continues. Some business leaders in Taiwan have recognized that their longer-run development interests lie in protecting property rights and ending piracy of software.

The final new area in the Uruguay round is trade-related investment measures. Many countries have begun to impose requirements on incoming foreign investment. Many of these measures are trade-related, such as local purchase requirements or preferential treatment for investment in sectors that export. The developed countries, the source of most foreign investment, naturally want restrictions on investment removed; the developing countries do not want to see their policies curtailed.

A grand overview of the issues on the table in the Uruguay round reveals what, in principle, looks like room for a deal. As a crude generalization, the developed and developing countries have different legitimate interests in liberalization. The developing countries want to see trade in agriculture liberalized. They are joined in this quest by some developed countries such as the United States, Canada, Australia, and New Zealand. The developing countries would also like to increase their access to markets for textiles and clothing in developed countries. The developed countries, on the other hand, have a new agenda in services, intellectual property rights, and trade-related investment measures.

The minimum requirement for a deal is at least some nominal progress in all these areas. But the sticking point has been agriculture and particularly the reluctance of the EEC to budge from its protectionist position. For the developing countries, this issue is the most critical. The United States has also become increasingly frustrated with the lack of movement on the part of the European Economic Community. Much to the chagrin of the internationalists, the Uruguay round has foundered on this issue.

One area that is not currently covered in GATT negotiations but that has been quite contentious is the link between environmental concerns and trade. U.S. environmentalists were particularly upset by a GATT ruling against a U.S. law that banned imports of tuna from Mexico that were caught using nets that also trapped dolphins. The GATT dispute settlement panel said that the United States could not embargo a product simply because the practices used to produce it violated U.S. domestic environmental laws.

The problem is that different countries have their own environmental codes, with the most strict in developed countries. If developed countries were to embargo products that do not fully meet their standards, imports from developed countries could virtually stop.

In general, more free trade could help the environment. For example, agricultural production in developing countries is much less intensive in the use of chemicals and fertilizers than developing countries. Environmental standards tend to increase with economic development. To the extent that trade promotes development, concern for the environment may tend to increase.

Still, there may be particular areas or problems in which environmental concerns are acute. A good vehicle for resolving these issues could be multilateral GATT negotiations that could lead to the development of general rules and prevent arbitrary actions by any one country to restrict trade.

The Nationalist Perspective

New Challenges to Free Trade

Opponents of free trade can be divided conveniently into two types. On the one hand are special interests who favor protection because it directly affects their own profits or employment. On the other are those who believe that it is important to limit free trade to improve a country's welfare. The second group has a long, distinguished history, ranging from the Mercantilists, who were attacked by Adam Smith;

to Frederick List, who advocated these policies for Germany; to the theoreticians of import substitution for the developing countries. In the 1980s a group of international economists began to discuss, and in some cases advocate, limits to free trade based on "strategic trade theory."

The new trade theorists essentially had two points. First, sometimes it does matter what a country trades. Countries should not be indifferent about whether they produce monkey wrenches or computer technology. Second, certain activities can generate monopoly profits or economic rents. Through appropriate government action, a country can steer these activities to its own borders and away from other countries. Both of these arguments have antecedents in the literature on trade. But in the 1980s they were developed fully and forcefully and found a sympathetic ear among traditional protectionist groups.

Why should it matter what goods a country produces for trade as long as the trade increases its consumption possibilities? The simple answer is that there may be externalities. This point, of course, had long been recognized by traditional trade theorists. But the new theory emphasized externalities arising from research and development and the development of high technology that could generate higher growth for an economy in the future. Thus, if a country failed to protect these high-tech industries, they might have additional consumption in the present, but they quickly would fall behind other countries and have reduced consumption prospects in the future.

What is special about industries that undertake extensive research and development (R&D) and produce high technology? Some economists have argued that in these industries it is impossible for a corporation to capture all the benefits of its research.[9] Despite protection from patent law, new ideas permeate out to other firms that benefit from the flow of innovative activity. But because a corporation engaging in R&D cannot capture all its benefits, it will not engage in the socially appropriate level on research. Subsidies are therefore needed and, if they cannot be given directly by the government, some protection might be necessary to insure that the industries flourish.

Governments, however, cannot subsidize all industries, so certain industries must be chosen over others. Picking winners and losers is not as easy as it seems. Even if we could, in theory, identify the industries generating positive externalities, it is extremely difficult to guide the political system in the proper direction. Politicians representing regions or interests adversely affected by these policies will not fade silently into the wind. They will find arguments—and often think tanks—to support the view that their industries also deserve subsidies.

But we are fooling ourselves if we believe that only an imperfect political system prevents us from finding an ideal industrial policy. It is not just the fashion industry that is subject to fads. Unfortunately, economic discourse is similarly plagued. Certain industries or products may appear to be the wave of the future and the basis of future technological development. Yet, if we are so prescient, why were there Edsels?

Even identifying industries that conduct intensive R&D is much more difficult than it sounds. While we are were accustomed to associating research with computers, the beverage industry devotes substantial resources to research in the search for new products. Should we subsidize Coca Cola and Pepsi? While we may admire the creative destruction of the computer industry in Silicon Valley, it bears a striking similarity to creative destruction in the rock and roll industry. Many new rock groups are launched, there is high turnover, and only a few successful innovative products make an impact on the market. Moreover, it is virtually impossible to prevent other rock and roll groups from copying a new style.

The second strand of the new strategic trade theory emphasizes unique activities that generate profits a country can capture for itself. A frequently used example is the market for commercial airplanes. Because of economies of scale, there is not room for more than a few manufacturers. Whoever enters the market will gain profits, but if too many firms enter, they all will lose.

Suppose, for example, that the commercial airline industry can only support one large firm. If two firms enter the market and compete, both will lose money. Under these circumstances, suppose that a country guarantees a profit (through subsidies, if necessary) to its domestic airline manufacturer. The domestic firm will always enter the market because it is assured of profits. The foreign firm, however, will not enter because it knows that the domestic firm will not leave and that, if they both enter, the foreign firm will suffer losses. The domestic manufacturer with its guaranteed subsidy therefore captures the market and the profits. And, best of all, the government does not have to pay the subsidy because the firm is profitable.

But there are at least two problems with this story. The first is that the other country could also offer a guarantee of profits. In this case, both firms will enter and incur losses for which the taxpayers of both countries will have to pay. In other words, strategic trade policy cannot work if there is retaliation. A second problem is that the policy still requires a country to pick winners. The Europeans captured the market for luxury, high-speed travel across the Atlantic. Unfortunately, the Concorde lost money for its sponsors.

In fairy tales, magic wands perform wonderful feats. There may be magic goods as well that perform wonders for a country that is fortunate enough to produce them. Our problem is that many claim to have the magic good, but we do not have the knowledge to choose among them. It would be foolish economics as well as foolish politics to try to do so.

The Problem of Japan

Trade relations between the United States and Japan have been strained throughout the 1980s and tensions are likely to remain in the 1990s. There are both legitimate and illegitimate reasons for concerns over trade with the Japanese, but the most publicized reason has little to do with trade policy.

Starting in 1982, the United States ran large trade deficits with the rest of the world. At the same time, Japan ran large trade surpluses. Moreover, bilateral trade between the United States and Japan during this period produced a pronounced surplus in Japan's favor. It was tempting to draw the conclusion that Japan was the source of our trade deficit and that Japanese economic policy was at the root of our trade deficit problems. Such a view underlay Congressman Richard Gephardt's proposal to levy progressively severe trade sanctions against Japan until the bilateral trade deficit disappeared.

But these views were not only mistaken but also implausible on their surface. According to most accounts—even by Japan's adversaries—the Japanese were engaging in their version of industrial policy and export promotion throughout the 1970s. Yet throughout this period the United States maintained a rough balance in its overall trade deficit and persistent deficits did not emerge until the early 1980s.[10]

Both Japan's trade surplus and the U.S. trade deficits were of macroeconomic origin. If a country spends more than it produces, it must obtain the additional goods from abroad. This trend characterized the United States in the 1980s. On the other hand, total spending in

Japan fell short of total production, and the remainder was available for net exports abroad. In the United States, the large fiscal deficits that emerged in the 1980s, fueled by consumer spending, contributed to the high level of domestic spending relative to output. In Japan, domestic spending has been low because of the high levels of private savings. These macro, or aggregate, effects are the source of the trade deficits or surpluses, not industrial policy.

Even if both Japan and the United States had overall balanced trade, an imbalance in the bilateral trade still would be likely. Japan, which has relatively few raw materials, must import more and thereby run trade deficits with the producers of those primary products. If the overall trade account between Japan and these producers is to be in balance, the deficits with producers of primary products must be met with trade surpluses in manufactured or finished goods. Because the United States is a large consumer market, the Japanese would still run a trade surplus with the United States even if their overall trade were balanced.

Still, critics are not satisfied by these arguments. Something must be wrong with the Japanese. It is alleged that the Japanese stubbornly resist importing U.S. goods. Is this true and, if so, is it a major problem?

Statistical studies tend to show that Japan imports less than would be expected from a country of its size.[11] Its exports are also relatively low—only 14 percent of GNP, a figure lower than in most developed countries except the United States. The contrast with Germany is striking. Until its recent problems with reunification, Germany had a larger trade surplus as a share of GNP than Japan, but its imports were relatively high. The trade surplus resulted because its exports were even higher. Japan, in contrast, achieves its trade surplus with a low level of exports and an even lower level of imports.

Standard measures of protection, however, do not demonstrate that Japan is sheltering its markets. While it does protect agriculture—as do all developed countries—its tariff rates on manufactured goods are low. Whatever barriers to trade do exist are infinitely more subtle than mere tariffs. Some observers point to social pressures to buy Japanese goods even if foreign goods are better value. According to this view, social customs in Japan are more powerful than capitalist motivations.

Other commentators point to structural features of Japanese society that make it difficult for imports to penetrate. Numerous regulations fetter large retailers that try to open shops in Japan. A lengthy process of consultation is necessary with small, local shopkeepers that can prevent or at least delay the opening of large retail outlets. The U.S. toy giant Toys R Us complained bitterly about these rules.

The Bush administration conducted structural impediment initiative talks with Japan to deal with both overall trade balance issues and the structure of markets. The talks recognized that the trade imbalances were primarily of macroeconomic origin. As usual in international meetings, the administration promised to take steps to reduce the deficit. Japan, on the other hand, was requested to increase its share of government spending by an entire percentage point. This request will probably be taken as seriously in Japan as the United States will take its promise to reduce its deficit.

The United States also proposed detailed steps for Japan to open its markets that included changes in urban policy and in distribution policies. By any standards, these discussions were highly intrusive talks aimed at changing many entrenched Japanese policies. The Japanese, however, offered suggestions to the United States. One list contained over a hundred policies that sould increase our savings rate and improve our international competitiveness. One item on the list gives the flavor and futility of these talks: to improve the U.S. savings rate, consumers would be limited to one credit card!

What is the harm to the U.S. if the Japanese market is not as open as U.S. markets? The main cost to the United States is a small reduction in our standard of living. To balance our trade—and over some interval we must—imports must be brought in line with exports. If some markets are closed to us, the only alternative method of balancing trade is to make imports more expensive to U.S. consumers through a depreciation of the dollar. The more export markets are closed to U.S. firms, the more the dollar will depreciate. Thus U.S. consumers will pay more for imported goods. This consequence is the cost of closed foreign markets.

A higher price for imports is a real cost to consumers, but it usually is not cause for paranoia. Other fears stir the imagination. Will the Japanese, as the new owners of U.S. corporations, behave differently by preferring their own managers and importing disproportionately from their own trusted suppliers? Will they keep all the good jobs in Japan and treat the United States as a third-world outlet? Very little evidence has demonstrated adverse effects from Japanese ownership. Yet these fears, along with frustrations by would-be exporters to

Japan, have led to a new aggressive stance in U.S. trade relations with the world.

The Japanese have started to mount their own public relations offensive against the United States. In 1992, a government-sponsored advisory council issued the first of a series of annual reports examining the trade practices of Japan's trading partners. The United States topped the list of countries with the most restrictive trade practices. The council cited four practices: a penchant for unilateral actions, abuse of dumping laws, the use of voluntary export restraints, and buy American laws. We should welcome these criticisms. The United States often adopts a holier than thou attitude on trade. But the Japanese should expect continued public scrutiny of their own trade practices as well.

Aggressive Unilateralism

Politics imitates movies. The Cold War spoof *Dr. Strangelove* has haunted U.S. politics in the 1980s. Congress and the administration have favored creating "doomsday machines" patterned after the movie. The logic of the doomsday machine is that policies are enforced by means of a terrible, binding threat that forces opponents to concede. In the case of the federal deficit, the Gramm-Rudman law (see Chapter 8) threatened to virtually shut down the government. In the trade area, the Congress forced the administration to adopt new trade procedures, coupled with strong threats, to open foreign markets. This trade policy is known as the Super-301 legislation.

Under this law, the Special Trade Representative must report to Congress any "act, policy, or practice of a foreign country" that unfairly restricts U.S. exports. After making this initial finding, the country is given a fixed period in which to negotiate with the United States to remove these impediments to exports. If the Special Trade Representative does not find that sufficient progress has been made, the United States must take unilateral action to punish the country. A typical action would be a 100 percent tariff against imports from that country.

The Super-301 law is clearly in violation of GATT. Under GATT Most Favored Nation status must be extended to all members. Under Super-301, imports from one country are singled out for tariff restrictions. Moreover, by making itself the judge of whether any policy or practice of a foreign country is unfair, the United States goes far beyond GATT guidelines with respect to dumping or other unfair trade practices spelled out in GATT.

Defenders of this policy claim that it is necessary to obtain action. Without severe threats, they argue, countries will not take any actions to open their markets. U.S. exporters will continue to be hurt by closed foreign markets.

While agreeing that the United States may have the power in some cases to force open markets, Jagdish Bhagwati decries what he calls "aggressive unilateralism."[12] Bhagwati believes that while the United States can use its power to gain some trade concessions, this policy ultimately will hurt the world trading system and, eventually, the United States as well.

Bhagwati outlined five objections to Super-301:

1. GATT has the force of a treaty in the United States. Because Super-301 clearly violates provisions of GATT, the United States essentially is violating a treaty.
2. Some proponents of Super-301 concede that it violates GATT provisions, but they claim that it is an example of justified "civil disobedience." In other words, with Super-301 the United States is adhering to the higher principles of GATT even if it is in technical violation of its provisions. Bhagwati rejects this rationale and notes that no one else seems to believe in the higher principles theory and that the past behavior of the Unites States with respect to GATT has not always been exemplary. He also believes that Super-301 eventually will generate cynicism toward GATT rules as other countries see that they can be altered when a powerful country feels constrained by them.
3. The political pressures applied under Super-301 can divert trade from its most efficient source. For example, a country may purchase U.S. goods to avoid sanctions, even though they could purchase the goods from a more efficient supplier elsewhere in the world. This diversion creates inefficiencies in world trade.
4. The political pressures can poison the sense of fairness necessary to reach other agreements in world trade.
5. Even if the United States were to use its power for altruistic purposes, Bhagwati challenges the notion that it should take on the role of the benevolent policeman.

In practice, Super-301 has not been as effective as its proponents had hoped nor as poisonous as its critics had feared. In the first year of the law, the Special Trade Representative named Brazil, India, and South Korea as guilty of restrictive trade practices. Negotiations were conducted satisfactorily with South Korea, and sanctions were applied only against India and Brazil. Although other countries may not have liked the U.S. law, there was not much doubt that India and Brazil did engage in restrictive trade practices. Japan was spared from the initial list, but the law clearly set the stage for the structural impediment initiative talks. The Super-301 law temporarily reduced the protectionist sentiment in Congress and has been more of an irritant than a disaster for international trade negotiations.

But with the EEC refusing to budge on agriculture and progress on the Uruguay round stalled, the biggest threat to multilateral negotiations is no longer Super-301. The growth of free-trade areas now is diverting attention away from multilateral negotiations.

Free Trade Areas

The original agreements in GATT recognized custom unions and free trade areas as legitimate departures from Most Favored Nation principles. Within both custom unions and free trade areas, there are reduced tariffs for the countries that belong to the union or area and common tariff barriers for nonmember countries. Custom unions allow free movement of factors of production—labor and capital—as well as the additional opportunities present for trade in free trade areas.

While the original GATT agreements recognized these groupings, they also tried to restrict them to countries that had eliminated all trade barriers among themselves. The implicit idea behind this rule was that countries willing to make these reductions would be attempting to achieve full economic integration. It would be foolish for GATT to stop this type of activity when economic integration was also a principal aim of GATT. However, in practice, GATT recognized custom unions and free trade areas that were much more limited in scope. The United States supported these arrangements largely because it approved of the general design of the European Economic Community. However,until recently the United States had refrained from engaging in these activities.

One might think that any reduction in tariff barriers would be welcome because it would be a step on the road to universal free trade. But economists have realized that custom unions or free trade areas do not necessarily improve either a country's welfare or the welfare of the world. Two different effects result when a group of countries reduces the trade barriers among them. First, prices will be lower within the bloc, so trade can expand. This result is called the "trade creation" effect, and it definitely increases consumer and producer welfare. The second effect, called "trade diversion," is not as benign. Suppose that, prior to the formation of a free trade area, a country outside the area was producing a good for sale within the countries. When the tariff barriers have been reduced within the free trade area, a country within the area may have an advantage because it faces a lower tariff rate. The reduced tariff shifts or diverts trade from the lowest-cost producer to a higher-cost producer within the free trade area.

Trade diversion clearly hurts the country that was the previous producer but lost its market to a country within the bloc. But if trade diversion is strong enough, it can overwhelm the gains from trade creation for a country within the union. A country that joins a union sacrifices tariff revenues when it switches its purchases to goods produced within the union. The loss of tariff revenues can be large enough to outweigh the gains from trade creation.

Proponents of multilateralism worry that the world will drift into three major trading areas that will conduct little outside trade. Europe will constitute the first; the United States, Mexico, and Canada will be the second;, and Japan and the countries of the far east will form the third. The nightmare of multilateralists is that the blocs will adopt extremely protectionist policies against countries outside the blocs. This result would lead to inefficient world production and trading patterns.

There are certainly some important concerns about the formation of large trading areas. When Europe first announced its plans for a unified market, there were fears that it would amount to a "fortress Europe." Regulatory policies and standards would essentially be rigged to prevent the entry of foreign firms. Fortunately, this scenario did not occur, perhaps because there was careful scrutiny of the early rounds in the process of creating the unified market. However, in the spring of 1991, GATT issued a report critical of some practices of countries within the EEC that had the effect of creating nontariff barriers to trade.

After first developing free trade arrangements with Israel and Canada, the United States turned its attention toward Mexico with the goal of forming a North American Free Trade Area. It is hard to believe that the United States would be interested in carving the world into trading blocs by forming this union. U.S. firms clearly have interests in trade outside of the limited North American market. However, the United States can use the threat of excluding other countries from the North American market if they fail to open their markets. This tactic would be another weapon in the aggressive unilateralism that Bhagwati deplored. While it is a dangerous weapon that potentially could backfire, it also could be used as a club in international negotiations.

There are two positive aspects of the creation of a North American free trade zone with Mexico. The first is simply the political dynamics of liberalization. If members of the Senate and Congress are focused on liberalization, traditional protectionists are put on the defensive. A similar phenomenon occurred with those seeking tax cuts in the 1980s. While they did not always prevail in their battles, they certainly took tax increases off the agenda.

The other positive factor is that the United States has clear interests in Mexico's economic development. Free trade has long been recognized by economists as a partial substitute for movements of factors of production. Translated into political terms, if Mexico can raise wages through their trade with the United States, there will be less incentive for illegal immigration across the border. The United States clearly would like to have some control over its immigration policy, but that control is severely threatened by immigration from below the border.

The politics of liberalization with Mexico has been somewhat predictable. Western U.S. states have welcomed the pact with an eye toward reduced immigration, while the midwestern and eastern states have been in opposition, fearing additional competition in manufacturing. The negotiations with Mexico have also focused on movements of capital from the United States into Mexico. This possibility promises even greater benefits for Mexico compared to simply lowering tariffs, but correspondingly raises additional concern among midwestern manufacturers.

Congress only undertakes major trade negotiations under "fast-track authority." This term means that once an agreement has been reached, there is only an up or down vote and no amendments are allowed. This tactic prevents special interests from tacking on so many amendments that the bill is killed on the floor. The lobbying, of course, does not disappear but goes behind the scenes and the negotiations. Limits may also be placed on the length of the fast-track authority; this step can be taken either by proponents to expedite or by opponents to try to sabotage any agreements.

This time the trade negotiations attracted some new players: human rights groups and environmentalists. The human rights groups saw trade negotiations with Mexico as a vehicle for their demands to end perceived abuses. The environmentalists had different fears. They had been reasonably successful with the passage of the Clean Air Act (see Chapter 4). They did not want companies to close down production in the United States and reopen factories under reduced environmental standards in Mexico. While relocation might reduce pollution in the United States, world pollution could increase. Thus, a strange political alliance between midwestern manufacturers, human rights groups, and environmentalists began to emerge.

In the short run, some firms perhaps would relocate to take advantage of more liberal environmental rules. But in the long run, environmental interests will be served by faster development for Mexico. The countries with the worst environmental records are poor or belonged to the former Soviet bloc. As development proceeds, there may be a long-run demand for cleaner air and water, as has occurred in developed countries. Mexico has already made important advances in this direction. Far-sighted environmentalists should welcome economic development and join the Western interests in supporting a pact with Mexico.

Do We Need New Institutions?

The growth of VERs and nontrade barriers in the United States and the rest of the world has prompted a number of proposals to revise the mechanisms for awarding protection against the consequences of free trade. Not only have politicians offered their own remedies, but economists have contributed to the debate as well.

Industries and workers that suffer when markets are opened are often able to exert political influence. Any realistic world trading system must recognize this. GATT, has an escape clause that is embodied in Article XIX:

If as a result of unforeseen developments and of the effect of obligations incurred by a contracting party under this Agreement, including tariff concessions, any product is being imported into the territory of that contracting party in such increased quantities and under such conditions as to cause or threaten serious injury to domestic producers in that territory of like or directly competitive products, the contracting party shall be free, in respect of that product, and to the extent and for such time as may be necessary to prevent or remedy this injury, to suspend the obligation in whole or in part or to withdraw or modify the concession.

In the United States, the escape clause is embodied in Sections 201 through 203 of the Trade Act of 1974. An industry seeking protection first must present its factual case to the International Trade Commission (ITC), which decides whether an industry has been injured by imports or not. If the ITC determines that the industry has been hurt by imports, final decisions on the form and nature of relief rest with the president.

The Trade Act of 1974 limited the definitions of "injury from imports" and, until recently, it was relatively difficult for industries to obtain protection from this procedure. From 1975 to 1985, fifty-seven petitions were brought to the ITC. They found injury in thirty-three—a success rate of 60 percent. However, of these thirty-three, the president only provided import protection in fourteen, so the final success rate was closer to 40 percent.[13] In 1988, trade legislation liberalized the definition of "injury from imports." Now, instead of having to be a "substantial" cause of injury to an industry, imports need only be a "significant" cause. The substantial cause criterion was interpreted to mean that imports had to be the most important cause of injury for an industry, an assertion that would be difficult to prove, for example, during a recession. We have not had much experience with the more liberal definition.

In their review of the escape clause prior to 1985, Robert Lawrence and Robert Litan argued that it worked relatively well. The purpose of the clause was to channel political pressure away from Congress or the president to an administrative agency where decisions could be made more on their merits and less on the political strength of the industries. According to these authors' review, the ITC successfully handled this pressure. Assistance was only recommended in cases in which there was clear evidence that the industry was adversely affected by imports; the ITC was not unduly influenced by political factors; and protection took the form of tariffs that, for the most part, remained temporary. From 1951 to 1985, thirty-one industries received protection through this mechanism. Only three industries remain protected.[14]

This record of successful temporary protection contrasts sharply with industries that have received protection through legislation, international quota agreements, or voluntary export restraints. In these cases, protection has tended to remain permanent. To take a few examples, textiles have received protections since 1957 through a variety of agreements; shipbuilding has had legislative protection since the 1920s; and automobiles from Japan have been subject to VERs since 1981.

The contrast between these forms of protection suggest that it would be desirable to shift more cases through the official escape valve channels of the ITC and away from legislation or quota agreements. Lawrence and Litan suggest a number of ways this may be accomplished. Trade adjustment assistance could be available to workers in industries in which the ITC found injury, even if the president did not award direct import protection. Although it is probably impossible to prevent the Executive and foreign governments from developing voluntary export agreements—because they are technically voluntary—the Congress could refuse to provide funds for the U.S. Customs agency to provide information to countries that would help them enforce their agreements.

While the goal of forcing more protectionist sentiment through the official escape valve mechanism is worthy, it may be difficult to accomplish. Powerful industries, such as the automobile industry, know that it may be difficult to obtain protection through the ITC and that protection probably will be temporary. That prospect is precisely why such industries prefer alternative arrangements through quotas or VERs. Or, to put it another way, industries that obtain protection outside of the escape valve procedure may be more powerful.

Voluntary export restraints were developed precisely because they were not pro forma illegal means of restraining international trade. It is difficult to envision any mechanism that could prevent VERs if the political will exists to protect the industry. In these circumstances, the only way to make progress is to change the political atmosphere so that protectionism is discouraged. This shift would require outspoken political leaders who could effectively demonstrate the high costs to consumers of saving an industry affected by trade. One recent study found that consumers paid $340,000 for each job that was saved by protective measures![15] Such change would also mean taking on powerful special interests like the automobile industry. Populism can be enlisted in good causes.

The trade economist Robert Baldwin has suggested that the public's concerns be aired during any proceedings about protection. Specifically, when the ITC and the president decide that an industry has been hurt by imports and recommend some protection, the public learns about the injury to the industry but not about the cost of protection to the consumer. Baldwin suggests that an agency in the executive branch should be given the task of outlining the costs of any protectionist actions and that these figures should be made available to the public. This move perhaps also could harness populist emotions under the free trade banner.[16]

Lawrence and Litan propose institutional reforms that possibly could lead to free trade in the long run. Their basic idea is that industries that now enjoy protection cannot suddenly have their protection stripped away. Some replacement must be found for the protection, but their current protection would be replaced with a more benign form that would eventually disappear.

Specifically, Lawrence and Litan suggest that all quotas or voluntary restraints be converted to tariffs that would be phased out gradually over a number of years. There are essentially three reasons for favoring tariffs over quotas or VERs. First, tariffs raise revenues. Existing quotas could be auctioned off to the highest bidder as another source of revenue. These revenues could then be used for worker assistance programs and, in some cases, to compensate other countries whose firms were benefiting from the quotas. Second, tariffs are preferable to quotas when there are monopolies or oligopolies in the domestic industry. With a tariff, domestic firms cannot raise prices too high on foreign firms will sell in the market. This potential competition limits the level of domestic prices. With quotas, however, domestic firms can raise prices because foreign firms can sell only a limited amount. Moreover, with tariff barriers there are always incentives for foreign firms to reduce costs to try to enter the domestic market; with quotas, these incentives do not operate. Finally, tariffs are more visible than quotas. It is easier for consumers and the general public to see that prices are higher because of the additional tax on imports. With quotas, the higher prices are largely invisible.

The tariffs would decline on a schedule so that protection would finish in a fixed number of years. Presumably, this arrangement would give the industry time to adjust. Some interim protection is unavoidable, but Lawrence and Litan argue that as long as it takes the form of tariffs and is temporary, it is a large improvement over the status quo.

The one difficulty with this scheme is its presumption that powerful industries that have arranged protection through quotas or VERs will acquiesce to a new arrangement in which their protection disappears. To put it bluntly, will the automobile industry allow this to happen, or will it carve out special exceptions for itself? The automobile industry has enjoyed voluntary export restraints for an entire decade and probably would resist any attempt to redesign its protection.

There are several ways to combat these entrenched interests. The first would be to engage in a massive reform that gains its own momentum and overwhelms the special interests. The Tax Reform Act of 1986 followed this model. The sheer momentum of a tax reform bill overwhelmed existing political interests. Perhaps Lawrence and Litan envision a similar process with their trade reforms.

Another way to combat special interests is for politicians to more effectively involve industries that are hurt by current restrictions in the political process. The GATT process currently brings in export interests that want open markets abroad. Many domestic firms are hurt by import restrictions. Rental car agencies would like lower car prices, and many large industrial enterprises would benefit if steel prices fall from their artificial levels.

In both cases, the ground swell must be led by politicians willing to take a long view of free trade. In the tax area, Senator Bill Bradley worked for a number of years to promote tax reform when the likelihood of a tax bill was remote. When the Tax Reform Act passed in 1986, he was rewarded for this work by tremendous praise from all quarters. The current economic environment is protectionist, and it is tempting for politicians to bow in this direction. More campaign money is probably available in the short run for those with protectionist views. But a risk-taking politician might gamble a big payoff from advocating free trade.

The free trade agreements with Israel and Canada and the potential agreement with Mexico may help channel politicians' attitudes toward free trade. If politicians find they can benefit from promoting free trade in these cases, the sheer momentum could carry over into other agreements. Principled free trade stands could then put the Europeans on the defensive and help insure that Europe after 1992 remains open. Perhaps advocates of free trade could even insure the complete success of the Uruguay round and strike that elusive deal that would benefit the world trading system.

Concluding Comments

The politics of international trade illustrate some of the difficulties inherent in collective action. Markets do not establish an international framework for trade—nations must establish the rules. But the best rules are often difficult to sustain in the face of domestic political pressures. Here are the key points to keep in mind when thinking about the intricacies of international trade.

1. With only a few minor exceptions, it is in the collective interests of all nations to have free and open trade.

2. However, within any country some interests always could profit from barriers to trade. It is not simply that special interests can gain from protectionism. The per-capita benefits they can reap through tariffs or quotas will tend to be very large, while the per-capita costs to others in the society will be much smaller as the costs of protectionism are spread widely over a larger group. This asymmetry in benefits and costs creates a political dynamic that encourages aggressive action by special interests.

3. To prevent the tyranny of special interests, nations in the postwar era have entered into multilateral agreements to maintain open markets. The Uruguay round of GATT negotiations stalled, largely because the Europeans insisted on high levels of protection for their agricultural industries. However, large gains could result from succeeding in these negotiations. Developing countries could find new export markets in agriculture and textiles, while developed countries would benefit from new rules for intellectual property, foreign investment, and services.

4. One new trend is the growth of regional free trade areas. Although this development is a departure from the strict multilateralism

of GATT, it can serve as a positive force for free trade. The danger of regional free trade pacts is that they can exclude other countries and thereby create inefficient patterns of world trade. On the other hand, they can create a dynamic for open trade and put the forces of protection on the defensive.

Further Reading

Jagdish Bhagwati is a world-renowned trade economist and an advisor to GATT. His book, *Protectionism* (Cambridge, Mass.: MIT Press, 1988), makes a strong case for the GATT process. Another GATT insider, Alex Oxley, provides a current perspective on the politics and economics of GATT in *The Challenge of Free Trade* (New York: Harvester Wheatsheaf, 1990).

Paul Krugman has played the devil's advocate against free trade and has been one of primary sources of arguments against completely unfettered trade. His article, "Is Free Trade Passé" (*Journal of Economic Perspectives*, 1987, pp. 131–44) is quite accessible. The reader can gauge the strength of Krugman's opposition to free trade.

The polital economy of GATT and trade policy is a fascinating subject. Robert Z. Lawrence and Robert E. Litan's *Saving Free Trade* (Washington, D.C.: Brookings Institution, 1986) is a source of many ideas. See also the article by Robert Baldwin, "The Political Economy of Trade Policy" (*Journal of Economic Perspectives*, 1989, pp. 119–36).

Notes

1. See Paul Krugman, "Is Free Trade Passé?" *Journal of Economic Perspectives* (1987): 131–44. Krugman is one of the key figures in the reorientation of trade theory in the 1980s. While his views will be discussed later in the chapter, he does argue that a general policy of free trade is a good rough and ready policy for a nation.
2. See Jagdish Bhagwati, *Protectionism* Cambridge, Mass.: MIT Press, 1988), 3.
3. Bhagwati, *Protectionism*, 5.
4. This example assumes a country can be competitive in some good. If not, the domestic price level would adjust either by exchange rate movements or wage changes. The result would be that the country would be competitive in the production of some goods.
5. L. Alan Winters, "The Road to Uruguay," *The Economic Journal*, 100 (Dec. 1990): 1289.

6. See Bhagwati, *Protectionism*, 11.
7. Alan Oxley, *The Challenge of Free Trade* (New York: Harvester Wheatsheaf, 1990), 200.
8. See Oxley, *Challenge,* 201.
9. This point is discussed in Krugman, "Is Free Trade Passé?"
10. During the 1970s, the United States had a slight deficit on its trade in goods and services, but net investment income from abroad roughly balanced the current account, the broadest measure of the private sector deficit with the rest of the world.
11. See Paul Krugman, *The Age of Diminished Expectations* (Cambridge, Mass.: MIT Press, 1990), ch. 10.
12. Jagdish Bhagwati, "Departures from Multilateralism: Regionalism and Aggressive Unilateralism," *The Economic Journal,* 100 (Dec. 1990): 1304–17.
13. This discussion draws on Robert Z. Lawrence and Robert E. Litan, *Saving Free Trade* (Washington, D.C.: Brookings Institution, 1986), ch. 3 and 5.
14. Lawrence and Litan, *Saving Free Trade,* 45.
15. Lawrence and Litan, *Saving Free Trade,* 48.
16. Baldwin also discusses alternative theories of why protection originates and the forms that it takes. See Robert Baldwin, "The Political Economy of Trade Policy," *The Journal of Economic Perspectives* (Fall 1989): 119–36.

7

Monetary Matters

Politics and Inflation

The decades of the 1980s and 1990s both started with deep recessions. The recession in the 1980s was caused by the high interest rates that were felt necessary to slow economic activity and bring down inflation. The origin of the 1990 recession is more controversial, but one cause was the reluctance of banks to extend loans because of pressure from regulators in Washington. In both cases, millions of individuals were directly affected by the rise in unemployment and bankruptcies that resulted and the monetary system was a key factor. It seems strange that we are still fighting the battles of business cycles that were identified so clearly by that brilliant analyst of capitalism, Karl Marx.

But not only technical issues are involved in combating business cycles through the use of monetary policy. Politics combine with our less-than-perfect knowledge of the macroeconomics of monetary policy to generate an important source of our difficulties. Monetary policy raises important issues in our pursuit of collective action. To understand the nature of these difficulties, a somewhat unusual analogy between money and drugs might be helpful.

Drugs are a ubiquitous part of the modern world. Used in proper doses and in proper circumstances, they work wonders. Infections that previously were fatal can now be cured easily; blood pressure can be reduced, prolonging life; and even the symptoms of the common cold can be made to disappear—for a while.

But drugs are easily abused. Tranquilizers can be addictive; morphine, which reduces pain, can lead to terrible addictions; and excessive use of diet pills can seriously disturb a person's equilibrium. Twentieth-century U.S. history illustrates that excessive drug use cannot continue unabated: the damage done to society simply becomes too great. Eventually, a reaction sets in and drug use becomes sharply curtailed.

Taken properly and in small doses, drugs are valuable, life-saving commodities. But they are easy to abuse and can cause immense harm.

In many aspects, monetary policy bears a close resemblance to drugs. Used properly, monetary policy can alleviate mass pain and suffering and even can help balance a budget. But when it is abused, monetary policy can quickly destroy an entire economy. Why does monetary policy have these effects?

To understand the somewhat complex role of monetary policy and its great potential for good and evil, it is necessary to digress into some basic principles of macroeconomics. The source of the difficulty with monetary policy is that the long-run effects of changes in the supply of money are very different from the short-run effects. The short-run effects of increases in the money supply can be benign, but the long-run effects can be malign.

In modern economies, wages and prices are somewhat "sticky"— that is, they change gradually over time. Wages for most workers, for example, are only changed yearly, while firms tend to be reluctant to change their prices too frequently. In this setting, if the supply of money is increased in the society and prices have not changed, the individuals with the extra money have additional command over real resources. They typically spend some of this money on financial assets and some on goods. When they buy financial assets (stocks, bonds, deposits in money funds), prices of financial assets tend to rise and interest rates fall. The fall in interest rates plus the direct demand for goods entices producers to increase their production. Thus, the economy begins to expand as new production takes place, new workers are hired, and unemployment falls. In the short run, an increase in the supply of money leads to an increase in economic output and a fall in unemployment. Conversely, bad times result when the money supply is decreased: output falls and unemployment increases.

But these effects only take place over some period of time, perhaps a few years. Over the longer run, an increase in the supply of money does not have any effect on output or unemployment but only leads to higher prices. The reason for this is fairly straightforward. People hold money in order to facilitate their transactions in the marketplace. The amount of money they want to hold naturally depends on the prices of the goods that they buy. If the prices of the goods double, an individual would require twice as much money to make the same real transactions. Imagine an economy starting with an initial supply of money and producing at full employment. Now let the supply of money be doubled and assume that after five years the economy will return to full employment. Because individuals have twice as much money, only if prices double will they have the correct amount to purchase output in the economy. If prices increase by less, individuals would have excess money and bid up the prices of goods. Similarly, if prices more than double, individuals would have insufficient money and prices for goods would tend to fall. In the long run, therefore, an increase in the supply of money leads to a proportional increase in the level of all prices.

Why are the short-run effects so different from the long-run effects? The key is the stickiness of prices in the short run. Initially, workers and suppliers of goods will keep wages and prices fixed and will supply more labor and more goods in the face of increased demand. But, over time, they will respond to the increase in demand for their services by raising wages and prices. Once wages and prices have fully adjusted, the economy returns to its original level of production, but prices have increased in proportion to the increase in money supply.[1]

The fact that wages and prices are sticky in the short run also means that, in the face of shocks, the economy can deviate from full employment and face severe recessions. Recessions would not last very long if wages and prices were fully flexible, but, in the face of stickiness, a recession can persist for a long period of time. In these circumstances, appropriate increases in the supply of money can be quite helpful. An increase in the supply of money during a recession will stimulate demand and lead to increases in production. With appropriate monetary policy, there is no need for a society to suffer through a prolonged recession.

But determining an appropriate monetary policy is very difficult. Because the long-run effects of an increase in the supply of money differ from the short-run effects, it is difficult to gauge the proper dose of monetary policy. If the dose is too large, the patient (the economy) eventually will suffer from other maladies (higher prices or inflation) that pose other important risks. Despite years of study and analysis, economists are not equipped to prescribe exactly the proper dose of monetary policy, and there is always the risk that too large a dose or an ill-timed dose will lead to longer-run inflationary consequences.

It is also easy to understand the political dangers of policies that have favorable short-run effects but unfavorable long-run effects. It would be easy for a political leader to succumb to the temptation of increasing the money supply to stimulate the economy prior to an election. The short-run effects of the increase in output and the fall in unemployment generally work to an incumbent's advantage. The long-run effects of higher prices will be felt later. Indeed, faced with higher prices in the future, the incumbent may become "addicted" to using monetary policy and engineer further increases in the money supply. This tactic may lead to a further expansion (unless the public catches on) but certainly will lead to even higher inflation later. After a while, the public no longer will be fooled by these monetary expansions, but by then the body politic will be left with deep-rooted inflation.

Up to this point, we have been discussing the problems of using monetary policy to change the level of output in the economy, either to avert recessions or to manipulate it for political advantage. But in developing countries with relatively undeveloped systems of taxation, money creation can serve another important function—it can be a source of revenue. A government can print money relatively costlessly and then use the new currency to buy goods or pay government salaries. The government acquires real goods and services in exchange for pieces of paper that cost almost nothing to print. But by continuing to put money into the economy, the government generates inflation, because the prices of all goods and services rise in proportion to the additional money that was created. Inflation is an inevitable consequence of raising government revenue through printing more money.

Governments easily can become addicted to printing money. In many developing countries, the so-called inflation tax amounts to nearly 10 percent of total government revenue. As inflation increases, however, people become more reluctant to hold on to money; they turn it over faster in their transactions and carry less in their purses or wallets. This response makes it more difficult for a government to raise additional revenue through higher inflation. Indeed, because the public responds to higher inflation by trying to hold less money, there is a limit to the amount of money that an addicted government can raise through the printing press. Monetary history is full of examples of governments that became too greedy in printing money and destroyed their economies with massive hyperinflation as they also witnessed a fall in the real revenues they collected.[2]

Some economists have theorized that all governments will pursue inflationary strategies. One theory recognizes that inflation can be a source of revenue and that governments generally will use all possible sources in order to raise revenue in a least-cost fashion. As long as the costs of inflation do not rise too quickly, governments inevitably will use inflation in their portfolio of tax instruments.

Another hypothesis is based on game theory. Suppose that the government has a preference for higher employment than would normally evolve in the labor market. This preference might arise for political reasons or could reflect the fact that distortions caused by labor taxation have led to too little employment. In any case, the government would like to increase employment and, in principle, can do so by fooling workers with higher inflation than they had anticipated. The workers, on the other hand, know the government's propensity and raise their wage demands to the point at which the government does not wish to incur higher inflation, even if it can fool the workers. The result of this process is inevitable—high inflation.

Despite the popularity of this view among economic theorists, very little evidence supports it. The United States, for example, has had a wide range of inflation rates in the postwar era. Monetary policy is important in controlling inflation and unemployment. But the diverse outcomes we observe are the result of a complex political process not inevitable tendencies of capitalist economies.

Because monetary policy has such important powers for good and evil in society, a host of important political and economic questions naturally surround monetary policy. The three principal ones are:

1. Who should control monetary policy? Should it be in the direct control of an elected government or turned over to a politically independent central bank?

2. How should the money supply be controlled? Should there be discretion in the conduct of monetary policy, or should it be conducted by fixed rules? And, in either case, by which principles should the money supply be controlled?
3. In an increasingly interdependent world economy, can a country still operate its monetary policy solely with regard to its own objectives, or must there be international coordination or agreement about policies? In addition, how should monetary policy be related to exchange rates?

Because there are at least three answers to each question, there are at least twenty-seven different permutations to the answers to these questions. Rather than tracing all the permutations, it is more efficient (and more informative) to highlight the key political and economic controversies within each question and to point out some of their important interrelationships.

Controlling the Sovereign

At least over short periods of time, monetary policy can have important differential effects on different groups in the economy. Debtors would prefer some unanticipated inflation so they can pay back their debts in inflated currency. Creditors, naturally would prefer to avoid these inflationary surprises. The unemployed also would like to see short-run expansionary policy to bring them back to work. Financiers and suppliers of capital prefer stable financial environments and dislike the disruptions that unstable monetary policy can bring.

In modern society, it is often unclear whether a particular individual would benefit from a short-run inflationary policy. A typical worker might like expansionary times, but if he or she has substantial assets in a pension fund, that retirement income could be endangered by an unstable financial policy. Unstable inflation eventually generates a countervailing policy response, and a typical worker may fear the future consequences of such an action.

Nonetheless, clear political interests are involved in monetary policy. In a perfect world in which the economy was not prone to recessions, there could be unanimity that a policy of constant money and minimal inflation would be the best for the long-run health of the economy. In this case, risks to the financial system would be minimized and the economy would be more productive without the extra disruptions of inflation. But this economic utopia is not the world we live in. Recessions occur, and monetary policy potentially can play an important role in ameliorating these downturns. But active use of monetary policy also carries with it the risk of excessive expansion and the resulting inflation. There are clear political interests in assessing the significance of these risks.[3]

The United States has a strange hybrid institution that deals with these real political conflicts. The U.S. Constitution gives Congress the power to "coin money, regulate the value thereof, and of foreign coins, and fix the standards of weights and measures." In 1914, Congress exercised these powers by creating the Federal Reserve System. After the collapse of the banking system in the 1930s, Congress made substantial changes in the Federal Reserve System in 1935 that gave it its present structure.

The Federal Reserve System is a mixed private–public institution. There are twelve Federal Reserve banks in the country whose presidents rotate to serve on the Federal Open Market Committee (FOMC) that determines the course of monetary policy. The other seven members of the FOMC are from the Board of Governors of the Federal Reserve. Members are appointed by the president for terms of fourteen years, while the chairman is appointed by the president for a four-year term.

Each regional Federal Reserve Bank also has a Board of Directors and is closely connected to the financial and business community in its area. The ability to summon influential local interests in times of political conflict is an important source of power for the Federal Reserve. Some members of Congress and the public have objected to the powerful role that the bank presidents from the private sector play in determining monetary policy. There have been lawsuits attempting to limit their role but, to date, they have not been successful. In 1991, legislation was introduced to limit the role of bank presidents in determining monetary policy.

In recent years, the bank presidents have represented "hard money" interests and have taken an aggressive posture against inflation and expansionary monetary policy. The appointees chosen by the Reagan administration, somewhat surprisingly, tended to favor rather easier money. These divergent views were the source of conflicts within the FOMC. But, stepping back from the workings of the

Fed for the moment, what is striking is that this rather peculiar organization is given political control of the money supply in a democratic country. Is this arrangement appropriate or desirable?

There are two popular views about the proper political control of monetary policy. One view, firmly in the populist tradition, is that monetary policy should be under strict democratic control. In the United States, that theory would translate into tight control of the monetary policy by the Congress or, perhaps, into more direct control by the White House. In either case, democratically elected officials would be held responsible for their monetary policy. In France and the United Kingdom, for example, the monetary authorities are under the direct control of the government. The other view is that monetary policy is too important to be left to popular control and should be placed under the control of a totally independent elite. The models in this case are the central banks of Germany and Switzerland, which historically have operated with a high degree of independence from their respective governments.

The dynamics of political developments are determined partly by the political structure of the monetary authorities. For example, by the fall of 1990 the economies of the United States and the United Kingdom both had plunged into recessions stemming from prior attempts to control inflation and from the rise in oil prices that immediately followed the invasion of Kuwait by Iraq. As the recession became obvious in both countries, the political leaders came under increasing pressure to prevent a further downturn. In the United States, George Bush had to use very indirect means to change monetary policy. His aids, of course, lobbied the Fed in closed-door meetings. But, at one point, President Bush held a press conference in which he expressed the "hope" that Alan Greenspan, the Federal Reserve chairman, would lower interest rates and encourage banks to engage in more lending. Bush clearly was trying to increase the political pressure on Greenspan, and he had to use all his resources—including his high popularity rating as a wartime president—to accomplish this aim. Greenspan did lead the Fed toward a policy of lower interest rates, but it is not clear that he moved as aggressively as the White House had desired nor that he would have changed his position at all without Bush's unusually strong public approval.

Across the Atlantic in the United Kingdom, the politics were quite different. John Major had taken over from Margaret Thatcher as prime minister and had an initial honeymoon period because the opposition Labor Party largely supported the Conservative Party's handling of the Iraq–Kuwait situation. But, after a time, the Labor Party began to make a political issue of the recession and the increase in unemployment. John Major could not blame an independent central bank for high interest rates. The Bank of England was under the effective control of his government. Instead, Prime Minister Major had to defend his own interest rate policy in the House of Commons. He decried the Labor Party for advocating the "soft option," which would lead to long-run inflation and further crises. Unlike President Bush, Prime Minister Major had to take full responsibility for the actions of the government.

In a democratic country, the initial presumption should be that the control of monetary policy should lie with democratically elected politicians. The burden of proof should be placed on those who claim that monetary policy cannot be made in the full glare of democratic government and requires the secrecy and isolation of an independent central bank.

Proponents of independent central banks believe that they have strong political rationales. Countries with independent central banks, they would argue, would have lower inflation rates on average and would be less susceptible to opportunistic short-run economic manipulation by politicians seeking electoral success. The Bundesbank of Germany (West Germany prior to unification) and the Central Bank of Switzerland are held up as models. After controlling for a variety of factors that may cause inflation, there is some evidence that Germany and Switzerland have lower inflation than a large group of comparison countries.[4]

But Switzerland, with its independent political posture, is not a good comparison for most countries. Germany also has a special legacy concerning inflation. Hyperinflation after World War I led to the destruction of the democratic Weimer Republic and helped to create the conditions that led to the ascendancy of Adolph Hitler. Even though Germany experienced very high unemployment in the 1980s, memories of the terrible inflationary past strengthened the hand of the Bundesbank. Other countries do not have the same historical nightmares to fortify a central bank.

Events in the 1980s and the early 1990s suggest that the Bundesbank may not be as fiercely independent as once imagined. The Bundesbank was quite reluctant to join the European Monetary System (EMS), which is the collective arrangement to fix exchange rates among most of the major European countries.[5] The Bundesbank feared that it would be under pressure from countries such as France and Italy that had high inflation rates prior to the formation of the EMS. Chancellor Helmut Schmidt decided to form the EMS against the advice of the Bundesbank but in support of the Ministry of Finance, which had official responsibilities for exchange rate arrangements.[6]

The unification of East and West Germany in the early 1990s also placed the Bundesbank under political pressures. As part of the political and economic unification of Germany, the East German currency had to be replaced by the deutsche mark. But what exchange rate would be used to convert East German marks into West German marks? The Bundesbank favored a low rate of exchange of East German for West German marks. It feared that if the exchange rate were too high, the East Germans would be given too much extra purchasing power and would spend this bonus on consumer goods in Germany, thus creating inflationary pressures. The Bundesbank wanted to avoid this outcome. A low exchange rate also would help to prevent the East German firms from collapsing under competition from the West. At a low enough exchange rate, wages paid to East German workers would be comparable to their low productivity.

The government and finance ministry saw the situation differently. They preferred a high exchange rate that would preserve the savings and purchasing power of the pensioners and those on fixed incomes. Too low an exchange rate would make pensioners wards of the state and inevitably lead to excessive government outlays. It was in their interests to let the Bundesbank provide the subsidy to the pensioners through a high exchange rate for their East German marks rather than through explicit government subsidies. The psychological impact of the reunification was also important. Too low an exchange rate could have been perceived as a signal that the new members of the Republic of Germany were not viewed as first-class citizens.

The Bundesbank lost this battle, and the rate of exchange for the East German currency was quite generous. Unfortunately, the high value of the currency coupled with aggressive wage demands by German workers led to a rapid rise in unemployment and to an increase in the rate of business failures in the eastern part of Germany. Moreover, the Bundesbank came under increasing pressure as the fiscal authorities were forced to transfer increasing amounts to fulfill the obligations that came with unification. The Bundesbank raised interest rates in the early 1990s in the face of government budget deficits, and it will face an increasingly adversarial relationship with the fiscal authorities. Other countries have also voiced opposition to the high interest rate policy of the new Germany. The power and independence of the Bundesbank will be sorely tested in the 1990s.

One of the tenets of proponents of an independent central bank is that the bank is able to withstand the political pressures surrounding electoral politics. There has been considerable interest in these "political business cycles" in the United States, and examining the evidence of political manipulation of the economy can shed light on the political role of a central bank.

There are two very different views of the relationship between political factors and economic policy in the United States.[7] According to the traditional political business cycle view, incumbents stimulate the economy just before the election in order to get elected. The result is that the economy grows rapidly just prior to the election, thereby boosting the incumbent's electoral prospects. The long-run result, however, is an inflationary legacy to the next administration. These boom and inflation cycles are socially wasteful and are generated solely by the electoral system.

Historical episodes clearly support the basic idea of electoral manipulation of the economy. Richard Nixon, for example, used a variety of methods to stimulate the economy just prior to his reelection in 1972. President Nixon believed that a sluggish economy at the end of the Eisenhower years had cost him a victory against John F. Kennedy in 1960, and he was determined not to let this happen again. It may have been fortuitous, but Ronald Reagan suffered through a recession in the beginning of his administration so that the economy was in a phase of rapid growth during his successful reelection bid.

But there are also obvious counterexamples to this theory. Both Gerald Ford and Jimmy Carter ran for reelection during a period of high inflation and sluggish economic growth. Carter pursued exactly the wrong economic policy according to the theory. He stimulated the economy just after his election and then, as inflationary pressures rose during his administration, he switched policies in midcourse to fight inflation. The second major oil shock of the 1970s, late in his administration, did not help matters. As the Carter and Nixon episodes illustrate, electoral manipulation is a possibility under our current system but not an inevitability.

The other political perspective suggests that political parties are much more important in determining economic outcomes than elections. According to this "partisan cycle" view, the Democrats pursue more expansionary (and hence inflationary) policies than the Republicans. Postwar U.S. economic history does indicate that unemployment tends to be lower, economic growth higher, and inflation higher under Democratic administrations.[8] This tendency may reflect the democratic process in action. At times voters prefer a more aggressive economic posture, one willing to risk possible inflation in order to stimulate the economy. If the gamble backfires and inflation rises, there may be a demand for a more sober, conservative government equipped to bring inflation under control, even at the risk of a recession.[9]

What role has the Federal Reserve played in these political minefields? The Federal Reserve, after all, is potentially in a position to offset any direct actions the government may wish to take to stimulate the economy. The emerging consensus among scholars of the Fed is that it tends, over longer periods of time, to be responsive to the president's general economic policy.[10] If, over the long run, an administration wants to fight inflation, the Federal Reserve tends to respond and conversely for economic stimulus.

During election periods, the Fed typically tries to avoid taking any actions that would draw attention to it, although there has been a considerable debate over the actions taken by Arthur Burns, chairman of the Fed under Nixon. Monetary policy was very expansionary just prior to President Nixon's reelection, but it was not clear whether this growth was politically motivated or a response to technical concerns in the conduct of monetary policy at that time. The notoriety of this episode, however, suggests that similar events are quite rare.

But one should not conclude that the president automatically controls the Fed over shorter periods of time. Jimmy Carter learned this lesson the hard way. Facing an inflationary crisis in his administration, he chose a hard money man, Paul Volcker, to be the new chairman of the Federal Reserve. Volcker delivered a severe antiinflation policy and interest rates soared. When Carter felt that an easing of policy might be in his interests prior to the election, the fears of Carter's advisers were realized and Volcker was unresponsive.

Volcker, not Carter, continued in office into the 1980s. After a brief recovery in the beginning of the Reagan administration, the economy again plunged into a steep recession in August 1981. As the recession proceeded, Volcker received mixed signals from the White

House.[11] President Reagan's pragmatic political advisers, such as James Baker, wanted to bring pressure to bear on the Fed to ease money, and Ronald Reagan participated in attempts to influence Volcker. His monetarist advisers, however, opposed these policies. Volcker continued his mission of reducing inflation until he became concerned about the possibility that Mexico might default on its debt and about the severe financial problems that were emerging in the banking sector. In the summer of 1982, he began to ease monetary policy.

From these and similar accounts, it is clear that the Federal Reserve does not instantly respond to demands from an administration and that this lack of unity often creates political frictions. These frictions may increase in election times when the Fed wishes to take a low profile and avoid partisan fire. It is also clear that Volcker could not have pursued a long-run policy of lowering inflation without the general support of Ronald Reagan. From this point of view, the Federal Reserve acts as a buffer between an administration's immediate desire for monetary policy and actual policy outcomes. Depending on one's perspective, this function is either a potential obstacle to short-run democratic control or a useful safety valve to prevent rash political decisions.

If the general consensus is that the president controls the policies of the Fed over the long term but not the short term, two questions still remain. First, how does the Fed muster the political resources to withstand the onslaught of the White House? And, second, where is Congress? Didn't they create the Fed, and don't they have official oversight?

The Fed acquires political capital in several ways. As noted before, the regional banks place the Fed in direct contact with key financial and business personnel throughout the country. These individuals can be called upon to exert pressure on their local member of Congress and sometimes on the executive branch. Washington politicians learn to deflect pressure from official lobbyists, but grassroots campaigns are often very effective. Through its connections with the regional banks, the Federal Reserve can call forth a grassroots response.

In addition to its responsibilities for the control of monetary policy, the Fed has important regulatory responsibilities and can gain political power through its supervisory role. As James Pierce has emphasized, the Federal Reserve controls actions of bank holding companies and thus indirectly touches every major financial power in the country.[12] Every large bank and financial institution is aware that the Federal Reserve, in its regulatory role, may approve or disapprove future key business transactions. This power is a potent source of political influence.

Pierce also suggests that the Federal Reserve has been using (and, in his view, abusing) its powers as "lenders of last resort" in times of financial distress. In recent years, the Federal Reserve essentially has provided continuing subsidies and finances to large banks that were in financial difficulties and facing large withdrawals. Examples of such banks include the Franklin National Bank in the 1970s and Continental Illinois in the 1980s. In both cases, the Fed lent vast sums to the institutions to prevent them from closing. The Federal Reserve has a duty to provide sufficient funds to the banking system as a whole to prevent runs on the entire banking system—that is, a wholesale contraction of the money supply as in the 1930s. But Pierce argues that in these cases, the banks could have failed without any disruption of the total financial system. When large depositors were withdrawing funds from these banks, they were depositing them in other financial institutions. By adopting a policy that effectively protects large banks from failures, the Fed acquires vast new political powers as the savior of the financial system.[13]

The apparent ineffectiveness of Congress in monitoring and regulating the Fed is somewhat puzzling. At times, Congress has attempted to create mechanisms to control monetary policy, such as requiring the Fed to outline targets for monetary growth and to report to Congress on its success in meeting these targets. But most observers of monetary politics note that the Fed has not been seriously restrained by these policies.

Nathaniel Beck suggests that monetary policy, as practiced in the United States, is not well suited for congressional interest. Political scientists view members of Congress as constantly looking for ways to steer government policies toward payoffs to their own constituencies. This goal can be accomplished in a variety of ways, from directing government contracts to local suppliers, to engineering tax bills favoring local interests, or even to securing loans and grants for profit or nonprofit institutions within the jurisdiction. Macroeconomic policy does not fit easily into this mold. Can a member of Congress take credit for convincing the Fed to lower unemployment without attracting blame if the inflation rate rises? It is much safer and easier to play the normal pork barrel game.[14]

In principle, monetary policy could be conducted differently, so that Congress would want to play an important role. The Fed controls the supply of money by buying or selling government securities, thereby increasing or decreasing deposits and loans at banks. An alternative policy would be to directly allocate loans or credits to particular corporations or particular sectors of the economy. Until reforms in the 1980s, this was the standard practice in France. In the United States, our policies favoring housing finance operate in this vein. Beck believes that if we had a system of direct credit allocation, Congress would be in its center. But it is difficult for any one member of Congress to try to change our system in that direction. Consequently, Congress does not have the incentives to be preoccupied with monetary policy under the current system.

We can summarize the salient political facts in four propositions:

1. There is occasional political manipulation of the economy for electoral purposes, but differences in control by political party are more salient in dictating economic outcomes.
2. In the short run, the Fed can operate macro policies independently of an administration, but over a longer period an administration can substantially influence the course of monetary policy.
3. The Fed has it own source of political power through local constituencies and its regulatory activities. It also has been increasing its clout through extensive loans to failing institutions.
4. Congress has little interest in monetary policy, although it is interested in regulatory activities that may directly affect individual member's constituencies.

Given these facts, should there be more democratic control of the Fed? If we wished to have more democratic control, it would have to rest with the executive branch. The president is held responsible for macro policy outcomes, and Congress does not have much interest in monetary policy. Allowing the executive branch to have more control raises the risks of some electoral manipulation, but it would prevent the Fed from pursuing a monetary policy at odds with democratic sentiment for a prolonged period of time.

Regardless of whether this direction would be desirable, it is unlikely under current political circumstances. First, Congress believes that it represents democratic sentiments, not the executive branch. This outlook is particularly important because the Democratic Party has dominated Congress in the postwar era, whereas the White House has often been Republican. Second, the relationships between Congress and the executive branch have been marked in recent years by battles over the separation of powers and the respective roles and duties of each branch of the government. These conflicts have been over important issues such as war powers and budgeting. In this environment, it is unlikely that any new powers would be turned over to the executive by Congress. But without congressional approval, no structural changes can be made.

The Mechanisms of Control

In one sense, the question of how central banks should operate is simple. Central banks always and everywhere set short-term interest rates. However, a policy of setting short-term interest rates is not a sufficient guide to monetary policy and can potentially lead a central bank into disaster.

To understand the problem, suppose a central bank sets short-term interest rates too low. Over time, this policy will cause a boom in the economy and lead to higher inflation. If the central bank keeps the interest rate constant, the real interest rate—the interest rate minus the inflation rate—will fall. Borrowers focus on the real interest rate because it measures the true cost of borrowing funds. If you can borrow at a 10 percent interest rate but inflation is also 10 percent, you will be paying back dollars that are worth 10 percent less. In this case, the real interest rate will be zero (ten minus ten) and the money is essentially free.

If the bank maintains the same market (or nominal) interest rate while the real rate falls because of higher inflation, there will be increased borrowing, a further boom in the economy, and further inflation. This process is unstable and must be curbed by the central bank raising interest rates.

There is a similar problem on the other side. If the central bank initially sets an interest rate too high, an economic slump and a fall in the inflation rate will result. The real interest rate rises and causes an increase in the real cost of borrowing. This process will lead to a further downturn, a further fall in inflation, and continued increases in the real rate of interest. Again, this process is unstable and can be stopped only with a fall in interest rates.

Of course, if the central bank sets exactly the correct real interest rate, these problems would not exist. But this policy is much easier to state than to execute. First, it is very difficult to estimate the correct real interest rate. Many factors, both domestic and foreign, affect the proper interest rate. For example, when East and West Germany were reunited, interest rates immediately rose in German capital markets because market participants recognized that there would be vast increases in borrowed funds in order to finance the reconstruction of East Germany. But world capital markets are linked, so as interest rates in Germany began to rise, they also began to rise in the United States. Domestic factors also are critically important in a large country such as the United States. During the 1980s, real interest rates on U.S. Treasury bills rose to over 4 percent after averaging nearly 1 percent in the pre-1980s postwar period. The most likely explanation for this sharp increase was the sustained budget deficits in the Reagan years.

Not only is it difficult for a central bank to determine the correct real interest rate, the proper interest rate is a moving target. As the experiences with Germany and U.S. fiscal policy indicate, many factors impinge upon interest rates, and changes can occur over rather short periods of time. Even if a central bank is determined to set the proper interest rate, it must be willing to alter that rate in the face of external changes. This responsiveness requires a flexibility and willingness to maneuver that may be beyond the scope of many banks. It is often especially difficult for central banks to raise interest rates. The building industry and homeowners do not welcome higher interest rates. These political difficulties impede a bank from rapid changes in interest rates.

In order to avoid the technical and political problems involved in setting interest rates, many economists have advocated using short-term interest rates only as a means of hitting nominal targets. Nominal or dollar targets include different measures of the money supply, total dollar credit, or even total dollar (that is, nominal) GNP.

The rationale for this policy is straightforward. If the central bank controls a nominal magnitude, there is generally less risk that inflation can get out of control. If the bank controls the money supply, for example, it effectively limits the extent to which inflation can deviate from its goals. Over long periods of time, the inflation rate roughly will track the growth in the supply of money. Thus, controlling the supply of money effectively puts boundaries around possible inflation rates.

But policies to control the money supply or the supply of total nominal credit in the economy only make sense if the money supply or credit supply has a stable relationship with the economy as a whole. Unfortunately, in the 1980s, the typical relationships that seemed to hold between the supply of money and credit and the economy broke down. This was not simply a U.S. phenomenon; it occurred throughout the developed world.[15] Many factors were responsible, but probably the most important were the vast changes in the financial system that occurred during the 1980s. As checking accounts began to pay interest and automatic teller machines began to dot the landscape, individuals and corporations changed the way they managed their money and finances. For example, as checking accounts began to pay interest, individuals no longer needed to monitor their checking accounts as carefully and would accumulate large balances. Moreover, money market accounts served both as vehicles for savings and for transactions. These changes were so radical that they effectively caused a breakdown in the relationship between traditional measures of money or credit and the economy.

While money and credit are no longer desirable instruments to control the economy, nominal or dollar GNP still remains a viable target. The growth of nominal GNP is the sum of the growth in real GNP and the growth of prices. Policies that control nominal GNP, therefore, are policies that control the sum of the real growth and the inflation rate. This policy may be reasonable, but it is not clear why the sum should be controlled and why targets cannot be set separately for growth and the inflation rate.

There is one important nominal target that we have not mentioned: the level of prices. A central bank could commit itself to a policy of engineering a stable price level. Indeed, Congressman Steven Neal of the House Banking Committee has introduced legislation that would compel the Federal Reserve to achieve a stable price level within five years. In testimony before this committee, Alan Greenspan, the chairman of the Federal Reserve Board, expressed support for the general goals of this legislation. Greenspan has stated on a number of occasions that price stability should be the ultimate goal of the Federal Reserve.

Unfortunately, reality intrudes into this dream. In 1992, inflation was running at about 3 percent. To reduce the inflation rate from three percent to zero, which would be required for price stability, would require a very severe recession. Unemployment would have to increase and remain near double-digit levels for some time. There is not the political consensus in the United States to deliberately engineer a sharp recession in order to meet a goal of price stability. Greenspan, of course, is quite aware of this sentiment, but perhaps he hopes to gradually ease down inflation over a longer period of time. Even more likely, Greenspan can use the goal of price stability to fend off demands for lower interest rates. He successfully pursued this policy until the recession of 1990 placed him under additional political constraints.

Greenspan's tenure at the Federal Reserve is evidence that a policy of controlling interest rates with sufficient flexibility to meet economic goals can be feasible. Greenspan took over the mantle of the Federal Reserve in a period of relative tranquillity. The economy was in the midst of its longest peace-time expansion, and the inflation rate was relatively low. His predecessor, Paul Volcker, had led the economy through a severe recession to curb the inflationary momentum that took hold in the late 1970s. By the time Greenspan took control of the Fed, there was also clear recognition that the supplies of money and credit were behaving erratically and were not suitable instruments of economic control.

During his tenure at the Fed, Greenspan steered the economy safely, avoiding too rapid growth or inflation until the recession of 1990. While real growth was sluggish during this period, the unemployment rate averaged about 5.5 percent, which was probably as low as could be achieved safely without a resurgence in inflation. The recession followed swiftly on the heels of Iraq's invasion of Kuwait. The economy had been slowing down previously because banks had become more reluctant to lend after the savings and loan debacle raised the level of scrutiny by bank regulators. It is not clear whether a recession would have occurred without the difficulties of the Middle East war, but the invasion did damage consumer confidence in a weakened economy and recession followed. Still, Greenspan deserves good marks for his tenure, which included other potentially turbulent episodes such as the October stock market crash of 1987.

The idea that a central bank could use wisdom and discretion in setting interest rates to guide the economy runs opposite the views that were held by many in the early 1980s. With the U.S. economy facing disturbing, accelerating inflation in the late 1970s, the opinions of the monetarists gained ascendancy. They argued that central banks could not be trusted to use short-term interest rates as a tool;

instead, central banks should control the economy through the growth of reserves at banks. In turn, the rate of growth of bank reserves was to be guided by the goal of maintaining a constant growth rate in the overall money supply.

There were several rationales for these policies. First, the Federal Reserve had shown itself incapable of keeping inflation under check. The monetarists viewed this not simply as the failing of a particular administration or chairman of the Federal Reserve but as a generic problem of a central bank operating with interest rate policies. By forcing the Fed to control reserves and hit nominal monetary targets, the Fed would be forced to bring inflation under control and not try to stimulate the economy. These policies would restore credibility to the Federal Reserve.

Central banks throughout the world adopted similar policies in the late 1970s.[16] In the United States, the Fed officially adopted this policy in October 1979. From the point of view of the Fed, a reserve policy had one important political advantage, which the monetarists had recognized. If the Fed controlled bank reserves, they could escape responsibility for high interest rates by blaming them on the market. And interest rates increased sharply during this period as the Fed fought inflation. The monetarist experiment was successful only in the sense that inflation was brought down through a severe recession brought on by these high interest rates. But the Fed was not able to precisely control the money supply during this period. By the summer of 1982, Volcker eased monetary policy and, at least in his own mind, abandoned the use of rigid monetary targets in favor of control by interest rates.

The United States was not alone in abandoning monetary targeting in the early 1980s. Other countries also experienced changes in their financial systems that made monetary targeting inappropriate. Canada, Great Britain, and France all abandoned targeting, while Germany and Switzerland let exchange rate concerns dominate their control over the domestic money supply.

Looking back at the episode in the United States, it appears that the monetarist prescription was useful as a mechanism for emerging from an inflationary cycle and restoring credibility in the Federal Reserve. But the credibility was restored not through rigid targeting of the money supply, which was abandoned in the early 1980s, but through the reduction of inflation through a painful recession. The experience of the Fed mirrored the experiences of the banks of Germany and

Switzerland: credibility did not come from following rigid rules but from a clear commitment to keeping inflation under control.

This gain in credibility enabled Alan Greenspan to manage the economy in the late 1980s through manipulating interest rates. Credibility gained can be lost easily, and Greenspan clearly was aware of the dangers of igniting inflation again. But as long as the markets can be confident in the overall direction of the Fed, they will give it some discretion in executing its policies. Discretion will disappear whenever inflation becomes a serious threat.

International Policy Coordination

Despite disruptions from OPEC and the breakdown of the Bretton Woods exchange rate system, world trade grew rapidly in the 1970s and again throughout the 1980s. The economies of the world were becoming open to trade again. The share of trade in GNP reached levels that were prevalent at the beginning of the century but that had plunged following the Great Depression. As even the large economies became more open to trade, cries for "policy coordination" began to be heard both in policy and in academic circles. According to this view, it was no longer possible for a country to conduct purely domestic economic policies. Countries of the world had become so interdependent that such actions would fail to yield desirable outcomes.

The basic idea behind policy coordination is straightforward and can be illustrated with a simple example. Imagine two large countries that are both operating below full employment and that are both concerned about the level of their exchange rate with the other country. Each country would like to expand its economy via monetary policy. But the countries know that if they increase the money supply and lower interest rates, asset holders will seek higher returns in the other country and their currency will depreciate as asset holders sell it to buy assets in the other country. The fear of this depreciation prevents each country from expanding. However, if both countries increase their money supplies together, interest rates will fall in both countries and neither currency will depreciate against the other. Collectively, they can pursue desirable, expansionary policies that they could not pursue if they took actions by themselves.

But policy coordination is not always so simple. Suppose that one country is operating below capacity and does not care about the level of its exchange rate. The other country is operating at full employment and wishes to maintain the current level of its exchange rate. The first country will want to expand using monetary policy; not only will the decrease in interest rates promote domestic spending but the exchange rate depreciation will stimulate the demand for its exports. The second country faces a dilemma. If it does not lower its interest rates, its exchange rate will appreciate and its exports will be hurt; if it does lower interest rates and maintains the initial exchange rate, the economy soon will operate above normal capacity and inflation will result. Policy coordination is not as simple in this case.

Policy coordination can lead to worse outcomes in both countries. Consider an example in which there is no policy coordination between two countries that both are concerned about their exchange rates. Suppose that aggressive unions want to increase their money wages. The unions know, however, that the central bank is limited in increasing the supply of money because the exchange rate would depreciate and promote further inflation. The unions, therefore, will moderate the wage demands because they know that the response from their central bank would be limited and that very aggressive wage demands would cause unemployment. With policy coordination, however, the unions know that increases in the money supply by their central bank would be met by similar actions abroad, so there would be no threat of currency depreciation. The unions thus know that they have more room to push wage demands because there is no longer the concern of a depreciating currency. If the domestic central bank increases the money supply in the face of union demands, a similar result will take place abroad. The final outcome is higher domestic inflation in both countries because of policy coordination.[17]

A further difficulty can arise when different countries have different views about how the global economy operates. Imagine the frustration of our European partners facing the abrupt shift in economic philosophy between the Carter and Reagan administrations. The Carter administration generally had a modern Keynesian viewpoint, while the Reagan administration was an amalgam of monetarist, supply-siders, and pragmatists.

Jeffrey Frankel and Katherine Rockett have illustrated how different views of how the economy operates can pose severe difficulties for policy coordination.[18] They conducted an interesting experiment. At a conference at the Brookings Institution, ten different econometric models were presented that all implied different responses to monetary and fiscal shocks of domestic and foreign origin. Frankel and Rockett used these different models to represent different "views of the world" of policy makers. They conducted the following experiment: from a given economic environment, each of two countries drew a view of the world and then tried to determine the best deal they could make in terms of mutually agreed-upon monetary and fiscal policies. The outcomes, however, were determined by a random draw from one of the ten models. Not only did the policy makers disagree, but they also were often misinformed about the true model. Frankel and Rockett found that in about one-half of all the cases, the outcomes of the policies adopted were inferior to the status quo.

Even in the best of all possible worlds, when there is no uncertainty about the correct view of the world, most estimates of the benefits from policy coordination are small. Typical estimates are usually less than 0.3 percent of GNP for the United States and Germany.[19] The basic reason for this minimal gain is that, despite the growth in international trade, the direct impacts of domestic monetary and fiscal policies of the United States and Germany on the other country are relatively small.

In the real world, policy coordination takes two forms. The first is explicit agreements about exchange rate policies. The best example of this is the Exchange Rate Mechanism of the European Monetary System, which today includes Germany, France, Spain, Italy, Ireland, Denmark, and The Netherlands. These countries essentially fix their exchange rates around rather narrow bands. The other form of policy coordination is periodic, opportunistic attempts to coordinate economic policy. It is worth considering some of the experiences with each type of coordination.

A country that belongs to the Exchange Rate Mechanism (ERM) essentially must use its monetary policy to maintain its exchange rate and not for purely domestic purposes. This priority can be beneficial in the long run but poses severe problems in the short run. Before joining the ERM, France had been known as a country with high inflation. But during the 1980s, its ties to the ERM and particularly to the dominant low-inflation Bundesbank of Germany led France to moderate its inflation rate. The ERM provided the discipline needed by the monetary authorities to keep inflation in check. Italy, Spain, and Great Britain all hope to emulate this performance over the long run.

Great Britain decided to join the ERM in 1990 under Margaret

Thatcher, despite her earlier objections and those of some of her advisers (especially Alan Walters) to surrendering "sovereignty" to Germany. Unfortunately, Britain entered the ERM at a bad time, in the midst of a recession with high interest rates, and it also entered at too high an exchange rate. To keep the exchange rate within the band prescribed for the ERM, Britain had to be very careful about lowering interest rates, despite the cries domestically to do something about the recession. At some points, the domestic debate almost became tragically comic. The financial press agonized over whether a small interest rate cut would cause the British pound to lose too much value against the Spanish peseta, which was at the top of the exchange rate band. As it turned out, Britain was able to lower interest rates a bit without running into a peseta problem.

For Great Britain, this episode was disturbingly reminiscent of their economic policies after World War I. They returned their currency to the gold standard, which had broken down during the war, but they returned at too high an exchange rate. The tight monetary policy that was necessary to maintain the exchange rate led to a dismal period of low economic growth and high unemployment. Critics of the ERM, such as Alan Walters, were keen to draw this analogy.

Great Britain was forced to abandon the ERM in 1992, although it vows to return. They were forced out of the mechanism because of the actions of currency speculators. The speculators saw that Great Britain was suffering from a severe recession yet was forced to maintain high interest rates because of Germany's high interest rate policy. When Germany refused to change its policies, the speculators gambled on the resolve of the British. They sold the pound in such massive amounts that the British could not cope. The British let the pound float and, at least temporarily, dropped out of the ERM.

But the British intend to rejoin the ERM. Why are they willing to suffer these difficulties and indignities? The answer is that British politicians and policy makers see their future as tied to the growth of Europe and intra-European trade. Just as the United States benefits from a single currency that is used without question throughout the country, so will the closely connected economies in Europe.

The European plan for a single European currency suffered in 1992 from these currency disturbances and from lack of progress in other European treaties. European business interests, however, will continue to push for a process leading to a common currency. These groups feel that they need a large domestic market with a single currency, just like the United States. Tying currencies together and forcing economies to converge to a common inflation rate is a first, necessary step in this process. Policy coordination in Europe is much more than a convenient agreement to make a deal; rather, it is the first step in an ongoing process of economic integration. Even Margaret Thatcher could not, by herself, stop this process.

U.S. involvement in policy coordination activities, on the other hand, has been more casual and episodic. After the breakdown of the Bretton Woods system in the early 1970s, there was very little policy coordination until the Carter administration. The Carter administration wanted to expand the economy but feared that this action would lead to too sharp a fall in the dollar. The United States proposed that Germany expand as well, thereby preventing downward pressure on the dollar—the so-called locomotive approach. Germany agreed to expand, but only if the United States took actions to end its dependence on imported oil by removing price controls on domestic oil and raising the domestic price of oil to the world level. In retrospect, decontrol of oil prices was a sensible free market policy, but the locomotive expansion in 1978 was not. By this time, world inflationary pressures had begun to rise, and within a year, the Carter administration was desperately seeking to dampen inflation. As the Reagan administration took over, the world plunged into a recession to cure the inflationary tendencies that had developed in the late 1970s.

During President Reagan's first term, there was an explicit hands-off policy toward exchange rates, despite the soaring dollar, and no interest whatsoever in policy coordination. This outlook changed, however, in the beginning of Reagan's second term. Two factors led to this change. First, because the high dollar was damaging to export industries, severe protectionist pressures arose in the Congress. While the Reagan administration was not keen to intervene in foreign exchange markets, they were even less excited about protectionist measures. The second factor was that James Baker, a strict pragmatist, replaced Donald Regan as Secretary of the Treasury, the primary official responsible for foreign exchange policy. Baker saw that something had to be done about the level of the dollar to fend off protectionists in Congress.

In September 1985, ministers for the G-5 countries (United States, Germany, Japan, United Kingdom, and France) met at the Plaza Hotel in New York and agreed to reduce the value of the dollar on world markets. Although this episode has been viewed favorably by some as the high point of policy coordination in the 1980s, it is not clear that the meeting and the subsequent actions were responsible for the subsequent fall in the dollar. The dollar had been declining from February 1985. Although it dropped sharply after the Plaza announcement, it then resumed its prior rate of decline.[20]

The next attempt at policy coordination did not even appear to be successful. By 1987, the dollar had fallen so far that there was general concern to stabilize it. As in 1978, the United States tried to get Germany and Japan to expand their economies, but these countries wanted to place the onus on the United States to get its house in order. At a Louvre meeting, the countries announced that the dollar was at an appropriate level. But when the October 1987 stock market crash occurred, U.S. monetary policy was geared solely to domestic concerns and the exchange rate was ignored.

Policy coordination efforts reached a low point in 1991 and 1992. At a time when the European central banks were intervening to try to prop up a sliding dollar, the Secretary of the Treasury of the United States, James Brady, was chastising U.S. banks for not lowering their interest rates. Lower U.S. interest rates, of course, would mean a lower dollar. Meanwhile, in the midst of a growing recession in the United States, the United Kingdom, and Canada, the Bundesbank was raising its interest rates because domestic deficits incurred to finance the reconstruction of its new eastern part were threatening domestic inflation. And, of course, economic policy coordination cannot be separated from ongoing political cooperation. Germany's initial reluctance to provide funds for the 1990–1991 Gulf War (in lieu of fighting forces) did not bode well for general economic policy coordination efforts.

Finally, preparations for a G-7 (the G-5 countries plus Canada and Italy) meeting in 1992 were marked by another conflict between the United States and Germany. On the eve of the meeting, a senior U.S. Treasury official blasted the Germans for running a loose fiscal policy (deficits) and a tight monetary policy (high interest rates). The Germans were angry and reminded the United States that this was the policy they had been running throughout the 1980s.

Henry Kissinger once observed that the Israelis did not have a separate foreign policy, only domestic politics. This observation rings true for the United States and many of its partners in international monetary policies.

But on balance, this policy is sensible. The United States is not going to quickly integrate its economy with Germany, greater Europe, or Japan. It would be best for international stability if we managed to tame our business fluctuations, gradually reduce inflation, and control our problems with the federal budget deficit. The rest of the world might prefer this as well. Would you want to live next to an unstable and erratic giant eager to join in your affairs or to a stable, quiet giant content to concentrate on its own economic affairs?

Concluding Comments

Monetary policy poses one of the classic problems that arise in collective action: delegation. Domestic and international monetary policy is so complex that it must be delegated to experts. Yet, poorly executed monetary policy can lead to excessive economic fluctuations and persistent problems with inflation. The costs of poor outcomes will be differentially felt throughout the society. How should monetary policy be structured so as to be efficient as well as sensitive to its differential impacts in the economy?

Three basic decisions must be made with regard to monetary policy:

1. How much democratic control should there be over monetary policy? In the United States, we insulate monetary policy from day-to-day political pressures through an independent Federal Reserve. Countries with independent central banks, like Germany and Switzerland, have better inflation performance, but the risks to workers of unemployment are not well represented. In the United States, Congress could, in principle, take a larger role, but monetary policy does not fit easily into their normal style of business.

2. Should monetary policy be governed by strict rules, or should policy makers be allowed to exercise discretion? Only when policy makers fail do we hear cries for tying their hands. In the United States, the strongest demands for strict rules came at a time when inflation appeared to be heading out of control. When policy makers have been successful and appear responsible, they are allowed significant discretion and flexibility to conduct their tasks.

3. Should monetary policy be aimed at domestic concerns, or should international policy coordination be a prime objective? Closely integrated economies, such as in Europe, must pay attention

to coordinating their policies. However, countries or groups of countries that are not so closely integrated do not gain much from policy integration. In particular, the United States, Japan, and Europe should, for the most part, try to conduct responsible domestic policies and let international coordination play a secondary role.

Further Reading

The politics of monetary policy and international monetary policy are fascinating but too often discussed in dreary technical language. The readings suggested here are, for the most part, relatively free of technical baggage.

A provocative book that raises interesting issues (even if the answers often are open to doubt) is William Greider's *Secrets of the Temple: How the Federal Reserve Runs the Country* (New York: Simon and Schuster, 1987). Greider strikes a populist note for control of the money supply and also provides inside detail about the making of monetary policy in the 1980s.

Two collections of academic essays on politics and monetary policy are worthwhile: Thomas Mayer, ed., *The Political Economy of American Monetary Policy* (New York: Cambridge University Press, 1990) and Thomas D. Willett, ed., *Political Business Cycles* (Durham, N.C.: Duke University Press, 1988).

Two chapters of my book *The Making of Economic Policy* (New York: Basil Blackwell, 1989) deal with monetary policy. One chapter analyzes game theory models and political business cycles, while another looks at the question of rules versus discretion in the conduct of monetary policy.

Finally, an excellent political-economic overview of international exchange rate policies is Jeffrey A. Frankel, "The Making of Exchange Rate Policy in the 1980s," in *American Economic Policy in the 1980s*, Martin Feldstein, ed. (Chicago, Ill.: University of Chicago Press, 1992).

Notes

1. This basic idea, that the short-run effects of monetary policy differ from the long-run effects, goes back at least to David Hume. Since then economists have worked to elaborate and refine this story with only modest

success. One approach allows workers and firms to have "rational" expectations about future changes in the supply of money. For an introduction to this literature see my book *Rational Expectations* (New York: Cambridge University Press, 1983), especially chs. 1–3.

2. This discussion leads to the question of what level of inflation raises the maximum revenue. Although precise answers are not possible, if a country has an inflation rate exceeding 1000 percent per year, there is a substantial risk that it has gone too far in printing money and could raise more revenue by printing less money. Certainly the famous hyperinflations (such as in Germany between the wars) were far in excess of revenue maximization.

3. In his spirited and lively book about the Fed, William Greider emphasizes the political role of the Fed. However, Greider comes very close to the position that permanent inflation would have beneficial consequences for workers and debtors. The benefits from inflation, however, are much shorter-lived. See William Greider, *Secrets of the Temple: How the Federal Reserve Runs the Country* (New York: Simon and Schuster, 1987).

4. The United States also has unusually low inflation according to this study. See King Banian et al., "Subordinating the Fed to Political Authorities Will Not Control Inflationary Tendencies," in *Political Business Cycles,* ed. Thomas D. Willett (Durham, N.C.: Duke University Press, 1988), 490–505.

5. The United Kingdom joined the system in the fall of 1990; Switzerland is not a member. The EMS will be discussed in more detail below.

6. For a perspective on the EMS, see Michele Fratianni, "The European Monetary System: How Well Has It Worked?" in *Dollars, Deficits & Trade,* ed. James A. Dorn and William A. Niskanen (Boston: Kluwer Academic Publishers, 1989), 263–88.

7. For a detailed discussion of alternative theories and evidence, see chapter 6, "Strategic Models of Policy Making," in my book *The Making of Economic Policy* (New York: Basil Blackwell, 1989).

8. There is also some evidence that recessions tend to start in the beginning of Republican administrations. The different theories and evidence are discussed in my book *The Making of Economic Policy.*

9. The "sober" Reagan administration brought down inflation but created a not-so-sober fiscal deficit crisis. See chapter 8 for an extensive discussion.

10. For a representative discussion, see Nathaniel Beck, "Political Monetary Cycles," in *The Political Economy of American Monetary Policy,* ed. Thomas Mayer (New York: Cambridge University Press, 1990), 115–30.

11. For a detailed account of the politics of this period, see Greider, *Secrets*.
12. See James L. Pierce, "The Federal Reserve as a Political Power," in *Political Economy of American Monetary Policy*.
13. Pierce believes that this policy is misguided and will lead to greater financial instability in the future as banks will feel free to take greater risks—witness the savings and loan debacle.
14. See Nathaniel Beck, "Congress and the Fed," in *The Political Economy of American Monetary Policy*. Beck also reviews and dismisses a revisionist view that Congress does control the Fed but in a subtle way, visible only when appointments to key committees change.
15. For a discussion of this issue with a broad focus, see Charles Goodhart, "The Conduct of Monetary Policy," *The Economic Journal*, 99(June 1989): 293–346.
16. See my book, *The Making of Economic Policy*, ch. 7, for an extended discussion.
17. This example originally comes from Kenneth Rogoff and is described, along with other cases, in Stanley Fischer, "International Macroeconomic Policy Coordination," in *International Policy Coordination*, ed. Martin Feldstein (Chicago: University of Chicago Press, 1988).
18. See Jeffrey A. Frankel and Katherine Rockett, "International Macroeconomic Policy Coordination when Policy Makers Do Not Agree on the True Model," *American Economic Review*, 78 (June 1988): 318–40.
19. See Fischer, "International Macroeconomic Policy Coordination."
20. For an interesting discussion of this and other international monetary episodes in the 1980s, see Jeffrey A. Frankel, "The Making of Exchange Rate Policy in the 1980s," in *American Economic Policy in the 1980s*, ed. Martin Feldstein (Chicago: University of Chicago Press, 1992).

8

Tackling the Deficit Problem

Checks and Balances

In the late 1980s, a group of influential Washington insiders argued that our political system had degenerated into paralysis and that radical constitutional reform toward a parliamentary system of government was required. In a parliamentary system, the executive branch is drawn from the majority party. This practice contrasts with the United States, which throughout the 1980s had a Republican executive branch and, for the most part, a legislative branch dominated by Democrats. According to advocates of the parliamentary system, this split in government had led to political and economic drift and could no longer be tolerated.

But Americans cherish their system of checks and balances and would not easily tamper with their political system unless there were overwhelming evidence of political dysfunction. The parliamentarians eventually lost the argument, and this issue has now disappeared from political debate. But there was one symbol of political dysfunction that even the strongest devotees of our constitutional system could recognize: the persistent federal deficits of the 1980s.

Those who followed the drama of U.S. politics in the 1980s will remember the renegade former Budget Director David Stockman's cry of "$200 billion deficits as far as the eye can see." This warning was dismissed as alarmist by many observers. But look at forecasts of the official on-budget deficit for the early 1990s. The Congressional Budget Office (CBO) estimates an on-budget deficit for fiscal year 1992 of $314 billion and by 1997, a deficit of $290 billion.[1]

What is most astonishing is that large deficits still persist, despite efforts lasting almost a decade to eliminate them. Looking back, it is not too difficult to understand how the deficit problem began. The Reagan administration proposed large budget cuts and large staged cuts in taxes. On paper, in the summer of 1981, these spending and tax changes appeared to lead to a balanced budget by 1984. However, there were two problems with this scenario. First, some of the spending cuts were fictitious; unable to find additional spending reductions, David Stockman specified some reductions as "cuts to be named later." Second, and more serious, was the recession that began in the summer of 1981—one of the most severe in the postwar era. The recession sharply decreased the amount of tax revenue accruing to the federal government as personal and corporate incomes fell dramatically.

The recession was caused primarily by an aggressive monetary policy implemented by the chairman of the Federal Reserve, Paul Volker, and implicitly endorsed by President Ronald Reagan. The recession raised unemployment to over 10 percent and, as a result, inflation fell. The overall economic strategy of the Reagan administration was to achieve this inflation reduction without a recession. This part of the plan was unsuccessful. Not only did unemployment rise, but hopes for a balanced budget faded as well.

The political system responded quickly to the emerging deficit. In 1982, significant parts of the Reagan tax plan were changed or repealed in a major tax bill. But the deficits still remained. In 1985, Congress took matters into its own hands and passed the Gramm-Rudman-Hollings law, which attempted to force the deficit down by threats of Draconian spending cuts. The Gramm-Rudman process is discussed extensively later in this chapter. From the continuation of our deficit problem it is clear that this process was not a total success.

The frustration with our deficit problem was compounded by the fact that other countries managed to cope with their problems. Under Prime Minister Margaret Thatcher, income tax rates in Great Britain were cut sharply and inflation was wrung out of the system, just as in the United States. But unlike the United States, income tax decreases were accompanied by increases in value-added taxes, and the government budget moved into surplus. Indeed, throughout Europe in the early 1980s there were major shifts in fiscal policy away from large deficits. Countries as diverse as Ireland and Denmark made important strides toward fiscal rectitude.

This chapter examines three aspects of the deficit problem. The first is purely economic. Why were there seemingly no adverse effects from the budget deficits in the 1980s? More importantly, does this absence mean that deficits do not matter or that troubles will be postponed in the future?

The second topic concerns the possibility of a strategic role for the deficit in the political battles of the 1980s. Some noted Democrats accused the Republicans of deliberately engineering the deficits in order to put a break on federal spending. At a more fundamental level, this issue becomes one of causality. What is a better description of the fiscal process: one in which spending initiatives create demands for financing—that is, spending causes taxes—or, one in which the tax revenue available to the government limits spending—that is, taxes cause spending?

The final topic concerns political control. Congress and the administration have been obsessed with mechanisms to bring spending and taxation into line. These attempts began with the Congressional Budget Act of 1974, continued with the Gramm-Rudman law and its modifications, and finally emerged as a new spending control process that began in fiscal year 1992. How, if at all, do these mechanisms work? Would a constitutional amendment to balance the budget be feasible or desirable?

The Economics of Deficits

If you had asked a typical economist at the beginning of the 1980s what would be the consequences of prolonged deficits in the federal budget on the order of 4 percent of GNP with the economy operating close to full employment, you would have received one of two answers, both of which would have been wrong. Some economists would have predicted high inflation, assuming that the government would have financed its deficits by increasing the supply of money. The government did not do that. Other economists would have predicted that government borrowing competing with private borrowing in the capital markets would result in sharply higher interest rates and reduced investment. In reality, the share of investment in GNP changed little in the 1980s. Where did these economists go wrong?

In the early 1980s, many economists would have ignored the fact that the United States had entered a large world economy with well-developed capital markets. This oversight would have been their key mistake. If the U.S. government needed to borrow funds to finance large deficits, these funds would be available on world markets. The availability of these funds would allow the government to borrow and private investment to continue at prior levels.

To look at this issue more closely, it is useful to consider a simple identity that must hold for all economies. In any economy, the government deficit and investment must be financed by total savings. In turn, total savings consists of two components: savings from domestic sources and foreign savings. To understand the role of deficits, imagine a situation in which there is no government deficit and no foreign savings, so that the level of investment equals domestic savings.

Starting from this situation, let the government deficit increase and domestic savings and investment remain at their prior levels. According to the identity, foreign savings must increase. But how do foreign savings originate? For foreigners to make funds available to the economy, they have to earn dollars in trading with us in order to lend them back to us. To put it another way, they must be selling more goods to us than we are selling to them in order to acquire the dollars to lend to us. Our trade deficit with them provides them with the funds to finance our government deficit and investment.

This pattern is essentially what happened in the 1980s. As the government deficit grew, interest rates rose in the United States. Higher interest rates caused foreigners to want to purchase U.S. securities, increased the demand for U.S. assets, and drove up the value of the dollar on world markets. Faced with a higher value for the dollar, U.S. exporters could not sell their goods abroad as easily and domestic consumers found imported goods cheaper. The result was a large trade deficit that, in turn, provided the additional foreign savings to finance the budget deficits.

The effect on the real economy was to shift the composition of domestic production away from goods produced for trade and toward those goods favored by the higher domestic budget deficit, specifically nontraded goods and defense-related products. After the economy recovered from the monetary-induced recession in the early 1980s, this shift occurred and led to an economy that was operating at full employment. While jobs were lost to international competition, jobs were found in sectors favored by the fiscal deficits.

According to this interpretation of the events of the 1980s, the United States enjoyed a binge of consumption, private and public, from the government deficits and financed these by foreign savings. Foreigners purchased U.S. assets: stocks, bonds, land, and other assets. In the future, they, not U.S. residents, will reap the benefits in the form of dividends, interest, income, and capital gains from these assets. Our consumption binge was thus financed by transferring ownership of our assets to foreigners. Because foreign owners increasingly will reap the benefits from our assets, we will pay for our consumption binge with reduced consumption levels in the future. This trend will be noticeable in the official government current account statistics as dividend and interest income increasingly flow abroad.

If U.S. budget deficits continue at current levels, transfers of assets to foreigners will continue. At some point, however, foreigners may become increasingly reluctant to provide further savings. If so, the dollar would fall on foreign exchange markets. While a weaker dollar would improve our trade deficit, it would deprive us of a source of financing for our deficit. If trade were balanced, domestic savings alone would have to finance the budget deficit and investment. Unless domestic savings increase, domestic investment would have to fall. The result would be lower productivity.

Either the transfer of assets to foreign sources or lower productivity growth has the effect of lowering our consumption possibilities in the future. This lower standard of living is the cost of budget deficits. From a political point of view, the threat is not dramatic enough to force the necessary action to control the deficit. Of course, it is possible that a crisis could happen. Suppose, for example, that a xenophobic Congress began to consider legislation to limit the flow of dividends and interest outside the United States. Foreign investors immediately would engage in a selling spree and the dollar would plummet on foreign exchange markets. A dramatic fall in the dollar would panic the monetary authorities, who would begin to fear the higher inflation that would arise as the price of imported goods rose from the fall in the value of the dollar. The Fed would raise interest rates sharply to prevent the dollar from falling and the result would be a sharp recession.

But barring this or a similar dramatic event, the damage from the deficit is slow and largely invisible. While political alarms have sounded, they have not rung loudly enough. As a global economic superpower, the United States has made the world adjust to its fiscal problems and probably can do so for some time.

Should we worry about the deficit? Essentially, this problem concerns intergenerational equity. We have enjoyed and continue to enjoy the consumption of goods, public and private, at the expense of future generations. There are three reasons why we may not wish to allow this practice to continue. First, this policy has not been deliberate; rather, we backed into it because of a series of accidents and an inability to face tough political choices. Second, the probability of a crisis may be small, but it certainly grows over time as our deficits persist. Finally, unlike in the past, it is no longer clear that future generations will be much wealthier than today's generation. Since 1973, productivity growth has stagnated and real wages for the average worker have not increased. While there may be a recovery in productivity growth, this is not inevitable. Thus, future generations may have lower living standards than the Japanese and Germans and have to pay interest and dividends to them as well. These three arguments suggest that we should tackle the deficit problem now.

Some groups of economists believe that deficits are not important. They can be classified into two groups. The first group believes that the private sector can and does undo any damage that the government appears to create with a deficit. The second group stresses that if we do our measurement correctly, there is no deficit.

Robert Barro is the intellectual leader of the first school. His basic argument is based on two premises. First, even governments eventually have to pay off their debts; if taxes are cut now, there will be tax increases in the future. Second, consumers understand this logic and, if taxes are cut now, they will increase their savings in order to have the funds available to pay the taxes in the future.[2]

The result of these two premises is that the total saving of an economy does not change if the government cuts taxes. The cut in taxes means that government savings fall as the result of the deficit, but private sector savings rise to fully offset this loss. Tax cuts, therefore, would have no effect on the path of investment or foreign savings in the society.

Economists have debated the precise conditions under which each of these conditions holds, and scholarly volumes are filled with the results. But the theory has a very simple prediction. If large deficits appear, as in the early 1980s, we should see a corresponding increase in private savings. But private sector savings were largely unchanged in the 1980s and, if anything, fell slightly. This finding is not consistent with the theory that the private sector will compensate for the federal deficit.

Barro recognized that the United States in the 1980s posed a problem to his theory, but he argues that increases in the stock market and in housing values may represent increases in savings. Savings can be defined as any action that increases your wealth. If your house increases in value, your wealth has increased. As long as you do not increase your consumption level to offset this increase in the value of your house, there will be a net increase in wealth and thereby increased savings. The same argument applies to stock market appreciation.[3]

But even if one accepts the difficulties of measuring savings, a further problem arises. Why was the increase in the federal budget deficit associated with an increase in the trade deficit? One argument is that the 1981 tax cuts increased U.S. productivity and led to an influx of investment from the rest of the world. But conventional investment figures do not show much change. Investment levels look high only if durable consumption goods (automobiles, refrigerators, etc.) are classified as investment. This definition clearly stretches the basic argument because durable consumption goods were not favored by the tax changes. All in all, it is difficult to overturn the view that the increased U.S. budget deficit in the 1980s caused the trade deficit of similar magnitude that emerged.

Robert Eisner has argued that, if the accounting is done properly, government deficits are much smaller than imagined and that there often have been surpluses.[4] Eisner's most important point is that the best measure of a deficit is the extent to which the real value of the government debt increases. In making these calculations, we have to control for the effects of inflation. Suppose there is an outstanding debt of $100 billion and a 10 percent inflation rate. Then the real value of the debt will decline by $10 billion (.10 x $100) each year. In order for the real value of the debt to increase, the budget deficit would have to be at least $10 billion. If the budget deficit fell short of this figure, the real value of the debt would decline. The apparent budget deficit, in this case, would be a surplus, because the real value of the outstanding government debt would have declined.

Making these and similar calculations, Eisner found that the country ran surpluses in the late 1970s and that the deficits in the Reagan years were much smaller than reported. He concludes from these calculations that deficit anxiety is unwarranted.

The problem with this argument is that the numbers for the budget deficit are not especially important, but the changes in these numbers are. By all measures, including Eisner's, the federal budget moved toward deficit in the 1980s. Although the level of domestic investment was not adversely affected, the trade deficit was, and the result was a transfer of the ownership of U.S. assets abroad. This result cannot be disputed by changing the way we measure the deficit. Thus, the essential problem remains the same: standards of living will fall in the future because of the transfer of assets abroad and the process will continue as long as persistent deficits remain.

The potential fall in productivity and the transfer of income from our assets abroad are particularly serious because they compromise our abilities to face the demands raised by our social insurance system. As noted in Chapter 3, the burden of Social Security on future workers will substantially increase if productivity growth continues at low levels. Our ability and willingness to make arrangements for long-term care also will be compromised.

Statistics comparing the United States to its major international competitors consistently show that we devote a substantially smaller portion of our GNP to investment. Typically, gross domestic investment (including depreciation) is about 17 percent of GNP. In Europe and Japan, the figures range from 20 to 32 percent. Even these figures are dwarfed by some countries, such as Singapore, which invests 47 percent of GNP.

Economists know that these figures are not always fully comparable. In the United States, for example, our relatively low levels of government investment are excluded from the investment series. Nonetheless, on an international scale of investment efforts, our performance more closely resembles the Philippines than it does Europe or Japan.

Given these low investment levels, we cannot afford to divert several percentage points of GNP from investment to consumption through deficit financing. No miracle cures for productivity are lying on the shelf. Education, literacy, and investment are all critical for economic growth. Deficits squander some of this investment.

Sand in the Sandbox or Tax Collector for the Welfare State?

In the fall of 1981, Donald Regan, the U.S. Secretary of the Treasury, was very pleased. The Congress had just passed the 1981 Reagan administration tax bill that Regan had shepherded through Capitol Hill. In a buoyant mood, Regan met with the staff of the tax policy group at the Treasury to congratulate them on their hard work and dedication. At this meeting, he made some intriguing comments.

He first declared that, "my favorite part of the tax bill was the indexing provisions." This statement was surprising. During the 1970s, inflation had pushed taxpayers into higher marginal tax brackets and real tax revenues had increased. The tax indexation provisions to which Regan referred would adjust the tax brackets and rates against inflation and prevent such rises from happening in the future.[5] What made Regan's statement surprising, however, was that the indexing provisions had not been part of the original Reagan tax package. They had been added later in the negotiations by the Senate Republicans. In a town where egos reign, it was surprising to see Regan implicitly giving credit elsewhere.

Regan then went on to explain why he felt so strongly about the indexing provisions. They will, he declared, "take the sand out of Congress's sandbox."[6] With this statement, Regan became one of the first politicians to argue that government spending could be controlled only if revenues were systematically withheld from the Congress. Tax revenues were the "sand in the sandbox," and the Congress would play with these revenues by creating new government spending programs.

Later in the decade, this view of the relationship between taxes and spending became quite conventional. Senator Daniel Patrick Moynihan even accused the Republicans of deliberately engineering deficits in order to slow the growth of government spending. Similar statements were echoed in other countries. For example, the conservative party in Denmark insisted that expenditure control (or what they called "stabilization") could not result without reducing tax revenues.

What is common to these views is the belief that taxes cause government spending. By cause we mean that if one controls the time path for taxes, then government spending will be controlled as well.

This is the common-sense view of causation. Other factors may affect government spending, but reducing tax revenues certainly will reduce government spending.

Another Republican politician, however, had an alternative perspective on the causal relations between spending and taxes. Congressman Newt Gingrich, a colorful "new right" Republican, found himself in political debate with Senator Robert Dole, a moderate Republican and, at that time, Senate Majority Leader. Dole was supporting revenue increases to close the deficit; Gingrich was opposed. Gingrich, a former history professor and skilled debater, turned up the rhetoric to criticize Dole. "Republicans have served too long as tax collectors for the welfare state," he declared.[7]

In this statement, Gingrich offered the view that government spending causes taxes. In his view, Congress (usually controlled by the Democrats) passes new spending initiatives. The Republicans are then called upon to be responsible and raise tax revenues to pay for the welfare state. The path of government spending controls the path of taxation.

This view of the causal relationship between taxes and spending is shared by the single most influential model of fiscal deficits in the macroeconomic literature. According to the "tax smoothing" model of Robert Barro, the path of government spending is determined by political factors. Taxes must be raised, over the long run, to finance this expenditure. However, it is costly to change the level of taxes too quickly in the short run. Thus, if government spending is temporarily high, the government will not raise taxes fully to finance the spending immediately but will incur a deficit and finance the deficit, plus the interest, at a later time. In this framework, government spending causes taxes.

To this point, we have discussed taxes causing government spending and government spending causing taxes. But there are two other possibilities. First, taxes and spending may be mutually interdependent—that is, any factor that controls one controls the other as well. This view has a certain surface plausibility because, in an ideal world, taxation and spending decisions should be considered jointly. Second, taxes and spending could be independently determined, with no causal relations between them. In this case, factors that change taxes would not necessarily have any effect on spending, and vice versa.

Knowledge of which causal relation has prevailed could be of more than academic interest. If, for example, taxes cause government spending, then Democrats interested in new social programs first would have to concentrate on obtaining new tax revenues. Also, taxes that are traditionally easy to raise, such as value-added taxes, should be avoided by those who wish to limit spending.[8]

How can one decide from the historical record which causal story appears to be true? Although many have attempted to disentangle the relationships between taxes and spending by looking at the historical time series, most of these attempts have been misguided. To see the difficulty, suppose that spending causes taxes but that budgets are always balanced, so that taxes and spending are always equal and there are no deficits. Because taxes and spending always move together, looking at the time series for taxes and spending will be uninformative. Without additional information, it would be impossible to determine the causal structure. The situation is not fundamentally changed if taxes and spending can diverge.[9] Without further information, you have a chicken and egg problem.

The key to disentangling the causal relations between taxing and spending is to combine a statistical analysis with additional information gained from the historical tax and spending record. To take an example, suppose we have estimated some statistical relations between taxes and spending that we call the normal tax and spending processes. Suppose some unusual historical events—such as a war or a change in the structure of spending committees in Congress—changes the normal spending process. If the tax process changes as well, we know that spending causes taxes. If the tax process fails to change, then spending does not cause taxes. Similarly, if a tax revolt changes the process for taxes but the spending process remains the same, then taxes do not cause spending.

The key idea is to use historical information along with the economic time series to interpret the data. We know that some events can be viewed as breaks in the process generating spending and that other events can be viewed as breaks in the process generating taxes. In principle, this additional information can aid us in solving the chicken and egg problem. Of course, our historical inferences must be reliable if we are to make any progress in this manner. But in many cases we have the additional historical or institutional insight to help us make progress in sorting out competing causal claims.

Using this approach, it is possible to scrutinize the causal relation between taxes and spending in the post-World War II era.[10] It appears that two different causal structures have operated in the postwar era:

one from the early 1950s to the later 1960s and another from the early 1970s to the present time. In the latter period, from a statistical point of view, the processes governing taxes and spending appear to be independent. Breaks in the tax process, as caused by the 1981 tax cuts, did not affect spending, while breaks in the spending process, as caused by the Reagan military buildup, did not affect taxes. The only interpretation consistent with this evidence is that taxes and spending are independent. We return to the fiscal implications of this discovery later.

In the earlier period, the situation is quite different. There are close statistical ties between taxes and spending. Specifically, government spending appeared to fall whenever the deficit in prior periods increased. While the time series for taxes and spending are clearly tied together, inferring causality is rather difficult because of the events surrounding the Korean War early in the period. Mild evidence, however, favors the view that taxes cause spending.

When the Korean War started, two tax bills were introduced, one for increases in personal taxes and the other for increases in corporate taxes. Both tax bills had built-in termination dates, and the taxes were scheduled to expire, presumably conditional on the war ending, at the end of 1953.[11] The war formally ended in early 1953, although the fighting had stopped somewhat earlier. Spending fell when the war ended.

The fall in spending when the war ended can be seen as a result of the tax legislation that was already on the books. The tax increases clearly had been envisioned as a means to finance the war; they were not meant to lead to a permanently higher level of government spending and so termination dates were built into the legislation. Spending does not always have to fall when wars end. Talk of peace dividends presupposes that the level of spending (and taxation) remains the same but that the composition of spending shifts to nonmilitary priorities. Clearly, no peace dividend was envisioned during the Korean War period. Taxes dictated the flow of revenue to the government or, in other words, taxes caused spending.

Thus, two different causal regimes have operated in postwar U.S. history. In the 1950s and 1960s, taxes caused government spending. Starting in the 1970s, however, taxes and spending appeared to become independent.

It is interesting to note that two quite prominent students of fiscal affairs, one an economist and the other a political scientist, also detected a switch in regime at about the same time. Robert E. Lucas, Jr., in a lecture delivered in 1984, noted that, "tendencies towards permanent deficit finance and inflation that have emerged in our economy in the *last fifteen years* have much deeper roots than a succession of transient external shocks and internal mistakes. They arose, I believe, because the implicit rules under which monetary and fiscal policy is conducted have undergone a fundamental change." (emphasis added).[12] This account places the break in the early 1970s.

Aaron Wildavsky, a well-known political scientist and scholar of the budget process, noted a similar phenomenon. In a chapter entitled "The Collapse of Consensus," in his book *The New Politics of the Budgetary Process*, Wildavsky discussed this change:

> Shortly after the standard accounts of classical budgeting were published in the early 1960s—Richard Fenno's *The Politics of the Purse* and the first edition of my *Politics of the Budgetary Process*—that process began to collapse . . . . In retrospect, the pattern is clear; Congress and the Presidents have trouble agreeing.[13]

In Wildavsky's initial book, he had argued that budgeting was incremental, in part because all parties agreed on fundamentals and adjustments could be made on the margin. At some point, however, this consensus disappeared.

This finding that taxes and spending are independent is important for understanding the fiscal history of the United States in the 1970s and 1980s. The Congress began to realize that spending and taxation decisions were becoming increasingly independent and sought remedies for this state of affairs. Unfortunately, as we have seen, these remedies were largely unsuccessful. But a closer examination reveals some important interactions between fiscal mechanisms to control spending and budgetary outcomes.

The Search for a Budget Process

Congress's first major attempt to unify the tax and spending process was the Congressional Budget Act of 1974. Prior to this act, spending and taxing were largely disjointed efforts. Authorization committees approved legislation, but appropriation committees determined how much could be spent. The appropriation committees, moreover, had no formal connections with the tax-writing committees in the House and Senate. Despite this rather disjointed structure, taxing and spending decisions seem to have been tied together until the late 1960s, perhaps by general taboos about deficit financing. But, by the early 1970s, this discipline began to disappear, and the result was the Congressional Budget Act, one of the first of several attempts to reunify taxes and spending.

The Congressional Budget Act created budget committees in the House and Senate. The purpose of these committees was to integrate spending and taxation through budget resolutions that would set forward the overall plans for spending, taxing, and the deficit. These committees were also given authority, which was not really used until the 1980s, to restrain the actions of other committees of Congress in order to meet the targets of the budget resolution. The act also created the Congressional Budget Office (CBO), which was designed as an intellectual counter-weight to the Office of Management and Budget (OMB) of the executive branch. The CBO provided the Congress with its own economic and budget forecasts and decreased its reliance on information provided by the executive branch.

The Congressional Budget Act provided some formal mechanisms to link spending and taxes, but, perhaps more importantly, it symbolized the rise of Congress as a significant player in budget policy. The CBO provided them with additional intellectual ammunition in the battle against the executive branch for fiscal control. It is important to keep in mind the political context at that time. The Congress had just impeached Richard Nixon, and the Democrats had made dramatic gains in the 1974 elections. The seniority system in the House was overthrown as the newly elected members sought greater powers. As the power of Congress grew throughout the 1970s, the discipline exerted in the past by the executive branch waned.

The budget committees failed to exert significant discipline in the 1970s. During this period, they essentially were just another layer of committees on top of the existing structure. Ironically, the real power of the budget committees was used first by the Reagan administration in the beginning of its first term. David Stockman, the director of OMB, used a procedure called "reconciliation" to impose the resolution of the budget committees on the other committees in Congress. This move led to significant budget cuts in the first year of the Reagan administration.

Despite the turmoil of the 1970s, the budget deficits—particularly when corrected for the business cycle—did not approach the large deficits of the 1980s. Earlier we chronicled the rise of the deficits in the 1980s through a combination of budget failure and severe recession. The large deficits, even by the mid-1980s, failed to create any noticeable economic harm. The stock market was rising, and the economy was in the midst of its almost decade-long expansion. Although the budget deficit was partly responsible for a rise in real interest rates, which raised the value of the dollar and hurt our tradeable goods industry, overall employment continued to grow as labor shifted to other sectors of the economy. As noted, the damage from deficits may emerge slowly.

There may not have been an obvious economic crisis, but a political crisis was about to emerge. The Congress became increasingly frustrated by its inability to control the deficit. In 1985, after the resignation of David Stockman and some failed political negotiations, several senators used a required vote on extending the debt ceiling as an opportunity to take matters into their own hands. Senator Phil Gramm, who had previously offered budget limitation proposals, enlisted a moderate Republican, Warren Rudman, and a Democrat, Fritz Hollings, to help pass the Gramm-Rudman-Hollings law (hereafter referred to as Gramm-Rudman).

The inspiration of the Gramm-Rudman law was the doomsday machine in the film *Dr. Strangelove*. Moviegoers will recall that this machine was a terrible, earth-destroying device that would go off if any nuclear weapons were exploded. It also was set automatically and could not be dismantled. The horror of the doomsday machine was supposed to prevent war.[14] The Gramm-Rudman law operated on a similar principle. The idea was to force Congress to reduce the deficit to preset targets. If Congress failed to do so, there would be unpleasant across-the-board cuts known as "sequestration." Ideally, the threat of sequestration would force Congress to meet its deficit targets.

The problems that arose in the design of Gramm-Rudman were intricate and sobering for those who favor a constitutional amendment to balance the budget. But Gramm-Rudman was a law, not a constitutional amendment, and this status influenced its structure. Laws, after all, can be changed easily by a future Congress. There was an important tension in Gramm-Rudman. Like a doomsday machine, the sequestration had to be dreaded by all parties so that agreements could be found to reach the deficit targets. On the other hand, if sequestration were too Draconian, it would not be credible because

members of Congress would know that they could pass new legislation in the face of dramatic protests.

As a consequence of the tension in creating a Draconian but credible punishment, the law exempted large parts of the budget from sequestration. In particular, Social Security payments and interest on
the debt were fully exempt, and there were limitations on other entitlement programs. As a result, the sequestration would fall on a relatively small part of the budget. This remaining part included both military and nonmilitary spending and still could create substantial
discomfort for all parties.[15]

One problem that all deficit limitation schemes face is the effect on
the targets of a slowdown in the economy or a recession. In a recession, deficits swell as tax revenues fall and social safety net spending
increases. One lesson remaining from Keynesian economics is that
wholesale cuts in spending during periods of recession can exacerbate
the recession. Yet, unless a deficit limitation scheme had some safety
valve provisions for a recession, the scheme could force spending cuts
at the wrong time.

There are two main ways to design these safety valve procedures.
The first is to adjust the targets according to the state of the economy;
that is, if economic growth is lower than anticipated, the deficit targets would be increased. The second procedure is to suspend the requirements of meeting the targets if certain economic conditions prevail. Congress chose this mechanism. Essentially, if economic growth
falls below 1 percent for two consecutive quarters or a recession (negative growth for two quarters) is forecast, the targets would be sus-
pended. Critics of these safety valve mechanisms noted that they were
unsuited for growth that is sluggish but fails to trigger the suspension
mechanisms.[16] As a practical matter, when a full-blown recession hit
in 1990, the entire Gramm-Rudman apparatus was replaced by a new
procedure.

How did the Gramm-Rudman law work in practice? The law was
in effect, in some form, from fiscal years 1986 to 1990, so there is
some experience with the difficulties of deficit limitation mechanisms
and their effectiveness. Because each year posed different problems, it
is worth looking at the history of the process.

When the first Gramm-Rudman law was passed, fiscal year 1986
was already underway. The Congress had intended sequestration to
occur that year as a mechanism to reduce the deficit. However, the
extent of sequestration was specifically limited for that initial year.

Essentially, this curb meant that cuts were spread over a limited part of the budget.

Fiscal 1987 was to be the first big test of the new mechanism. However, while Congress was planning for fiscal year 1987, the Supreme Court declared that the Gramm-Rudman law was unconstitutional. The court ruled that the automatic trigger provisions were an executive function and that the head of the Government Accounting Office (GAO), an appointee of Congress, played too important a role in the procedure, thereby violating the separation of powers doctrine. As a result, the threat of sequestration was removed from the law.

Yet, despite the lack of a credible threat, the Congress went to extraordinary lengths to meet the deficit goals set forward in the legislation. So much public awareness had been created by the Gramm-Rudman process that the Congress felt constrained to meet the goals. However, in order to meet these goals, the Congress used an extraordinary range of budgetary loopholes. First, there were asset sales totaling $8.7 billion that did little for the solvency of the government but certainly improved its cash flow. Second, eliminating some prepayment penalties on loans also led to a rash of repayments and to an improvement in the government's cash flow and, thus, in the measured deficit. Finally, and most outrageously, the government essentially backdated payments to the states for revenue-sharing in order to ascribe those payments to fiscal year 1986, when there were no penalties, rather than to fiscal year 1987. Budget hypocrisy was the tribute the Congress paid to fiscal solvency.

As the fiscal year 1988 approached, Congress passed a new version of Gramm-Rudman that gave the OMB more authority in the sequestration procedure so that it would be constitutional. They also increased the deficit targets and stretched them out over several additional years. Despite this relaxation of the goals, in the fall of 1987 it appeared that a major sequestration would occur. However, in October 1987, the stock market crashed. Wall Street pointed a finger at Congress and the Congress was prompted to act. The Gramm-Rudman goals, however, did set a floor for the negotiations and probably led to slightly higher budget cuts than would have occurred in their absence.

Fiscal 1989 witnessed a conspiracy between the White House and the Congress. Elections were coming up and no one wanted budget difficulties to keep them in Washington in the fall before an election. The White House and the Congress agreed on the OMB forecast for the economy, which was substantially more optimistic than that of the CBO or other private forecasters. With the higher forecast, sequestration could be avoided. When the economy grew faster than anticipated and the OMB forecast proved close to the mark, sequestration was avoided.

When George Bush campaigned for president in 1988, he claimed that he would meet his budget obligations by the ambiguous device of a "flexible freeze." Essentially, this tactic meant trying to limit spending where possible and letting a growing economy provide additional tax revenues. Some observers noted that this strategy probably would work for one year but would be difficult to enforce in subsequent years. This prediction proved correct. The Gramm-Rudman targets were met in fiscal year 1990, but in large part this success resulted from the growing surpluses in the Social Security accounts. The problems that arose in fiscal year 1991 became fatal for Gramm-Rudman when the recession hit and the deficit soared.

Looking back at the Gramm-Rudman experience is sobering for those advocating deficit control through constitutional mechanisms. Safety valve mechanisms were difficult to formulate, and a deep recession helped kill the entire process. Congress viciously exploited every loophole and showed every propensity to continue these activities. The deficit control that was accomplished was largely because of the symbolic value of explicit goals. When Congress was close to previously set targets, it tended to meet them, even if it had to resort to a variety of loopholes.

The fall of 1990 brought another round of deficit panic. This time failures in the savings and loans industry necessitated substantial infusions of cash from the Treasury. The recession sharply limited tax revenues. The Gramm-Rudman targets were no longer feasible, and the President engaged in long, acrimonious negotiations with Congress. The result was a new budget mechanism.

New Budget Procedures

In the fall of 1990, the Congress and the president agreed to a multiyear plan to reduce the deficit. At the time, the CBO forecast that if this plan were successfully implemented and no economic surprises occurred, the budget deficit (inclusive of the surplus in Social Security) would be reduced from 5.3 percent of GNP in 1991 to 1.8 percent of GNP by 1996. By 1992, the CBO already had raised its estimate for 1996 to 3.5 percent of GNP. But we have heard such promises before; what mechanisms insure that the deficits actually come down?

The current budget procedure has the title "The Budget Enforcement Act of 1990," and it clearly emphasizes the critical role of enforcement in multiyear budget agreements. The agreement is very complex. In an explanation of the act, the CBO commented, "The act is long and complicated and was written hurriedly, and most of its provisions have not been tested."[17] Bearing in mind these reassuring words, how does the new law work?

Three components of the budget procedures pertain to limits on discretionary spending, rules for entitlements, and flexible deficit targets. Sequestration provisions apply separately to each component of the process.

There are preset limits on discretionary spending—that is, spending that must be appropriated annually. The spending targets are adjusted for inflation, changes in budgetary definitions, and emergencies; they also can be changed in the event of a recession. These limits have been set to gradually reduce the deficit over a five-year period. If Congress fails to meet these targets, there is broad-based sequestration provision to insure that total spending meets the targets. Until 1993, there are separate subtotals, and sequestration provisions, for defense, international, and domestic programs. For 1994 and 1995, these programs are put into one category.

Entitlements, or so-called mandatory spending, are handled in a different manner. Instead of trying to reduce entitlement spending, a theme of past budget summits, the new law essentially prohibits any changes in benefits or taxes that would increase the deficit in any year over a five-year period. The law can be changed to increase benefits, but only if taxes are raised to finance the increase. Similarly, if taxes are cut, other taxes must be increased or benefits decreased. This arrangement has been termed a pay-as-you-go system. These provisions freeze the status quo on entitlements.

Social Security, the largest entitlement program, is treated differently and is not subject to the pay-as-you-go policies. The law explicitly removes Social Security from the official deficit and from all enforcement procedures of the act. This provision has two consequences. First, the official on-budget deficit is significantly larger than in previous years because the Social Security element in its calculation had been running a surplus. For example, for fiscal year

1991, the official deficit was $321 billion, but the consolidated deficit, including Social Security, was $269 billion. In prior years, Social Security had been included in the budget. For most macroeconomic purposes, the appropriate deficit measure is the consolidated fiscal picture and not the official measure, which excludes Social Security.

Second, and perhaps more important, removing Social Security from the enforcement provisions of the new budget law opens up the possibility that Congress could increase Social Security benefits or cut taxes, particularly because the fund currently shows a surplus. The budget act tried to control this temptation by amending voting procedures to make it more difficult to change the Social Security surplus, but there is no experience with these provisions.

The sequestration procedures for the pay-as-you-go component of the budget are quite weak. Most mandatory spending is excluded from the sequestration, there is a low maximum level of sequestration, and Medicare is largely exempt from sequestration. It remains to be seen whether these provisions provide important deterrents.

Finally, there are highly complex separate targets for deficits. Unlike those under the Gramm-Rudman laws, however, these targets are not fixed but can be adjusted for economic conditions and for any changes in discretionary spending targets. The CBO, in fact, concluded that the deficit targets would be irrelevant (given the other parts of the program) for fiscal years 1992 and 1993 and might be irrelevant for subsequent years as well.[18] Under the new law, control of the federal deficit is to be accomplished by controls on discretionary spending and by pay-as-you-go rules, not by explicit attempts to control the deficit.

It is too early to assess the procedures adopted in 1991, but it is possible to highlight the key differences in style with the prior Gramm-Rudman laws. In its favor, the new law puts much more emphasis on multiyear budget targets. This orientation removes the incentives to shift funds from one year to the next that plagued Gramm-Rudman. It also removes one-time payments, such as additional expenses for the Gulf War or the savings and loans bailout, that would distort a system based on deficit targets. In the discretionary spending area, the law puts direct ceilings on spending over a five-year period. For entitlements, it eschews all attempts at reducing promised benefits but contains provisions that attempt to curb the growth of new programs.

Because the provisions of the bill are so complex, it is a true insiders bill. Unlike Gramm-Rudman, in which the deficit targets were fixed and visible to the general public, the new law contains intricate provisions that only insiders can interpret. There appears to have been a trade-off between a potentially more workable law and a more complex one. The complexity of the new law makes it more difficult for the public to bring pressure upon Congress.

As the history of Gramm-Rudman revealed, public deficit targets put pressure on Congress. The new law makes it more difficult for the public to continue its pressure on Congress. On the other hand, Congress became adept at manipulating the law for its own goals. Perhaps a more carefully written insiders bill can be more effective. But there is a nagging suspicion that without public pressure Congress will find a way out of the trap it has laid for itself. Congress almost surely will do so if fundamental disagreements over budget priorities and the size of government continue.

A New Budgetary Constitution?

Despite these years of tortuously complex budget agreements and interminable political battles, the long-run deficit projections still look bleak. Table 8–1 contains the long-run budget forecasts of the Congressional Budget Office. These forecasts assume that the current budget arrangements remain in place, that the economy recovers and growth resumes at its normal level, and that no new major policy

Table 8–1
The Budget Outlook Through 2002 (by Fiscal Year)

	1992	1993	1994	1995	1996	1997	1998	1999	2000	2001	2002
In Billions of Dollars											
Revenues	1,088	1,162	1,242	1,323	1,390	1,455	1,534	1,612	1,693	1,779	1,870
Outlays	1,402	1,493	1,511	1,567	1,644	1,745	1,845	1,962	2,093	2,233	2,384
Deficit	314	331	268	244	254	290	311	350	400	454	514
As a Percentage of GDP											
Revenues	18.6	18.8	18.9	19.1	19.0	18.9	19.0	19.0	19.0	19.0	19.0
Outlays	24.0	24.1	23.0	22.6	22.5	22.7	22.8	23.1	23.4	23.8	24.2
Deficit	5.5	5.3	4.1	3.5	3.5	3.8	3.8	4.1	4.5	4.8	5.2

Source: Congressional Budget Office, "The Economic and Budget Outlook: Update" (Washington, D.C.: Congressional Budget Office, Aug. 1992).

initiatives are forthcoming from the Congress. Nonetheless, by the year 2002, the CBO forecasts the deficit to be 5.2 percent of GNP.

Why is the long-run forecast so dismal? The answer lies on the spending side, and the causes of this problem were discussed in Chapter 2—health costs are out of control. Through its Medicare and Medicaid programs, the federal government is fully exposed to this rise in health costs. As long as health costs continue to rise at current levels, there is little hope of reaching budget balance without a dramatic increase in new revenues.

Years of frustration with the budget problem and these gloomy long-run projections have led to a resurgence in interest in a balanced budget amendment to the U.S. Constitution. In the 1980s, a balanced budget amendment fell just short of being passed by the required number of states. But the process could start afresh. Richard Darman, the director of OMB under President Bush, had opposed such an amendment, but later declared his support of one in 1992.

A typical balanced budget amendment would require Congress to pass a balanced budget unless a majority or supermajority (for example, 60 percent) voted to waive the requirement in face of a national emergency or severe recession. Some versions of the amendment would make it more difficult to balance the budget by raising taxes than by cutting expenditures. Others would try to exempt some parts of the budget—for example, Social Security.

The experience with the Gramm-Rudman legislation illustrated some of the difficulties that also would be inherent in a constitutional amendment. Loopholes always can be exploited, the courts are likely to be drawn into the budget process, safety valve mechanisms need to be designed, and the budget itself needs to be defined carefully—for example, perhaps by distinguishing between current expenditures (consumption) and capital expenditures (investment). All these areas are plagued by pitfalls and difficulties. We can be sure only of one thing—new and unforeseen problems will arise with any constitutional amendment.

Darman, a veteran of budget battles, fully understood all these problems and knew from firsthand experience the limits of budgetary controls. Why did he become a supporter of a constitutional amendment to balance the budget?[19] There may have been narrow political motives, but—putting those aside—it is interesting to examine Darman's own rationale. According to his perspective, entitlements (mostly health-related) are driving the budget. Although waste and duplication exist throughout the government, constant budget pressures have eliminated the most visible and prominent examples of these inefficiencies. The burgeoning deficits are not caused by growth in discretionary programs but by the virtually uncontrollable entitlement budget.

Congress and several administrations have not had the political will to curb the growth in entitlements. It is not that they have proliferated new programs. Rather, growth in existing programs and sharp increases in health costs have predominantly increased spending growth.

A balanced budget amendment, in Darman's view, would be an opportunity to develop a new political stance toward the budget. Darman suggested working toward a total cap on all entitlement spending by limiting spending in this category to a certain percentage growth rate. With an expenditure cap on entitlements, progress can be made on the overall budget deficit.

Expenditure caps are not policy decisions or policy solutions; they would, however, force policy changes. Darman and other budget observers recognize that, ultimately, no progress can be made on the budget deficit without progress in controlling health costs. As a society, we will have to confront the difficult choices outlined in Chapter 2 on health costs.

We have come full circle. In the end, solutions to our macroeconomic deficit problems depend on resolving the microeconomic problems in health care. A macroeconomic solution is necessary to reduce the deficit, increase investment spending, raise productivity, and ease the burden of our social insurance programs. Whether we like it or not, solutions to these problems must come from Washington.

Concluding Comments

The U.S. budget deficit is the single most visible symbol of a failure of collective action. Although there are some important criticisms of using the federal budget deficit to judge the success of our economic policy, very few observers believe that large, persistent deficits are totally benign. Because the United States is a relatively low-saving country, any diversion of funds away from investment to consumption (private or public) reduces our productivity and rate of growth.

The seemingly inexorable rise in health care costs means that the deficits will not disappear. Action needs to be taken on either spending or taxes to prevent the problem from growing worse over time. Careful examinations of the current budgetary process suggest that tax and spending decisions are not fully integrated and are made largely independently. There are no natural forces leading to budgetary balance.

In these circumstances, there has been increasing interest in mechanisms to tie the hands of policy makers and force a process that would eventually lead to budget balance. Two important considerations must be kept in mind when thinking about these mechanisms:

1. Budget laws written by the Congress and the president (such as Gramm-Rudman) only work within narrow limits. Our experience with this type of legislation suggests that it can provide only a limited amount of discipline. If the going gets tough, the law is changed.
2. Health costs, not waste or military spending, are principally responsible for current forecasts of persistent deficits. Should a budget discipline measure be directed solely at health costs or at the budget as a whole?

Further Reading

The economics of deficits are discussed from a variety of perspectives in the spring 1989 issue of the *Journal of Economic Perspectives*. Articles by Robert Barro, Robert Eisner, and Edward Gramlich are all worthwhile. Gramlich discusses the question of whether taxes drive spending or spending drives taxes. My favorite treatment of this issue is Kevin D. Hoover and Steven M. Sheffrin, "Causation, Spending, and Taxes: Sand in the Sandbox or Tax Collector for the Welfare State?" (*American Economic Review*, March 1992, pp. 225–48).

Two political science books treat budgetary politics and the deficit in depth. See Aaron Wildavsky and Joseph White, *The Deficit and the Public Interest: The Search for Responsible Budgeting in the 1980s* (Berkeley: University of California Press, 1988). Allen Schick is one of the foremost authorities on budgeting. His book, *The Capacity to Budget* (Washington, D.C.: The Urban Institute, 1990) is a sobering assessment of our current budgetary problems, with some possible solutions.

Finally, two prominent economists, William Niskanen and Charles Schultze, discuss whether federal spending has gone out of control in a symposium in the *Journal of Economic Perspectives*, spring 1992.

Notes

1 Unless otherwise specified, all the numbers in this chapter are drawn from *The Economic and Budget Outlook: Update* (Washington, D.C.: Congressional Budget Office, Aug. 1992).

2 For a full discussion of his view, see Robert Barro, "The Ricardian Approach to Budget Deficits," *Journal of Economic Perspectives* (Spring 1989), 37–52.

3 Barro, "The Ricardian Approach," 50.

4 See Robert Eisner, "Budget Deficits: Rhetoric and Reality," *Journal of Economic Perspectives* (Spring 1989), 73–94.

5 The indexation provisions were not scheduled to go into effect until 1985. They were subsequently repealed but later reinstated in the 1986 tax bill.

6 The source of this quote is the author's recollection of that meeting.

7 This quote is very famous—*Washington Post*, Nov. 19, 1984. Gingrich and Dole later tangled over the budget in the early 1990s, when Dole appeared to be the victor.

8 This is slippery territory. Once we have theories that proclaim how government works, it is often difficult to see what role the individual actor plays in the story. The difficulties are similar to those encountered in general discussions of free will versus determinism.

9 The approach taken to causality in this section as well as its conclusions are drawn from Kevin D. Hoover and Steven M. Sheffrin, "Causation, Spending, and Taxes: Sand in the Sandbox or Tax Collector for the Welfare State?" *American Economic Review* (March 1992) 225–48. This paper provides justifications and references for the discussion of causality as well as the empirical conclusions.

10 This analysis draws on sections 3–6 of Hoover and Sheffrin, "Causations."

11 Initially the corporate tax increase was scheduled to end in June 1953, but it was extended to December 31, 1953, to coincide with the termination of the personal tax increase.

12 The lecture was published two years later: Robert E. Lucas, Jr., "Principles of Monetary and Fiscal Policy," *Journal of Monetary Economics* (Jan. 1986): 133.

13 Aaron Wildavsky, *The New Politics of the Budgetary Process*, (Glenview, Ill.: Scott, Foresman, 1986) 120.

14 The reader should recall that in the movie the Doomsday machine was activated and could not be turned off.

15 For a more extended discussion of Gramm-Rudman, see my book, *The Making of Economic Policy* (Cambridge, Mass.: Basil Blackwell, 1989), ch. 7.

16 For a more detailed assessment of the safety valve mechanisms, see Sheffrin, *The Making of Economic Policy*, 193–94.

17 Congressional Budget Office, The Economic and Budget Outlook: Fiscal Years 1992–96 (*Washington, D.C.,* Jan. 1991), 44. A more complete description of the new budget process can be found in Chapter 2 of that document.

18 Congressional Budget Office, *The Economic and Budget Outlook: Update (Washington, D.C.: Congressional Budget Office, Aug. 1992) 38–39.*

19 Eric Pianin, "Darman: Amendement Only Way to Control Deficit," *Washington Post VII5*, May 7, 1992: A4.

9

Principles for Reform

Washington is a city of details. Lawyers, lobbyists, staffers, and bureaucrats scurry through town with the latest details of bills, proposals, and regulations. Specialty publications, whose growth seems unbounded, bring daily tidbits of fast-breaking developments to all interested partisans. As the complexity of the Washington money-go-round continually grows, each interest group finds it imperative to hire its own lawyers and lobbyists to keep track of the nuances of legislation, court rulings, or regulations. Citizens or interested parties not privy to all the details feel excluded from the process and are viewed as naive by the Washington crowd.

Senators and members of Congress are also pinned in by the details. Lobbyists and campaign contributors do not care about defense or social policy as such; they care about their own contracts and programs. Groups seeking to get their way in Washington are quite willing to peddle policies that further their own interests at the expense of the public interest. They want legislators to use special provisions or loopholes that typically are hidden in the complexity of legislation.

The villains in this process are not necessarily the groups that have gained public notoriety. Charitable organizations, for example, were unhappy about the reduction in personal income tax rates brought about by the 1986 Tax Reform Act. They feared that lower income tax rates would reduce the tax incentives that encourage high-income individuals to make gifts to charities. They preferred the old system with high tax rates but many loopholes. General charities could do little to oppose the 1986 law; however, art museums were eventually able to make a deal. They strongly objected to provisions of the alternative minimum tax in the 1986 law that had the effect of limiting the deductions allowed for contributions of art works that had appreciated in value. After several years of persistent lobbying, they were successful in having this detailed provision of the law changed. Only tax experts and those in the museum business followed this debate carefully. As usual, the action was in the details.

Readers of the previous chapters also must have been struck by the details and complexity of economic policy. The rules and regulations for Social Security are intricate and difficult to understand. Environmental regulations are particularly detailed. And few citizens have any idea of the regulations surrounding trade policy or the self-imposed budget rules that the Congress has adopted. With this complexity, how can members of the general public monitor policy developments and evaluate candidates and new ideas?

The public cannot surrender economic policy to the experts. Without general monitoring of the political process, the Washington money-go-round will conduct business as usual, immersed in the details, with legislators and bureaucrats cutting deals for the insiders. Experts pursue their own interests—sometimes financial, sometimes ideological, and sometimes just the quest for self-importance.

The general public cannot compete with the experts on the details of policy, but they can evaluate outcomes based on a set of guiding principles. Politicians can be judged by the extent to which they adhere to the spirit of these principles. Such principles can serve as an organizing framework for assessing economic policy. Equipped with some basic ideas, the public can listen to the experts or politicians debate particular issues without becoming overwhelmed by the details.

I, of course, advocate principles based on an understanding of the tensions between market failure and political obsessions, the organizing theme of this book. But, as the previous chapters indicate, the application of these ideas is subtle and every area of economic policy has its own contours. To assist the reader in keeping the major themes in mind and not becoming lost in the details, I now return to the key areas of economic policy—from health care to fiscal policy—and highlight the major findings of the preceeding chapters. Rather than reviewing all the arguments and findings, I concentrate on the basic issues that are likely to emerge in future policy debates.

The health care debate is one of the most complex areas and one in which the stakes are perhaps the highest. As the Clinton administration recognizes, sharply rising health care costs are crippling federal and state budgets, and the public views uneven access to basic care as generally unacceptable. Proposals for reform range from a radical nationalization of the entire health care system to an increased emphasis on competition, although managed.

The first principle to keep in mind is that the health care debate is largely about access, not health. There is abundant evidence that lifestyles, individual choices, and general social conditions are far more important to health than any medical treatment. The social costs of the spread of AIDS through sexual activity and drug abuse keenly illustrate this point. Even in prenatal care, a healthy lifestyle for the mother dwarfs the benefits of medical care. Nonetheless, timely access to medical care is increasingly viewed as a general right (perhaps because of our propensity to engage in unhealthy activities), and the health care system must respond to these demands. But there should be no illusion about the efficacy of medical care by itself.

We should also abandon the illusion that the United States could ever adopt a completely state-run, Canadian-style health system. Four factors work strongly against such a possibility. First, the United States has a strong tradition of choice and freedom of access that a state system could not provide. The rich and the upper-middle class have access not only to a level of care but also to many options and varieties of care that could not be sustained in a state system. Second, under a state-run system, private health insurance would largely disappear. It is impossible to envision Congress or a president demolishing such a powerful industry. Third, the penchant for litigation in our society would make fully centralized cost-control decisions difficult to implement. Finally, American citizens, who harbor deep-rooted suspicions about bureaucratic efficiency, are not likely to hand over an entire industry to the state.

The two broad options that remain are managed competition and regulatory control. Insights and strategies from both approaches will be necessary. Consumers must have some incentives in the system. These incentives must work through the choice of health plans or insurance, not by forcing decisions at the point of care. The easiest way to restore some incentives into the system is to limit the tax benefits associated with health care. Employees should pay taxes on employer-paid health care benefits after these benefits exceed a basic allowance. Paying in after-tax dollars, consumers would be forced to evaluate whether, for example, a health maintenance organization would be preferable to a more expensive system in which they had free choice of health care providers.

Including employer-paid health insurance in taxable income, once these payments reached a certain threshold, would also have beneficial effects on the Social Security system. Because of the favorable tax treatment for health insurance and other benefits, taxable wages have grown less quickly than total employee compensation—that is, wages plus benefits. A reversal of this trend, through limits on the exclusion of employer-paid health benefits, would raise taxable wages and strengthen the Social Security system.

The additional tax revenue that would be raised through this proposal should be allocated for tax credits to low-income households to buy medical insurance. States and insurance firms can also be given incentives to provide basic, bare-bones insurance coverage to recipients of these tax credits.

The other insight from managed competition is that the insurance market must be regulated to prevent adverse selection. The government can facilitate healthy markets and prevent abuses through several mechanisms. They can sponsor and subsidize insurance pools for small businesses and uninsured individuals; require that employees retain the option to purchase insurance after leaving employment; restrict the ability of insurance companies or employers to rewrite insurance contracts after the fact; and reform U.S. pension law so that states can regulate self-insured firms.

A more radical version of managed competition would be based on competition among insurance providers for a fixed geographical population. This system, known as community rating, would require the government to set geographical boundaries, provide detailed definitions of the rules for competition, and choose the winners based on these criteria. While community rating could, in principle, solve the adverse selection problem, it has several fatal drawbacks. Community rating is incompatible with insurance coverage organized through employers. This system would mean that millions of individuals, fully satisfied with their existing employer-provided health coverage, would be forced to change to a new system. In addition, writing rules for competition, selecting winners, and enforcing both the rules of competition and the subsequent performance would be complex and daunting tasks for the government to undertake. To the naive listener, a program with the government as the final arbiter sounds just like the defense contracting industry. But in defense, there are no other options than government monopoly. In health care, we have a choice.

Managed competition by itself cannot prevent the rapid escalation of health costs. Consumers still have a penchant to overinsure, and most policies still provide catastrophic coverage. As long as the government and the private sector provide complete reimbursement once individual expenditures reach a certain threshold, the system will provide incentives for research and development in high-cost technology and drugs. This spiral between insurance and technological innovation needs to broken if there is to be any hope of reducing the growth rate of costs in this industry.

The federal government, through Medicare and Medicaid, can use its influence to slow the adoption of high-cost technology and drugs. The government can limit reimbursement for treatments using drugs and technology that have not met prior cost–benefit tests. Moreover, it could extend its regulatory reach to the private sector through legislation that would prevent any hospital or doctor receiving funds from Medicare or Medicaid from using nonapproved treatments. Through these policies, the government would accomplish two goals: It would prevent the use of existing inefficient high-cost technology or drugs, and, more important, it would reduce incentives for costly innovations. The government could still encourage low-cost innovations by signalling that it would liberally approve cost-effective treatments.

These regulatory steps are a natural evolution of increasingly aggressive federal policy. In the 1980s, hospitals were regulated through diagnostic-related groups. Doctors fees were rearranged through relative-value scales. Recently, Medicare has tried to reduce costs by paying only a single fee to hospitals for major operations, such as heart bypass surgery, and letting the doctors and hospitals fight over the fixed fee. The natural next step is for the government to begin to intervene in decisions to reimburse high-cost procedures and to extend its reach to transactions within the private sector.

As the largest entitlement program, Social Security is always under examination. The latest proposals to reform Social Security are to tax or even deny benefits to high-income individuals. In the policy jargon, Social Security should be "means tested." While these proposals may be tempting revenue-raisers, they could endanger a very successful and popular program.

Social Security has achieved its overwhelming approval largely because it is a universal program. In its current form, it will continue to enjoy support despite an inevitable rise in costs. Throughout its history, proponents of Social Security have carefully balanced two opposing concerns: adequacy versus equity. Adequacy means providing sufficient benefits for the poor; equity means paying a fair rate of return on contributions. Both are crucial to obtaining long-run popular support. While the Social Security payroll tax is regressive, the structure of benefits is highly progressive. The result is that higher-income individuals today already are promised a much lower rate of return than lower-income individuals. Policies that apply high taxes to Social Security benefits or even threaten to confiscate them would drastically alter the balance between equity and adequacy. As the experience with the ill-fated catastrophic health insurance plan demonstrated, successful social programs must have the allegiance of politically active upper-middle-class individuals. An attack on wealthy Social Security recipients would be an attack on Social Security itself.

The other lesson from the catastrophic health debacle was the tendency of social programs, especially entitlement programs, to grow without bounds. This lesson is critical for plans for government-sponsored long-term care for the elderly. Long-term care is a prepackaged, ready-made policy disaster. No government can distinguish between the truly disabled elderly and those suffering the infirmities of old age and led or pushed to an independent existence. Nor can the government easily distinguish between necessary care and luxury accommodations. We can encourage individuals to purchase long-term insurance as part of their retirement packages, but the government must not be in the business of parenting the elderly.

Environmental policy in the United States has one obvious defect: it suffers from the neglect of basic economic principles. It is hard to believe that in some areas we could construct such tortuous policies. We evaluate health risks for raw foods on rational cost–benefit grounds but, for processed foods, we use zero-risk approach whose scientific foundation is, at best, insecure. Development can be disrupted by the discovery of an obscure species inhabiting the area. On the basis of warnings from scientists whose motives may be mainly political, we contemplate radical changes in our industrial policy.

Basic economic thinking calls for recognizing that the environment is typically an unpriced resource and that ideal environmental solutions should put a price back on the environment. Determining the appropriate price for the environment is equivalent to deciding how much environmental protection to purchase. This evaluation naturally will be the subject of legitimate debate. But viewed in this way, there clearly are trade-offs between protection of the environment and the production of other goods.

There is a natural temptation to deny these trade-offs. For some, environmental protection is a moral issue and thus not suitable for the economic calculus. For far too many educated individuals, economics begins and ends with Malthusian fears. Other environmentalists offer economic myths in the form of costless energy conservation. From the opposite side, business sometimes challenges legitimate environmental protection as a threat to its competitiveness and fails to recognize that environmental resources are not free.

Fortunately, there are some hopeful signs that economic common sense may play a greater role in policy. Markets in emissions are beginning to grow in an attempt to achieve least-cost solutions. Environmental advocates now recognize that the Endangered Species Act does not work well to protect a broad range of species. And there is recognition in some quarters that a gradual, market-based approach to the possibility of global warming is the best tactic.

Perhaps some can find a silver lining in recent environmental regulation, but they will be hard-pressed to find any good news about the liability crisis. As the *Wall Street Journal* noted, at a recent meeting of the Association of Trial Lawyers special groups gathered to discuss the new hot areas of litigation: diet plans, breast implants, aquatic industries, automatic teller machine security, dry-cleaning fluid exposure, the sleeping pill Halcion and the antidepressant drug Prozac, lead paint, power saws, tapwater burns, and others.[1] State courts throughout the country, where the real action takes place, routinely adopt new theories from other states about causes of accidents, standards for proof, and liability for related parties. Contrary to wishful thinking in some segments of the legal community, the boom in liability claims will not simply run its course.

The solutions to the liability crisis lie in common-sense federal or state legislation that places reasonable limits on litigation. These measures might include, for example, limits on pain and suffering claims, protection from litigation if federal or state approvals have been given for production of drugs and medications, and reasonable limits on statutes of limitations and deep-pocket coverage. What stands in the way of such legislation is the potent political power of lawyers, who often align themselves with public interest groups. The fact that many legislators are lawyers does not help. Business interests must continue to press politicians for reform and constantly remind the public of the true cost of our distorted legal system.

Special interests are also at center stage in our difficulties with trade policy. Free trade benefits society as a whole but can hurt particular individuals or industries. These interests' skill in fighting for protection makes free trade very difficult to sustain. Even when business is good, some industries want protection. For example, despite having 85 percent of the market for minivans, U.S. car manufacturers lobbied hard to have foreign minivans classified as trucks so that they would be subject to higher tariffs.

Partly to circumvent domestic protectionist pressures, nations have entered into GATT agreements to gain reciprocal tariff reductions and to harness export interests in favor of free trade. Unfortunately, domestic interests, especially powerful farm lobbies in Europe, have impeded productive international agreements. In part because of the slow progress of international organizations, the United States and other countries have turned to free trade agreements among neighboring states. While free trade arrangements can be beneficial, such negotiations can turn into mutual protection pacts and drift away from free and open trade. U.S. textile interests allegedly tried to interest Caribbean nations in joining the United States–Mexico free trade pact if they would in turn help sabotage the GATT negotiations that would have liberalized trade in textiles. But ideally the momentum of free trade negotiations will keep protectionist forces on the defensive.

Protectionism can disguise itself in many forms. Some in Congress have proposed taxes on imports from Japan and Europe as a payment for our defense spending abroad. Others want taxes on imports as environmental fees. Whatever their label, taxes on imports are simply tariffs that distort the domestic market and favor domestic producers. Tariffs are ineffective environmental taxes—they do not encourage foreign firms to adopt cleaner technologies or more environmentally efficient means of production. Noble-sounding rationales for barriers against free trade should be regarded with suspicion.

Elaborate rationales are also given for monetary policy. With fiscal policy in a straightjacket, monetary policy determines the risks of recession and inflation. The Federal Reserve and the financial community often insist that monetary policy is their technical preserve and that the Congress and the president are too political to handle the responsibilities of monetary policy. While the details of monetary policy are technical, the risks involved in stabilization policy must be faced by elected officials who ultimately will be held accountable.

As the world economy grows and economic integration increases, the fate of the U.S. economy becomes increasingly tied to world developments. Who would have thought that German unification would lead to slow economic growth in the United States? As Germany engaged in U.S.-style deficit spending, its central bank raised interest rates, forcing its European partners, whose currencies were pegged to the German mark, to raise their interest rates. The result was slow economic growth abroad and a limited market for U.S. exports. While there were cries for economic policy coordination, the United States did not have a high moral ground from which to criticize the Germans for engaging in the same policy United States pursued for a decade. We should be thankful that, unlike some European countries, the United States is not on a fixed exchange rate with Germany, so we can conduct our own monetary policy.

The federal budget deficit is both a symbol and a source of our economic problems. As our relations with Germany indicate, persistent budget deficits have damaged our international standing and prestige in economic affairs. As the proximate cause of our large trade deficits, it has hurt our relations with Japan and strengthened the hand of domestic protectionists. Finally, as the federal government has absorbed private savings, it has displaced resources from domestic and foreign investment, reduced our productivity growth, and transferred ownership of U.S. assets abroad.

There have been numerous attempts to find hidden virtues in deficits. These virtues remain stubbornly invisible. Unfortunately, increased deficits do not lead to increased private saving; they no longer keep federal spending in check; nor can they be justified because of inflation or because the government is engaging in investment, not consumption, spending.

Solving the deficit problem means adhering to a few key principles. These principles are not surprising, but few politicians are willing to embrace them all. First, deficit reduction should be gradual. We are not sufficiently at risk and we are too central to the world economy to roll the economic dice with Draconian cuts. Second, health care reform is an essential component of any strategy, preferably along the lines suggested previously. Third, we cannot launch any new major social initiatives until we have solved this problem. Long-term care, massive infrastructure investments, and other plausible ideas must remain ideas. Finally, we need to find some additional revenue while doing the least damage to the economy.

One tax would raise considerable revenue without doing much harm to the economy. Some economists believe that this tax would be beneficial. A fifty-cent tax on gasoline would raise nearly $50 billion dollars a year and would improve air quality through reduced vehicle use. Measured as a share of total consumption, a gasoline tax would be roughly proportional to income and certainly would be no more regressive than a basic sales or value-added tax.

There is only one problem with a gasoline tax: it is the tax the public hates the most. In a survey, U.S. residents were asked which taxes they would object to a great deal even if they were sure the proceeds would be used to reduce the deficit.[2] Only 20 percent objected to an increase in corporate income taxes, and only 22 percent objected to an increase in cigarette or tobacco taxes. On the other hand, 60 percent strongly objected to a twenty-cent tax on gasoline.

But all is not lost, even for the most poll-sensitive politicians. Only 31 percent objected to a five-dollar-a-barrel oil import fee. This tax would raise about $10–12 billion dollars a year. This amount would not solve the deficit problem, but it would not be a bad start. With a bit of discipline, a tiny bit of courage, and a willingness to address the issue, the federal deficit can be brought under control. Hopefully, we can find a modicum of leadership within the Washington money-go-round.

Notes

1. Christi Harlan, "Lawyers Focus on Product-Liability Suits," *Wall Street Journal* (July 31, 1992): B6.
2. These findings are from a 1987 Harris poll. *Index to International Opinion* (New York: Greenwood Press, 1987), 112.

APPENDIX

Annotated Guide
to Washington Think
Tanks and Sources
of Policy Information
(With the Assistance of Jean Stratford)

We take pride in the fact that this listing of think tanks and sources of policy information is both selective and subjective. It is based on our experiences with organizations and their publications: the good, the bad, and the boring. Some important think tanks or policy sources are not mentioned here, and to them we apologize. But our intent was to prepare a useable listing of the most important sources reflecting our personal perspectives. Here are a few of the basic principles we followed in preparing our list:

1. Think tanks should have a commitment to intellectual inquiry and be more than mere mouthpieces for the ideology of a particular political group.
2. No organization that routinely engages in litigation is included.
3. When in doubt, we included an organization if it widely disseminates the results of its work (via conferences, lectures, etc.) through such forums as C-SPAN.

Inside the Beltway Independent Think Tanks

American Enterprise Institute for Public Policy Research
1150 17th Street NW

Washington, DC 20036
(202) 862-5800

The AEI is one of the preeminent think tanks in Washington. Its roster includes many stars ranging from Robert Bork to Herbert Stein. On the political scale, it takes "responsible" conservative positions. This stance means that it urges deficit reduction, for example. A true heavy-hitter. The AEI produces research monographs, conference papers, and other information on a variety of public policy topics, including international economics, and it publishes a bimonthly journal, *The American Enterprise*, which replaced a variety of prior publications.

Brookings Institution
1775 Massachusetts Avenue NW
Washington, DC 20036
(202) 797-6000

The oldest and most famous Washington-based think tank. Charles Schultze, Alice Rivlin, and Henry Aaron are some of the stars who have been on its roster. Brookings is known for taking the "responsible" liberal position. Like responsible conservatives, it urges deficit reduction. Brookings produces a variety of publications, including journals, annuals, and research reports. Of special note are the *Brookings Review* and *Brookings Papers on Economic Activity*.

Cato Institute
224 Second Street SE
Washington, DC 20003
(202) 546-0200

The Cato Insitute was started by libertarian activists, but it has broadened it scope to become an important force advocating free markets, liberty, and personal freedom. Its conferences and forums are first rate and reach an international audience. They publish the *Cato Journal* (three times a year), and *Policy Report* (bimonthly) and produce a public affairs radio show, "Byline."

Center for Strategic and International Studies
Georgetown University
1800 K Street

Washington, DC 20006
(202) 887–0200

Formerly affiliated with Georgetown University, this think tank now claims fifty senior researchers and a large budget. It traditionally has been associated with powerful thinkers in the military-foreign policy establishment, including Edward Luttwack and Walter Laquer. It is now broadening its reach into international economic affairs.

Center on Budget and Policy Priorities
777 North Capitol Street NE
Suite 705
Washington, DC 20002
(202) 408–1080

Founded in 1981 by Robert Greenstein, the center is widely regarded as a clear-thinking advocate of the poor and children. It produces research reports, is visible in testimony before Congress, and publishes the monthly newsletter *Women, Infants and Children.*

Economic Policy Institute
1730 Rhode Island Avenue NW
Suite 200
Washington, DC 20036
(202) 775–8810

Founded in 1985, the Economic Policy Institute is known for advocating a traditional Democratic agenda—for example, more activist government policy and increased investment in infrastructure and education. They produce occasional research reports tied to policy issues and organize conferences and forums.

Heritage Foundation
214 Massachusetts Avenue SE
Washington, DC 20002
(202) 546–4400

The Heritage Foundation dramatically rose to national prominence in the 1980s. Unlike other conservative think tanks, its members saw themselves more as advocates than as traditional policy scholars. They prepared a detailed policy and organizational plan for the Reagan administration that was very influential. They understood the need for quick policy response in Washington and prided themselves on their ability to affect outcomes. Hertiage produces a wide variety of reports, newsletters, and a quarterly journal, *Policy Review*.

Institute for Policy Studies
1601 Connecticut Avenue NW
Washington, DC 20009
(202) 234-9382

The Institute for Policy Studies was founded in the early 1960s and earned its reputation as a think tank for the (old) new left. One of its most famous publications was *A Vietnam Reader* by Marcus Raskin and Bernard Fall, which was a bible for antiwar activists in the late 1960s and early 1970s. The institute is affiliated with the Transnational Institute in Amsterdam, an organization devoted to seeking solutions to disparities between the rich and poor throughout the world.

Progressive Policy Institute
316 Pennsylvania Avenue SE
Suite 555
Washington, DC 20003
(202) 547-0001

A new entrant onto the Washington scene (1989), the Progressive Policy Institute has tried to move the Democratic party to the center of the political spectrum. It has close ties with the Democratic Leadership Council, an organization of moderate Democrats.

Urban Institute
2100 M Street
Washington, DC 20037
(202) 223-1950

Established in 1968, the Urban Institute relies heavily on contracts with the government, providing intellectual firepower on a wide range of social issues. They have specialized in assessing the efficacy of government policies and strategies. They also publish a wide range of books through their own press.

Government Sources of Policy Analysis

Advisory Commission on Intergovernmental Relations
Suite 2000, Vanguard Building
1111 20th Street NW
Washington, DC 20575
(202) 653–5540

This commission develops offical positions and conducts research on the interrelations between local, state, and the federal government. It also commissions studies and reports on intergovernmental finance.

The Board of Governors of the Federal Reserve
20th Street and Constitution Avenue NW
Washington, DC 20551
(202) 452–3000

The Federal Reserve System was established to serve as the nation's central bank and to execute monetary policy. The Board of Governors collects a wide variety of statistical data and conducts research in areas relating to monetary policy. It published the *Federal Reserve Bulletin.* In addition, the member banks collect and disseminate statistical data and publish research findings in their own journals. The articles in the journals of the member banks are often quite clear and informative.
The member banks are:

Federal Reserve Bank of Atlanta
Research Department
P.O. Box 1731
Atlanta, GA 30301
(404) 521–8500

Publishes *Economic Review* and *Working Paper Series.*

Federal Reserve Bank of Boston
Bank and Public Information Center
600 Atlantic Avenue
Boston, MA 02106
(617) 973–3000

Publishes *Conference Series, New England Economic Indicators, New England Economic Review, New England Economic Indicators, Monthly Update, Regional Review.*

Federal Reserve Bank of Chicago
Publications Division
P.O. Box 834
Chicago, IL 60690–0834
(312) 322–5322

Publishes *Economic Perspectives, Economic Commentary, Economic Review, Working Papers.*

Federal Reserve Bank of Cleveland
Research Department
P.O. Box 6387
Cleveland, OH 44101
(216) 579–2000

Publishes *Economic Review.*

Federal Reserve Bank of Dallas
Research Department
Station K
Dallas TX 75222
(214) 651–6111

Publishes *Agricultural Highlights, District Highlights, Economic Review, Energy Highlights, Financial Industry Studies, Roundup.*

Federal Reserve Bank of Kansas City
Research Department
925 Grand Avenue
Kansas City, MO 64198
(816) 881–2000

Publishes *Economic Review, Regional Economic Digest.*

Federal Reserve Bank of Minneapolis
Office of Public Information
Minneapolis, MN 55480
(612) 340–2345

Publishes *Fedgazette: Regional Business & Economics Newspaper, Ninth District Conditions, Quarterly Review.*

Federal Reserve Bank of New York
33 Liberty Street
New York, NY 10045
(212) 720–5000

Publishes *Perspective, Quarterly Review.*

Federal Reserve Bank of Philadelphia
Public Information Department
P.O. Box 66
Philadephia, PA 19105–0066
(215) 574–6000

Publishes *Business Review.*

Federal Reserve Bank of Richmond
Bank and Public Relations Department
P.O. Box 27622
Richmond, VA 23261
(804) 697–8000

Publishes *Economic Review.*

Federal Reserve Bank of San Francisco
Research Information Center
P.O. Box 7702
San Francisco, CA 94120
(415) 974–2000

Publishes *Economic Review.*

Federal Reserve Bank of St. Louis.
Research Department
P.O. Box 442
St. Louis, MO 63166
(314) 444–8444

Publishes *Annual U.S. Economic Data, Federal Budget Trends, International Economic Conditions, Monetary Trends, National Economic Trends, Review.*

Congressional Budget Office
Second and D Streets SW
Washington, DC 20515
(202) 226–2621

The CBO provides Congress with budget estimates and conducts a wide range of policy studies as well. It issues a wide range of reports that are available to the public. Its *Economic and Budget Outlook,* published yearly, is an excellent source of information about the economy and the budget.

Congressional Research Service
Library of Congress
101 Independence Avenue SE
Washington, DC 10540
(202) 707–7904

The CRS provides objective nonpartisan research, analysis, and informational support to Congress. It is divided into various divisions, including American law, economics, and environment and natural resources policy. Its research reports are frequently published under congressional imprint or in CRS's own publications series. CRS materials are indexed in *Major Studies and Issues Briefs of the Congressional Research Service.*

Intergovernmental Organizations

International Monetary Fund
700 19th Street NW
Washington, DC 20431
(202) 623–7000

World Bank (International Bank for Reconstruction and Development)
1818 H Street NW
Washington, DC 20433
(202) 477–1234

These two organizations were formed after World War II to facilitate international economic management and to spur economic development. Both organizations produce statistical data and research reports.

ORGANIZATIONS OF STATES

National Governors Association
Hall of the States
444 North Capitol Street
Washington, DC 20001
(202) 624–5300

National Association of State Budget Officers
Hall of the States No. 295
400 North Capitol Street NW
Washington, DC 20001
(202) 624–5382

Housed in the Hall of the States near the Capitol Hill, these two organizations (and others like them) represent the collective interests of state governors, legislatures, budget offices, and so on in Washington. Typically, these organizations hold conferences and meetings and collect the most current data to share with their members and the press. They are the best source for up-to-minute trends in state economic and budget developments.

Outside the Beltway Think Tanks

Conference Board
845 Third Avenue
New York, NY 10022
(212) 759–0900

The board produces a montly *Statistical Bulletin* and a variety of reports and surveys on economic topics.

Hoover Institution on War, Revolution, and Peace
Stanford University
Stanford, CA 94305
(415) 497–1754

Founded by a gift from Herbert Hoover and located at Stanford, the institution has a unique combination of scholars and policy analysts with a conservative and free market emphasis. The scholars associated with Hoover are world-renowned and have included Milton Friedman, George Stigler, and Seymour Martin Lipset.

Hudson Insitute
5395 Emerson Way
Herman Kahn Center
P.O. Box 26-919
Indianapolis, IN 46226
(317) 545-1000

The Hudson Institute was founded by Herman Kahn and colleagues in the early 1960s. For most of its existence it was dominated by the personality and perspective of Herman Kahn, who became known as a "futurist." After Kahn's death, the institute moved to Indianapolis, and it is starting to establish a post-Kahn identity.

National Bureau of Economic Research
1050 Massachusetts Avenue
Cambridge, MA 02138
(617) 868-3900

The NBER is an influential voice in economic research today. Several hundred of the top academic researchers are affiliated with the programs and activities of the NBER. Its main activities are in Cambridge, Massachusetts. The NBER publishes a number of conference volumes on cutting-edge economic issues. A committee from the NBER officially determines when recessions begin and end.

Rand Corporation
1700 Main Street
Santa Monica, CA 90406
(213) 393-0411

Rand was the prototypical think tank. It grew out of contract research with the Department of Defense after World War II. Over the years it has expanded its operations to include programs in justice (both criminal and civil) as well as medical economics. Interdisciplinary activity has always been its forte. Rand also publishes the *Rand Journal of Economics* and operates a graduate school in in public policy.

Subject-Specific Think Tanks

The following think tanks focus on a smaller range of issues than the general think tanks described above. As policy issues become more complex, there is a growing role for these organizations. Subject-specific think tanks can be located outside the beltway and the listing includes those as well as Washington organizations.

American Medical Association Center for Health Policy Research
515 North State Street
Chicago, IL 60610
(312) 464–5022

Publishes research results in journals. Also compiles several statistical annuals.

Council on Competitiveness
900 17th Street NW
Suite 1050
Washington, DC 20006
(202 785–3990

Produces an annual *Competitiveness Index* that provides data the United States' comparative position in terms of industrial competitiveness relative to other industrial nations.

Institute for Civil Justice
Rand Corporation
1700 Main Street
P.O. Box 2138
Santa Monica, CA 90406
(213) 393–0411

Disseminates its research through the Rand Corporation's publications series.

Institute for International Economics
11 Dupont Circle NW
Suite 620
Washington, DC 20036
(202) 328–9000

Publishes research reports, books, and a journal, *International Economic Insights*.

Resources for the Future
1616 P Street

Washington, DC 20036
(202) 328–5000

Publishes the quarterly journal *Resources,* as well as research reports and books.

World Resources Institute
1709 New York Avenue NW
Suite 700
Washington, DC 20006
(202) 638–6300

Produces the biennial report *World Resources,* which provides statistical data and analysis on world resource topics such as population and health; human settlement; forests, rangeland, and habitat; fresh water, oceans, and coasts; and global systems and cycles.

Sources for Further Inquiry

The following related sources may be valuable for policy research.

Organizations

Bureau of National Affairs
1231 25th Street NW
Washington, DC 20037
(202) 452–4200

The BNA publishes a wide range of daily, weekly, and biweekly updates on policy developments and legislation, with an emphasis on legal, labor, and economic matters. BNA materials are quite in-depth and are designed for the policy insider.

Tax Analysts
6380 North Fairfax Drive
Arlington, VA 22213
(703) 533–4400

Tax Analysts comprehensively reviews all federal tax developments. The group also produces specialized publications on state and foreign taxation issues. Its major publication, *Tax Notes,* is a weekly guide to the inside world of tax policy. Tax Analysts also produces on-line services for up-to-the-minute information on taxation.

Publications

The Idea Brokers: Think Tanks and the Rise of the New Policy Elite by James A. Smith is an interesting history of think tanks that highlights their origin and their changing role in our society. The book was published by The Free Press in New York in 1991.

Major U.S. Statistical Series: Definitions, Sources, Limitations by Jean Slemmons Stratford and Juri Stratford, Chicago, Illinois: American Library Association, 1992. This book provides readers with a framework for locating and understanding statistical data. It describes the sources, construction, and publication of a number of basic statistical measures in several broad categories.

National Journal (1730 M Street NW, Washington, DC 20036) is a weekly journal devoted to policy issues and politics. *National Journal* is an excellent and timely source of in-depth reporting on policy issues.

The Research Center Directory, now in its sixteenth edition (1992), is an excellent source for information on university-related and other nonprofit research organizations. The directory is divided into broad subject categories and provides addresses, phone numbers, and background information. The directory is currently edited by Karen Hill and is published by Gale Research of Detroit, Michigan.

INDEX

Carter, Jimmy, 207, 208, 218,
221–222
Central banks, 201, 212–213,
215–216, 218, 222, 223
England, 205
Germany, 205–207, 219, 222
Switzerland, 205
China, 119, 121
Clean Air Act, 101, 103, 104–107,
189
1990 amendments, 107–109
Cline, William, 118
Clinton, Bill, viii, 57, 255
Cold War, 102, 184
Collective action, 197, 223,
249
Collective goods (public goods),
4, 7, 11, 130
Competition, 1, 9–10, 146, 164,
169, 176–177, 183, 230–
231
Congressional Budget Act of
1974, 229, 239–240
Congressional Budget Office
(CBO), 17, 57, 159, 228,
240, 243–244, 246, 247
Conservation, 97, 98
Consumption, 8, 84–85, 176–177,
179, 231, 233, 234, 248,
249, 261, 262
Currency market, 183, 230, 231,
241, 261
Cutler, David, 85

Danzon, Patricia, 153
Darman, Richard, 248
Denmark, 219, 235
Developing countries, 118, 119,
120, 172, 176–178, 194
monetary policy in, 200–201
Diamond, Peter, 53
Dole, Senator Robert, 236

Easterlin, Richard, 66
Economic development, 30, 164,
178
Economic efficiency, 10, 33, 169–
170, 171, 173, 185
Economic growth, 107, 159, 179,
234, 242
Solow growth model, 38
Economic policy, 1, 3, 4, 10, 11,
12–13, 181, 208, 254,
258, 261
Eisenberg, Theodore, 149–150
Eisenhower, Dwight D., 207
Eisner, Robert, 233–234
Employee Retirement Income Se-
curity Act (ERISA), 53
Employment, 28, 66, 201
full employment, 199, 217, 229,
230–231
Endangered Species Act, 128,
132–133, 259
Enthoven, Alain, 51
Entitlement programs, 17, 18, 90–
91, 245, 246, 248–249,
258
Environmental Protection
Agency, 101–104, 106,
109, 111–112, 122, 124–
126, 127–128, 132–133
Environmentalism, 4, 6–7, 9, 10,
11–12, 178, 258–259, 260–
261
Equity, 2, 8, 10, 27
Erlich, Paul and Ann, 129–130
Europe, 73, 85, 110, 114, 165,
166, 175, 181, 187, 260
Europe, Eastern, 1, 2, 119, 121
European Community, 165–166,
172–176, 177–178, 186,
187
EMS (European Monetary Sys-
tem), 205–206, 219–221
Exchange rate agreements, 219–